patsy

MYSTERY HIDDEN YET REVEALED

A Study of the Interrelationship
of
Transcendence, Self-actualization
and Creative Expression,
with
Reference
to
the Lives and the Works
of
Thomas Merton and Georgia O'Keeffe

Marie Theresa Coombs

Cascade Books
A division of *Wipf & Stock Publishers*
199 West 8th Avenue, Suite 3 • Eugene OR 97401

Cascade Books
A division of Wipf and Stock Publishers
199 West 8th Avenue, Suite 3
Eugene, Oregon 97401

Mystery Hidden Yet Revealed
By Marie Theresa Coombs
Copyright©2003 by Marie Theresa Coombs
ISBN: 1-59244-381-4

To

Christ Jesus,

the

Mystery Hidden yet Revealed
of God,

in

heartfelt appreciation
of
the beloved children of God
who journey with me
in contemplative-eremitical community at
Lebh Shomea House of Prayer

Now your life is hidden with Christ in God.
When Christ, our life, is revealed,
you too will be revealed with him in glory
(Col 3:3-4).

Contents

Part I: Transcendence, Self-actualization and Creative Expression

Part II: Thomas Merton
(1915-1968)

Abbreviations

Writings by Marie Theresa Coombs and Francis Kelly Nemeck

Called by God HAVE	*Called by God: A Theology of Vocation and Lifelong Commitment.* Eugene, OR: Wipf and Stock Publishers, 1992.
Contemplation	*Contemplation.* Eugene, OR: Wipf and Stock Publishers, 1982.
Discerning Vocations	*Discerning Vocations to Marriage, Celibacy and Singleness.* Eugene, OR: Wipf and Stock Publishers, 1994.
Exploring the Catechism	*Exploring the Catechism.* Jane E. Regan, et al. Collegeville, MN: The Liturgical Press, 1995.
O Blessed Night	*O Blessed Night: Recovering from Addiction, Codependency and Attachment, based on the Insights of St. John of the Cross and Pierre Teilhard de Chardin.* Staten Island, NY: Alba House, 1991.

Spiritual Direction	*The Way of Spiritual Direction.* Collegeville, MN: The Liturgical Press, 1985.
Spiritual Journey	*The Spiritual Journey: Critical Thresholds and Stages of Adult Spiritual Genesis.* Collegeville, MN: The Liturgical Press, 1987.

Part II: Writings by Thomas Merton

A Search for Solitude	*A Search for Solitude: Pursuing the Monk's True Life (Journals III).* Ed. Lawrence S. Cunningham. New York, NY: HarperCollins Publishers, 1996.
Asian Journal	*The Asian Journal of Thomas Merton.* Eds. Naomi Burton, Brother Patrick Hart and James Laughlin. New York, NY: New Directions, 1973.
Bread in the Wilderness	*Bread in the Wilderness.* New York, NY: New Directions, 1953.
Collected Poems	*The Collected Poems of Thomas Merton.* New York, NY: New Directions, 1977.
Conjectures	*Conjectures of a Guilty Bystander.* Garden City, NY: Image Books, 1968.
Contemplative Prayer	*Contemplative Prayer.* Garden City, NY: Image Books, 1971.

Courage for Truth	*The Courage for Truth: Letters to Writers.* Ed. Christine M. Bochen. New York, NY: Farrar, Straus and Giroux, 1993.
CWA	*Contemplation in a World of Action.* Garden City, NY: Doubleday and Company, Inc., 1971.
Dancing in the Water	*Dancing in the Water of Life: Seeking Peace in the Hermitage (Journals V).* Ed. Robert E. Daggy. New York, NY: HarperCollins Publishers, 1997.
Disputed Questions	*Disputed Questions.* New York, NY: Farrar, Straus and Cudahy, 1960.
Entering the Silence	*Entering the Silence: Becoming a Monk and Writer (Journals II).* Ed. Jonathan Montaldo. New York, NY: HarperCollins Publishers, 1996.
Hidden Ground of Love	*The Hidden Ground of Love: The Letters of Thomas Merton on Religious Experience and Social Concern.* Ed. William Shannon. New York, NY: Farrar, Straus, Giroux, 1985.
Honorable Reader	*Honorable Reader: Reflections on My Work.* New York, NY: The Crossroad Publishing Company, 1989.
Learning to Love	*Learning to Love: Exploring Solitude and Freedom (Journals*

	VI). Ed. Christine Bochen. New York, NY: HarperCollins Publishers, 1997.
Literary Essays	*The Literary Essays of Thomas Merton.* Ed. Brother Patrick Hart. New York, NY: New Directions, 1981.
Love and Living	*Love and Living.* Ed. Naomi Burton Stone and Brother Patrick Hart. New York, NY: Farrar, Straus and Giroux, 1979.
Merton in Alaska	*Thomas Merton in Alaska.* New York, NY: New Directions, 1988.
MZM	*Mystics and Zen Masters.* New York, NY: Farrar, Straus and Giroux, 1967.
New Seeds	*New Seeds of Contemplation.* New York, NY: New Directions Paperbook, 1972.
No Man Is An Island	*No Man Is An Island.* New York, NY: Harcourt, Brace and Company, 1955.
The Other Side	*The Other Side of the Mountain: The End of the Journey (Journals VII).* Ed. Patrick Hart, OCSO. New York, NY: HarperCollins Publishers, 1998.
Road to Joy	*The Road to Joy: Letters to New and Old Friends.* Ed. Robert E. Daggy. New York, NY: Farrar, Straus and Giroux, 1989.

Run to the Mountain	*Run to the Mountain: The Story of a Vocation (Journals I).* Ed. Patrick Hart, OCSO. New York, NY: HarperCollins Publishers, 1995.
School of Charity	*The School of Charity: The Letters of Thomas Merton on Religious Renewal and Spiritual Direction.* Ed. Brother Patrick Hart. New York, NY: Farrar, Straus, Giroux, 1990.
Secular Journal	*The Secular Journal of Thomas Merton.* New York, NY: Farrar, Straus and Cudahy, 1959.
Seven Storey Mountain	*The Seven Storey Mountain.* New York, NY: Harcourt, Brace and Company, Inc., 1948.
Sign of Jonas	*The Sign of Jonas.* New York, NY: Harcourt, Brace and Company, 1953.
Thoughts in Solitude	*Thoughts in Solitude.* Garden City, NY: Image Books, 1968.
Turning Toward the World	*Turning Toward the World: The Pivotal Years (Journals IV).* Ed. Victor A. Kramer. New York, NY: HarperCollins Publishers, 1996.
Vow of Conversation	*A Vow of Conversation: Journals: 1964-1965.* Ed. Naomi Burton Stone. New York, NY: Farrar, Straus and Giroux, 1988.

ZBA	*Zen and the Birds of Appetite.* New York, NY: New Directions, 1968.
Witness to Freedom	*Witness to Freedom: The Letters of Thomas Merton in Times of Crisis.* Ed. William H. Shannon. New York, NY: Farrar, Straus and Giroux, 1994.

Part III: Writings on or by Georgia O'Keeffe

A Woman on Paper	Anita Pollitzer, *A Woman on Paper: Georgia O'Keeffe.* New York, NY: A Touchstone Book, Simon and Schuster, 1988.
Art and Letters	Jack Cowart, Juan Hamilton and Sarah Greenough, *Georgia O'Keeffe: Art and Letters.* Washington, DC: National Gallery of Art, 1987.
CR	Barbara Buhler Lynes. *Georgia O'Keeffe: Catalogue Raisonné (Volumes I and II).* London and New Haven: The Yale University Press, The National Gallery of Art, The Georgia O'Keeffe Foundation, 1999.
Georgia O'Keeffe	Georgia O'Keeffe, *Georgia O'Keeffe.* New York, NY: Penguin Books, 1976.
Lovingly, Georgia	Clive Giboire, ed., *Lovingly, Georgia: The Complete Correspondence of Georgia*

O'Keeffe and Anita Pollitzer. New York, NY: A Touchstone Book, Simon and Schuster, Inc., 1990.

O'Keeffe...and the Critics   Barbara Buhler Lynes, *O'Keeffe, Stieglitz and the Critics, 1916-1929*. Chicago, IL: The University of Chicago Press, 1991.

O'Keeffe: In the West   Doris Bry and Nicholas Callaway, eds., *Georgia O'Keeffe: In the West*. New York, NY: Alfred A. Knopf in association with Callaway, 1989.

One Hundred Flowers   Nicholas Callaway, ed., *Georgia O'Keeffe: One Hundred Flowers*. New York, NY: Alfred A. Knopf in association with Callaway, 1989.

Some Memories   Georgia O'Keeffe, *Some Memories of Drawings*. Albuquerque, NM: The University of New Mexico Press, 1974.

General Remarks

Notes

1. All translations from the Hebrew and Greek Scriptures are my own. I adapt most biblical texts to reflect gender inclusive language.

2. I have left as they stand quotations from the writings of Thomas Merton and Georgia O'Keeffe that do not employ gender inclusive language.

3. Georgia O'Keeffe has in her writing certain peculiarities of style; for instance: often not using an apostrophe in contractions of words (*dont* instead of *don't* and *Im* instead of *I'm*); dashes instead of a period at the end of a sentence; incomplete sentences; misspellings or rarely used spellings. I have let O'Keeffe's stylistic preferences stand as they are, without indicating them.

Acknowledgments

Grateful acknowledgment is made to the following for permission to use previously published material:

The Doubleday Broadway Publishing Group, A Division of Random House, Inc., for excerpts from *Conjectures of a Guilty Bystander*, by Thomas Merton. Copyright 1968 by The Abbey of Gethsemani.

Harcourt Brace Jovanovich, Inc., for excerpts from *The Seven Storey Mountain*, by Thomas Merton. Copyright 1948 by Harcourt, Brace

Introduction

This work is a reflection upon a reality central to each human life and basic to every branch of theology; namely, mystery hidden yet revealed. This study explores that theme from the perspective of the interrelationship of transcendence, self-actualization and creative expression.

My interest in this subject arose out of the ministry of spiritual direction. I first formulated for myself the question of the interrelationship of transcendence, self-actualization and creative expression some years ago during a period when I was privileged to accompany three women artists through significant thresholds of their spiritual journeys. I was struck by two commonalities in their experience: *first,* how each one's coming into her own in terms of emerging self-identity was inexorably linked with her experience of transcendence; and, *second,* how each one's artistic expression, together with her philosophy of art, became radically refined and personalized as a consequence of her deepening encounter with God and her unfolding self-actualization. In the ensuing years the question of the interrelationship of transcendence, self-development and creative expression so intrigued me that I felt impelled to explore in depth this subject. Thus, I chose this theme as the topic of my doctoral dissertation in theological studies at the Graduate Theological Foundation then located in Donaldson, Indiana (1996). In this book, I present a revised edition of that original work.

Transcendence refers to God forever beyond creation and always more than it. Yet, God's transcendence is also immanent. That is, God hidden yet revealed shines forth from within all creation. The depths of each person and each living thing open out in some way to the depths of God concealed yet manifest.

Self-actualization denotes the unfolding of our personal identity. From a Christian viewpoint it refers to the lifelong process

of becoming fully our unique self in Christ Jesus.   Three
interconnected vocational components bear upon the actualization of
our identity. They are: (1) the development of our hidden self (*who*
God calls us to be); (2) the living out of a combination of Christian
lifestyles (*how* God calls us to become ourselves); (3) the increase of
God's reign in this world through our mission and ministry (*what*
God calls us to be and to do).

   Creative expression denotes the use of word, image, sound
or movement in order to name for ourselves and to communicate to
other persons something of our experience of mystery hidden yet
revealed, both within ourselves and within the world around us.

   This study consists of three parts. In *Part I*, I examine the
three notions of transcendence, self-actualization and creative
expression as they relate to human life and interconnect with each
other.   Then, from that foundation I proceed to flesh out the
interrelationship of those realities in the lives and in the works of
two well-known persons: Thomas Merton (1915-1968) in *Part II* and
Georgia O'Keeffe (1887-1986) in *Part III*.

   My methodology throughout this study embodies the
following characteristics:

*   It has as its starting point reflection upon human experience.
*   It recognizes relationality – that is, intimacy, interactiveness and
    communion – as the core of that experience.
*   It approaches mystery as embracing *both* interiority *and*
    exteriority; that is, it addresses the within and the without of a
    person's life as a whole (in contrast to reducing the reference
    point of spirituality to *either* the inner realm *or* the outer world).
*   It is evolutionary – that is, developmental and process-oriented –
    in its approach.
*   It is interdisciplinary. I integrate into my theological perspective
    insights from biography, history, science, psychology, sociology
    and art.

   As for the scope of my consideration of Thomas Merton and
Georgia O'Keeffe, I set certain boundaries. I limit my theological
reflection upon them to the theme of the interrelationship of
transcendence, self-actualization and creative expression within each
one's life and work. The study of each one stands on its own. I
make no direct attempt to compare Merton and O'Keeffe, although
points of convergence and divergence become apparent in the course

of my reflections.

I have chosen Thomas Merton and Georgia O'Keeffe for a number of reasons. They are contemporary and contemporaneous. Each one has a body of work that gives firsthand testimony to his/her personal experience. Both the similarities and the differences between them serve to enrich this study. Among their similarities are values such as individuation, creativity, solitude and simplicity of life. Among their differences are these factors:

- One is a man and the other is a woman.
- Merton's mode of creative expression was primarily verbal. O'Keeffe's form of creative expression was mainly visual.
- Merton's transcendent experience unfolded within the context of institutional religion. O'Keeffe's encounter with transcendence occurred outside any organized religious framework.

Although Thomas Merton and Georgia O'Keeffe were singularly gifted individuals, their experiences have commonalities with the life quest and the human struggle of most people. In the course of their lives both Merton and O'Keeffe had to contend with joy and pain, success and failure, growth and diminishment. Thus, the lives and the works of these two persons can encourage, enlighten and challenge us as we ourselves undergo mystery hidden yet revealed. Their sense of integrity and their fidelity to their respective spiritual journeys can inspire us to be true to ourselves and to God indwelling us.

I have come to see that the interrelationship of transcendence, self-actualization and creative expression has significant bearing on each human life and every spiritual quest. Thus, it is my hope that this study will assist people earnestly searching for "an I-don't-know-what,"[1] whatever their starting point – science, spirituality, psychology, sociology or the arts. In a special way, I believe this work will help those persons who have sought out spiritual guidance, as well as the spiritual directors who minister to them.

---

[1] St. John of the Cross, *The Spiritual Canticle,* stanza 7.

Part I:

Transcendence,

Self-actualization

and

Creative Expression

CHAPTER 1

Face to Face with Mystery

Mystery – or the transcendent, or the numinous – holds us in its warm embrace from our coming into being unto our personal death. Our life journey unfolds along its pathway. In joy we surrender to its touch; in pain we seek to acquiesce to its wisdom.

Mystery is the ground of all being and becoming. Creation comes forth from transcendence, and into the numinous creation is moving.

Mystery reveals itself to us immediately and directly. The transcendent reveals itself also through our seeing, hearing, touching, feeling, imagining, thinking and loving. The numinous exists at the heart of all human experience. *

We begin our study of the interrelationship of transcendence, self-actualization and creative expression by setting out certain foundational truths; namely:

- The human person is an enfleshed being who is becoming.
- Acting in and interacting with the world around us, we gain experience.
- Within our human experience we discover transcendent depths.
- Our encounter with mystery is laden with paradox.
- That mystery hidden yet revealed in human experience is none other than God's immanent transcendence.

A. Enfleshed Beings Becoming

As humans we are enfleshed beings. Our body is formed from the matter of the universe. Thus, we have a physical

* an unseen but majestic presence that inspires.

interconnectedness with the entirety of creation. It is as embodied persons situated in a tangible world that we encounter the transcendent dimension of life. The depths of our inner mystery call unto the depths of mystery within other persons, things and events. Those depths emanate even through the physicality of our body and the materiality of the world around us.

The human body stands open to the numinous, the mysterious, the transcendent in a four-dimensional manner. Two of those dimensions are vertical: one relates to what is *above* us, while the other relates to what is *below* us. Two of those dimensions are horizontal: one relates to what is *within* us, while the other relates to what is *outside* us.[1]

With the *above* dimension, we associate rising up or ascending, as in "going up in an airplane" and "lifting up one's heart." With the *below* dimension of our physical self, we associate concepts like grounding and descending, as in: "with feet planted firmly on the ground" and "a dive into the deep." While that which is above draws us toward the heavens, that which is below grounds us to the earth. The correct balance between above and below enables our physical body to remain upright or vertical. That balance makes it possible for us to stand our ground.

Our horizontal body perspective pertains to relatedness. With respect to the *within* of our embodied self, we tend to use words like receptivity, openness, interiority, accessibility. To designate our relatedness to what is *outside* us, we employ words such as expressiveness, interaction, activity.

As embodied persons then, we function in this manner: From the center or axis of our enfleshed being we engage in a dance of four-dimensional movement: upward-downward-within-without. This motion is a fourfold energy resource that enables us to relate to the world in a space/time continuum. This bodily movement is a catalyst facilitating our penetration of the heights and the depths of the mysterious, the transcendent, the numinous within us and around us. In that process of movement we develop and mature. Thus, we are not only embodied beings, but also embodied beings becoming.

---

[1] See Charles M. Johnston, *The Creative Imperative: A Four-Dimensional Theory of Human Growth and Planetary Evolution* (Berkeley, CA: Celestial Arts, 1984), 103-255.

B. Human Experience

Our activity as enfleshed persons forms the basis of human experience. The following elements constitute "an experience":

- an encounter of a subject with a reality (e.g., During a walk in the woods I come upon a deer.);
- influence of the person and the reality upon each other (e.g., I am impressed by the gracefulness of the deer as it stands there looking at me.);
- the individual's incorporation of the encounter into his/her personal history (e.g., I return home and write in my journal about the beauty of the deer.);
- interpretation of the meaning of the encounter (e.g., I reflect upon how much simple beauty exists all around me.).

Human experience denotes the convergence of a series of interactions into a comprehensive whole. The phenomenon that we call an experience consists of a meaningful synthesis of a sequence of events in which we are participants.[2]

Once we attain that point of unification, an experience recedes into the realm of the past. Yet, past experience influences the configuration of our present. That experience places at our disposal energies which we can convert into practical skills and value implementation. Past experience can launch us toward expanding horizons and new enterprises. It can be a source of ingenuity and creativity, a wellspring of wisdom and insight.

Interpretation of experience occurs with reasonable accuracy only when a series of events have reached a point of unification. The cultures and sub-cultures to which we belong condition our experience as well as our interpretation of it. The various communities in which we participate provide sets of beliefs, values and norms to guide our experience. They furnish language, symbols and rituals to help us comprehend it. Communal wisdom and collective experience serve as standards by which to test discernment of personal experience.

Early in life we form frameworks of understanding in regard to personal experience. Initially, we use those basic structures in a

---

[2] See Philip N. Joranson and Ken Butigan, eds., *Cry of the Environment: Rebuilding the Christian Creation Tradition* (Santa Fe, NM: Bear and Company, 1984), 324-326.

pre-conscious and a pre-reflective way to name and to assess our experience. As time goes on, we employ those guidelines consciously and reflectively. With continued experience we engage in a critique of cultural norms. That evaluation results in modification of the personal points of reference for assessing experience.

C. Experience of Mystery

All human experience has a transcendent aspect. In fact, transcendence is the depth dimension of human experience. From a phenomenological viewpoint transcendence or mystery refers to the inexplicable and enigmatic, the unfathomable and incomprehensible which we encounter within ordinary living. When we reach our limits, we find limitlessness awaiting us. When we stand at a boundary line, we discover boundlessness before us. When we reach a goal, we yearn for something beyond that attainment.

Mystery is the name that we give the unnamable aspect of our experience. Thus, mystery is not ignorance of truth or confusion of thought. Nor is mystery the same as a problem.[3] Knowledge replaces ignorance. Clarity dissipates confusion. The discovery of a solution marks the cessation of a problem. Mystery, on the other hand, always remains mysterious. Moreover, the more deeply we encounter mystery, the more ineffable it seems to us.

We are embodied persons who actively participate in the numinous. Mystery is present in every encounter, whether or not we advert to it. It precedes our involvement with it. It exists prior to our awareness of it.[4] Our actual encounter with the transcendent is on the level of the pre-conceptual, pre-emotional, pre-imaginal. That is, we have first a living experience of mystery. Only in reflection upon the event do we name something of the transcendent.

D. Mystery: Fraught with Paradox

Our experience of transcendence sets before us many apparent contradictions.

Mystery contains the revealed and the concealed, the

---

[3] See Kenneth T. Gallagher, *The Philosophy of Gabriel Marcel* (New York, NY: Fordham University Press, 1962), 30-49.

[4] See Karl Rahner, "The Concept of Mystery in Catholic Theology," in *Theological Investigations*, vol. 4, trans. Kevin Smyth (New York, NY: Seabury Press, 1974), 36-73.

manifest and the hidden. It pervades the familiar and the unfamiliar, the ordinary and the extraordinary. It holds both the question and the answer, the problem and the solution, the known and the unknown. It is operative in both our growth and our diminishment. It manifests itself in light and shadow, in clarity and obscurity, in illumination and darkness.

In mystery we can be simultaneously at home and restless. The numinous transcends our seeing, hearing, feeling and understanding, yet all the while touching us in our beholding, listening, loving and knowing. Mystery draws us out of ourselves, while introducing us to our true self. It bonds us with another person, while keeping that other beyond us. It filters through the details of our daily lives, even as it draws us toward the cosmic. Mystery thrusts us beyond the safe and the familiar, as it directs us securely along untrodden paths. It dispossesses us of all things, even our very selves, while imparting communion with the universal. It unites us with all, while bringing our individuality to its fullness.

On the one hand, we never know where we will encounter mystery. On the other hand, we can be sure that it awaits us everywhere and in all things, if we but listen, behold and receive.

Mystery can be subtle in its coming, drawing us gently into its embrace. It can be also assertive and at times overpowering. Mystery is capable of shaking us up, overturning our judgment and demolishing our sense of control. It baffles our knowledge, upsets our plans, confounds our expectations, stops our arrogance dead in its tracks. It reduces our world of illusions to a heap of ashes.

As we encounter mystery, opposite responses arise simultaneously within us. We find ourselves drawn irresistibly to it even as we are frightened by it. We welcome mystery even as we seek to evade it. We pursue mystery even as we try to run from it. We find peace in mystery even though we cringe at the changes it demands of us. We feel both exhilaration and dread before the mysterious.

E. Mystery: The Immanent Transcendence of God

From a spiritual perspective, what is this mystery that shows its face to us in our activities and shines through the countenance of every living creature? What is this mystery that once it touches us awakens in us insatiable longing to plumb its depths? What is this mystery that instills in our hearts restless yearning for "an-I-don't-know-what"?[5] What is this mystery that having captivated us makes us pilgrims and seekers, always straining forward toward the unattained and the unattainable?

This mystery, which pertains to the essence of our humanity and our experience, is ultimately God. It is God so close to us as to abide within us, yet so other than us as to remain beyond us. It is the immanent transcendence of God within all creation.

The concept, "immanent transcendence," is born out of the truth of God's secret inmost essence (what the Hebrews called "holiness") and God's free self-revelation and self-communication to humankind (what they called "glory"). Immanent transcendence describes how we experience God when God's holiness and divine intimacy converge upon us. Our experience of God consists of increasing darkness and illumination, night and light, mystery and communion. The interplay of God's transcendence and self-revelation does not cease in the resurrection. Rather, we see God face to face in such a way that God remains forever mystery to us.

What we term the immanent transcendence of God is relative to our perspective. It describes how we designate God as a consequence of our experience of the numinous. We intuit a name emerging out of namelessness, a form coming out of formlessness, a shape appearing out of shapelessness. We perceive light emanating out of darkness and directing us toward a future as yet unknown. We call that mysterious presence to us "God."

In the Christian tradition mystery is ultimately God who is Love, Spirit and Truth indwelling each person, indeed, all creation; God whose ways are unsearchable and whose decisions are inscrutable (Rom 11:33-36); God who is Father, Son and Spirit. Immanent transcendence is ultimately Christ Jesus, the Word made flesh (John 1:14) and our participation in God's life through him. The mystery hidden yet revealed is Christ within us, our hope of glory (Col 1:26-27).

---

[5] St. John of the Cross, *The Spiritual Canticle*, stanza 7 of the poem.

CHAPTER 2

The Cosmic Dance

The universe witnesses to mystery. The numinous pours forth from the depths of creation. Shining through the cosmos – both from within it and from beyond it – is something vast, incomprehensible and transcendent.

From a faith perspective, the mystery transparent in the universe is ultimately the one we call God. God dwells in some way within each creature, sustaining it in existence. God weaves all times, places and seasons into the fabric of salvation history. The cosmos itself is a self-revelation of God.

Various images portray this mystery of God's immanent transcendence; for instance: the web of life, the world soul, the sacramentality of creation. From among those images we highlight in this chapter that of the cosmic dance.

We focus our attention now on these aspects of God's mystery revealed in creation:

- the ordinary world around us as revelatory of immanent transcendence;
- the scientific reality of cosmic evolution;
- creation as one living organic whole;
- evolution as God's way of creating.

A. Mystery Transparent in the Ordinary

A perceptive person cannot but sense in the most ordinary events of life something of the mystery that resides within the cosmos.

When we gaze upon a newborn baby, mystery moves us.

When we listen to a favorite piece of music, mystery fills our soul. When we embrace a loved one, mystery enfolds us. When we share our most cherished hopes with another person, mystery bonds us. When we satiate our hungering and thirsting, mystery nurtures us.

Looking up at the star-studded night sky, we behold mystery. Listening to sounds of laughter and pain, we hear mystery. Holding in our hands newly turned soil, we touch mystery. Reveling in the brilliant colors of autumn, we feel mystery. Drinking water from a cold spring on a hot day, we taste mystery.

Mystery is written in the line, shape and color of every living thing. It is in the sunrise and in the sunset. It is in the faces of children, young people, strangers, elderly men and women. It shines through the convergence of light, feeling, thought and activity that makes up each moment. It keeps all in a state of constant change, evolving form, unfolding life. It permeates the uniqueness of each moment, every encounter, each person.

Mystery reverberates in the silence of the expansive universe, in the sound of human voices, in bird songs, in animal calls. It echoes in the wind, the oceans, the mountains and the streams. It fills the wide-open space of plain or prairie and the dark enclosed space of caves and crevices. Mystery awakens within the deepest recesses of the earth, sprawls across the boundless seas and stretches upward to touch the sky.

Mystery rests within the snow-covered world of winter. With a single touch mystery awakens spring. Mystery sustains the fruition of summer and is at work in autumn decline.

Mystery leaves its traces in the footprints of deer, cattle, kittens and people, etched in the earth's sandy skin after another day of living.

Mystery nurtures the earth, seen from outer space as a blue bulb of light and life surrounded by vast cosmic darkness and silence. Mystery holds in itself good and evil, life and death.

Mystery sustains us in our endeavors. It is manifest in the exhilaration of new possibilities and fresh beginnings. It shines forth in the courage and the perseverance with which we complete our undertakings. It permeates our fidelity to our commitments. It abounds in the fruits of our labor. It intensifies our joy and makes bearable our suffering. Mystery instills hope in time of loss.

We behold mystery in the microcosmic world and in the macrocosmic universe. Mystery reveals itself in the interconnectedness of all living creatures. It animates the world soul. It is the music of the cosmic dance.

B. Cosmic Evolution

Each day the mystery that we are as unique persons encounters mystery transparent in the ordinary people and events of our world. Yet, that experience is but a recapitulation of a lengthy development. Our now has roots in the far distant past. Time, space, matter and energy have their origin in the birth of the cosmos, and they evolve along the trajectory of history. Moreover, present experience thrusts us toward the future. Our now orients us toward eternity itself.

Scientists today accept the fact of evolution, although they subscribe to differing theories of the origin and the development of the universe.[1] Currently, the most widely accepted theory of the cosmic beginning is the Big Bang hypothesis. That is, approximately 13.7 billion years ago the universe began with a fireball explosion of energy. Existing at its inception in a very hot dense state of energy, the cosmos then began expanding outward. Galaxies became scattered around the cosmos in a pattern that includes some patches of numerous constellations and other stretches with very few clusters. Scientific observation indicates that even now the universe continues to expand.

Many physicists maintain that from the beginning the universe seems calibrated for the existence of life. The conditions and the dynamics of the original fireball were geared toward the emergence of life. Thus, life is not a quality of one species or one planet, but a principle innate to primordial cosmic structure.[2]

The earth, around 4.55 billion years of age, originated contemporaneously with the solar system, which occupies a tiny space in the Milky Way galaxy.[3] That constellation itself consists of a cluster of stars, immensely vast in comparison to the solar system

---

[1] The above estimates in relation to the age of the universe, the end of the universe, and the amount of matter in the cosmos are based on information attained by the NASA satellite known as WMAP (the Wilkinson Microwave Anisotropy Probe, launched in June 2001).

[2] See, for example, Brian Swimme, "Science: A Partner in Creating the Vision," in *Thomas Berry and the New Cosmology*, eds. Anne Lonergan and Caroline Richards (Mystic, CT: Twenty-Third Publications, 1987), 81-90.

[3] For a brief outline of salient features of the evolution of life on planet earth, see G. Ledyard Stebbins, "Evolution and Religion," in *Cry of the Environment: Rebuilding the Christian Creation Tradition*, eds. Philip N. Joranson and Ken Butigan (Santa Fe, NM: Bear and Company, 1984), 181-197.

but minuscule in relation to the expanse of the whole universe.

Biochemical evolution on earth began when temperatures on the earth's crust became cool enough for organic chemical reaction to occur.   In an initial stage small carbon-containing molecules (nucleotides and amino acids) formed. In a second stage there came from these carbon-containing molecules the construction of nucleic acids and proteins, of which living systems primarily consist. Those molecular structures became over time increasingly complex, leading eventually to nucleic acids that contain informational messages coded in the order of their units (i.e., DNA and RNA). One estimate puts the time span of pre-biological chemical evolution between one hundred million and four hundred million years.

Biological evolution began approximately three and a half billion years ago. The first forms of biological life, whose habitat was water, were microscopic and structurally simple, comparable to modern-day bacteria and algae. Over many hundred millions of years multi-celled microscopic organisms appeared, which were followed by the first animals (jellyfish, sponges and worms) and the first plants (seaweeds) of sufficient size to be seen by the naked eye. It took approximately seventy million years for the development of the major subdivisions of the animal kingdom and another one hundred to two hundred million years before the evolution of the phyla of land plants.

Scientists have identified the following as components of the evolutionary process: hereditary variation in groupings; the specific nature and faithful transmission of the variation; differential survival and reproductive rate of better adapted individuals; and occasional mutations which enrich the gene pool. In the animal kingdom the thrust of biological evolution was toward the development of a nervous system encased in bone. That basic structure would become increasingly complex as in the case of dolphins and whales.

Like other species, humankind also underwent evolutionary development. Scientists cite certain ancestral primates as the origin for the line of evolution leading to humanity. Even after the appearance of distinctly human features, human evolution continued over the course of millions of years before arriving at what is known as biologically modern peoples.

The nature and the functioning of the human brain allowed for three distinctive biological traits: (1) the creativity to design and to use tools, (2) the capacity to plan for the future by remembering past experience, and (3) the ability to use imagination in cognitive processes. With those traits humankind has been able to adapt to environment primarily by means of cultural rather than biological evolution.

Cultural evolution denotes the transmission and the modification of past societal traits, together with the acquisition of new characteristics. Cultural evolution occurs mainly by teaching and learning. It has at least three advantages over biological evolution: (1) more possibilities for adaptation, (2) increased speed in adapting, and (3) the ability to be goal-oriented in undertakings.

As people of all times and places have reflected upon the origins of the universe, so also have they pondered the ultimate fate of the cosmos. People have grappled with the question not only of where creation came from, but also the issue of where it is going.

Albert Einstein described the universe as a space-time continuum that could theoretically take one of three geometric forms: (1) closed space/positive curvature (like the surface of a ball); (2) flat (like a sheet of paper); or (3) open space/negative curvature (like the seat of a saddle). The actual shape of the universe is dependent upon the amount of matter and energy that it contains. Recent studies estimate that the cosmos contains 4% ordinary matter (i.e., heavy elements, neutrinos, stars and free hydrogen and helium), 23% dark matter (i.e., invisible matter whose gravitational effects can be seen on stars), and 73% dark energy (i.e., a force of an undetermined nature that expands the universe). From that data most physicists conclude that the shape of the universe is flat.

Those estimates give indication also of the probable ultimate destiny of the cosmos. The total amount of matter in the universe does not have enough gravity to halt cosmic expansion. Furthermore, the antigravity effect of dark energy is actually accelerating the rate of expansion. An increase in expansion brings with it an increase of dark energy. Thus, the effects of dark energy become more dominant as expansion continues.

Based on that data, physicists conjecture that the final end of our universe will be ice rather than fire. The Big Bang will end in a Big Lingering Death rather than in a Big Burn-out or a Big Crunch. The galaxies will slip further and further out of sight of each other. The stars will twinkle out. Dead matter will collapse into black holes. The black holes will disintegrate into stray particles. Those particles could bind loosely to form individual atoms bigger than today's universe, which in turn would eventually decay. Finally, only a cold, dark, infinitely vast void would remain.[4] But, assuming that is a generally accurate prediction of the ultimate fate of the universe, would the dark void really be the end, or would it be a creative ferment from which a new creation would evolve?

C. The Interconnectedness of All Creation

From the initial Big Bang, creative activity has continued rippling through time and space to the present. This vibrant moment in history is part of one movement stretching all the way back to the cosmic beginning, extending outward in every direction to include the entirety of creation and thrusting all toward the future. Each person exists in the midst of interconnected historical trends that embrace all time, space and creation. Those trends include one's personal life trajectory, one's family tree, the unfolding events of the cultures and sub-cultures of which one is a member, the history of one's nation, global history, cosmic history.

Everything and everyone in the universe, even on its most physical level, is bonded together in a communion. Gravitational attraction unites all the galaxies. Electromagnetic interaction binds all molecules. Genetic coding connects all the generations that compose the tree of life. Every living creature on earth, including human beings, is a descendent of the original supernova explosion.[5] As human beings, we are children of the universe, no less than the stars in the sky. We are all participants in the great cosmic dance.

Each creature engages in some way in the process of shaping the energy that burst forth in the cosmic beginning. For instance, with respect to the earth, each of us affects the functioning of this planet as a whole, and this planet as a whole influences the functioning of each life system. Yet, as interconnected as all creation is, every living thing retains its singularity. Union differentiates. Oneness with the whole enhances the uniqueness of each person and thing.

Many thinkers see the relationship of humankind to the rest of creation in terms of the earth – indeed, of the entire universe –

---

[4] See, for example, Fred Adams and Greg Laughlin, *The Five Ages of the Universe* (New York, NY: Touchstone Books, Simon and Schuster, Inc., 2000).

[5] See Swimme, "Science: A Partner in Creating the Vision," in *Thomas Berry and the New Cosmology*, 89.

having become conscious of itself.[6] Humanity is thus comparable to a global brain and to a world soul. Exteriorly, humankind epitomizes the earth or the universe reflecting upon itself. Interiorly, humankind represents the conscious endeavor of all creation to seek ultimate fulfillment beyond itself. (Many thinkers maintain that the future of the evolutionary process is linked to further development by humankind of its capacity for reflection, freedom, spirit and love.[7])

From the perspective of the cosmos as an interconnected whole, there exists a certain fluidity or permeability of boundaries between creatures. The human person is not merely a skin-encapsulated ego or an autonomous self. Each human being retains the uniqueness of his/her personhood, while being a member of one body. Moreover, each human being is also a personalized mode of the functioning of planet earth in particular and of the cosmos as a whole. Besides being the expression of an individual talent or gift, each person's undertaking is a planetary and a cosmic activity. When an artist writes, sings, dances, paints or carves, the earth also – indeed, the entire universe – is attaining consciousness and expressing itself.[8]

D. Evolution as God's Way of Creating

Beholding the cosmos, we cannot but stand in awe at its beauty and magnificence. Each creature and the universe as a whole bespeak the mystery from which all creation came into being-becoming. How do we express even what we see and know, let alone that numinous realm which we intuit beyond our observation and cognition?

Peoples of all times and places have shared something of their encounter with the transcendent dimension of the cosmos, and in particular of the earth, through their creation myths.

---

[6] See, for example: Pierre Teilhard de Chardin, *The Phenomenon of Man*, trans. Bernard Wall (New York, NY: Harper and Brothers, 1959) and *Man's Place in Nature,* trans. René Hague (New York, NY: Harper and Row, 1966); Peter Russell, *The Global Brain* (Cos Cob, CT: Hartley Film Foundation), VHS video cassette, 35 minutes; Brian Swimme, *The Universe Is A Green Dragon: A Cosmic Creation Story* (Santa Fe, NM: Bear and Company, 1984), 34-36, 58-60.

[7] See, for example, Pierre Teilhard de Chardin, *Human Energy,* trans. J. M. Cohen (New York, NY: Harcourt Brace Jovanovich, Inc., 1969).

[8] See Pierre Teilhard de Chardin, "The Function of Art as an Expression of Human Energy," in *Toward the Future,* trans. René Hague (New York, NY: Harcourt Brace Jovanovich, Inc., 1975), 88-91; Swimme, "Science: A Partner in Creating the Vision," in *Thomas Berry and the New Cosmology,* 88.

The Judaeo-Christian tradition has its own myths.[9] The Priestly and Yahwistic creation stories in the Book of Genesis (Gen 1-2) affirm these truths: God alone is the creator of all that exists. Creation is good. Man and woman hold a privileged place in God's creation of the cosmos. The reality of evil, especially human failure in the face of temptation, is counter to God's desire for the world. When we sin, God calls us to conversion.

Certain prophets, such as Deutero-Isaiah and Ezekiel, proclaimed that God exerts salvific power for the benefit of not only the Jewish people, but also the entire world. The Israelites thus realized that their God of the covenant was also God the Creator of the universe.

Biblical Wisdom literature, which emerged largely from the experience of the Jewish people in the Diaspora, contains explicit reflection on the mystery of creation. Basically, this literature presents creation as transparent with its Creator. This literature invites the beholder of the created world to encounter its Maker and Sustainer (e.g., Wis 13 and Job 38-42).

Those biblical insights arose centuries before the scientific discovery of evolution. How then does faith in God as Creator accord with the fact of cosmic evolution? From a Christian perspective, evolution is God's way of creating.[10]

The Johannine and Pauline biblical writings in particular suggest a faith experience which perceives creation as an ongoing work of God. Those traditions re-present the teaching of the Hebrew Scriptures and the biblical Wisdom literature in light of God's self-revelation as Father, Son and Spirit. Jesus is simultaneously the human, the divine and the cosmic Christ.

In Johannine theology it is through God's Word that all creation came into being. That Word became flesh in the person of Jesus (John 1:1-18). God thus became human, and in so doing entered into physical interconnectedness with the entire universe. Jesus came forth from the Father and returned to the Father, whose will it is that Jesus draw all creation to himself and transform it (John 6:39). Therefore, creation itself has an inner thrust toward fullness in God. It is the Spirit of Jesus and of the Father who leads creation

---

[9] See Werner Foerster, *ktízo...* (to create), in *Theological Dictionary of the New Testament*, eds. Gerhard Kittel and Gerhard Friedrich, trans. Geoffrey W. Bromiley, 10 vols. (Grand Rapids, MI: William B. Eerdmans Publishing Company, 1965), 3:1000-1035.

[10] See Pierre Teilhard de Chardin, *Christianity and Evolution*, trans. René Hague (New York, NY: Harcourt Brace Jovanovich, Inc., 1971).

to that consummation (John 16:6-15). Jesus remains the Alpha and the Omega of the entire process (Rev 1:8).

The Letter to the Colossians speaks of Jesus as the firstborn and the head of all creation. In him, through him and for him were created all things in the heavens and on earth. He holds all things together, for in him all fullness dwells (Col 1:15-19).

The Letter to the Ephesians refers to God's election of us in Christ even before the creation of the world. It proclaims God's revelation to us of the mystery of God's purpose: "that God would bring everything together under Christ as head, everything in the heavens and everything on the earth" (Eph 1:9-10). This letter sees the Christian community, the *ekklesía*, as the Body of Christ (Eph 1:23).

Theoretically, evolution could proceed in a number of possible directions. However, the Christian viewing the process from a faith perspective perceives all evolution as moving in a single direction. It is converging upon the point of ultimate consummation: Christ, Omega. Thus, the evolution of the universe – cosmogenesis– is in reality also Christogenesis.[11]

---

[11] See *Spiritual Direction*, 27-31; *O Blessed Night*, 118-120, 124-126.

CHAPTER 3

The Hidden Self

Who am I? Whence did I come? What is the meaning of my life? Where am I headed?

Those questions arise in reflective persons throughout the course of life. Sometimes, those questions impress themselves with urgency in the forefront of consciousness. At other times, they simmer in the background of awareness. In any case, those questions persist. In living them out and in trying to respond to them, we discover the inescapable truth that we are mystery even unto ourselves.

To reflect upon that mystery of our personhood, we consider in this chapter the following points:

- community as the matrix of our self-actualization;
- ways in which the transcendent dimension of ourselves manifests itself to our consciousness;
- the self as hidden with Christ in God;
- three concepts related to discovering our hidden self;
- the wisdom of the hidden self.

A. Self-actualization within Community

It is as members of a living whole immersed in history that we grow toward the full stature of our individuality. At any moment we confront ourselves in the context of a personal, a collective and a cosmic history, as well as in the configuration of events and people who constitute our immediate world. We become ourselves as we engage in an intricate web of relationships that span the entirety of the universe. The quest for self is thus not an individualistic undertaking accomplished in isolation from creation. Self-actualization occurs in the context of an ensemble of communities that are all part of the one cosmic community.

From the perspective of creation as an interconnected whole, the quest for self has four basic characteristics:

- *Individuation*: We move in the direction of becoming the unique person that we are capable of being.
- *Relationality*: We attain individuation as we engage in a network of relationships.
- *The undertaking of a lifework*: Our lifework can consist of a number of responsibilities taken on simultaneously (such as spouse, parent and doctor), or it can comprise diverse tasks engaged in sequentially (for example, passing from being a student to a full-fledged professional and finally to retirement). Our undertaking of a lifework fosters our self-actualization and enables us to give service to the world around us.
- *Engagement in a lifelong process*: Throughout our life span we remain in a process of becoming. We continue forward on our specific way.

In short, we become ourselves over the course of our human journey as we interact with creation in diverse ways and make a unique contribution toward the advancement of the whole. Integral to this task of self-actualization is the balancing in our lives of certain apparent opposites; for instance: interaction and action; receptivity and activity; relationships and work; intimacy and separateness; community participation and personal solitude.

B. The Transcendent Dimension of Personhood

As persons, we are ever unfolding and taking shape. We stretch toward a fullness of identity that we cannot even begin to envision. We stand in openness to a depth of personhood that far transcends our current self-concept. Thus, we tend spontaneously to image human life as a journey to the beyond, as a pilgrimage toward something more.

The human person has an innate bent toward mystery. No matter where we find ourselves on the journey at any given moment, we experience a longing for the more that is beyond us. Sometimes we do not associate that yearning with anything specific. If we attempt to name it at all, we can call it only a gnawing "I-don't-know-what."[1] Often, however, we describe that propensity in terms of a desired achievement or an ideal relationship. The pursuit of those directions never completely satisfies us. On the contrary, our ventures – even when they yield some measure of success or fulfillment – increase our hungering and thirsting for something more.   Instead of alleviating that perplexing emptiness, our involvements intensify it.

That experience of ourselves as innately oriented toward mystery comes about especially through these three factors:

- the ecstatic quality of certain human processes;
- the developmental aspect of those processes;
- the finite nature of creatures.

(1) The Ecstatic Quality of Certain Human Processes

The noun "ecstasy" has its origin in two Greek words: *ek* (out of) and *stásis* (existence or being). Thus, the word denotes the activity of going out of oneself, surpassing oneself or losing oneself.

Certain processes characteristic of us as human beings have an inherent ecstatic aspect in that ultimately those activities both emerge from and guide us toward a mysterious depth which surpasses the functioning of our empirical self. Three examples of those processes are loving, desiring, knowing.

The experience of love for another person is ecstatic. When we are attentive, sensitive and compassionate toward a loved one, we surpass vested self-interest. If we trace our loving to its inner source, we discover a transcendent dimension of our personhood. Moreover, the activity of loving leads us outwardly to a surrender of ourselves to what is most mysterious in the beloved.

Similarly, the experience of discovering our most heartfelt desire is one of awesome wonder at having tapped into the numinous aspect of self-identity. That desire leads us to give ourselves outwardly to the pursuit of something greater than ourselves.

The experience of attaining insight is one of marvel at somehow having touched deeply the mystery of truth residing within us and within the world around us. Knowing, imagining and intuiting launch us beyond the utmost bounds of human thought into

---

[1] St. John of the Cross, *The Spiritual Canticle*, poem, stanza 7.

a numinous wisdom.

The transcendent realm of our personhood and of life itself that we feel our way into by loving, desiring and knowing is open-ended. Moreover, we discover in those depths of ourselves the fontal source of the union and communion of all creation.

Viewing our loving, desiring and knowing from a faith perspective, we recognize that those processes arise from within us but originate far beyond us. We experience those energies as graced participations in God's own loving, desiring and knowing. Thus, the mystery of ourselves becomes the point of encounter with God as mystery. In the transcendent realm of our unique personhood we encounter the immanent transcendence of God. We find the transcendent God so near to us as to abide within us, yet so other than us that we can never grasp the fullness of the divine presence. Moreover, our loving, desiring and knowing stretch us outward to encounter the immanent transcendence of God in the world around us.

(2) Processes as Developmental

A process consists of a dynamic unfolding toward a point of consummation. Implicit to process is movement from incompletion toward completion, imperfection toward perfection, limitation toward integration.

As human processes, loving, hoping, believing, knowing and desiring remain at any given moment incomplete, imperfect and limited, even at their best. Each process contains an innate thrust toward more. For instance, we love a person truly, yet we discover ourselves growing in love for that person. We believe in a loved one, yet find our faith deepening. We hope, even as we discover our longing is moving toward a boundless hoping against hope. We know, only to find that our insight catapults us beyond all understanding. We desire, only to find we yearn for more and more. The open-endedness or incompletion of those dynamics points us toward the transcendent dimension of our personhood and of life itself. Our experience of them as processes reveals to us in a striking way the unfinished aspect of our being-becoming.

Human processes of loving, believing, hoping, knowing and desiring reach their consummation only in the resurrection. The developmental aspect of those activities manifests to us that while we are already children of God we have, nonetheless, only the foggiest notions of what is yet to be revealed in the resurrection (1 John 3:1-2).

(3) The Finite Nature of Creatures

In daily living we exercise human processes such as loving, knowing and hoping ordinarily with reference to some person or thing. That created being plays a significant role in our awakening to transcendence. Personal and non-personal creation teaches us through our involvement with it that it cannot fulfill all our desires. While creation is *of* God, *from* God and *to* God, it is not God and cannot give us the fullness of God. Thus, the innate finiteness of each creature confronts us with our inability to be totally satisfied by anyone or anything but God alone. The limitation of creatureliness opens our hearts to the numinous. The creature as creature points us to mystery.[2]

In the awareness of our finiteness we feel ourselves oriented toward the infinite. In encounter with our limitation we intuit ourselves being swept toward limitlessness. Perception of the numinous depths within us awakens joy-filled awe. Nonetheless, the transcendent dimension of ourselves, even when experienced, remains ineffable to us. Having come in touch with the ultimate ground of our identity, we remain a mystery unto ourselves. We realize that we can never in this life grasp fully who we are or who we are becoming.

C. The Self Hidden with Christ in God

The first account of creation in the Book of Genesis refers to the transcendent dimension of selfhood in terms of God creating man and woman in God's own "image and likeness" (Gen 1:26-27). In the Johannine writings the theme of the divine indwelling applies to the numinous aspect of personhood. Jesus calls us to remain in him as he abides in us and as he and the Father live in each other (John 14-17). The Pauline Corpus refers to Christ Jesus as "the image of the unseen God" (Col 1:15). By being conformed to Jesus, Son of the Father, we participate in God (Rom 8:29-31). Our transcendent self is Christ living in us (Gal 2:20). The mystery of personhood pertains to our life "hidden with Christ in God" (Col 3:3).

---

[2] See *O Blessed Night*, 47-68.

That hidden self is not yet fully formed. Each day through whatever events come our way, God fashions us ever more in the divine image and likeness. We are co-workers with God in that activity of forming our hidden self.

Another biblical notion that relates to the process of becoming our Christ-self is calling.[3] When God brings us into being, God gives unique meaning to our life. We term that meaning "vocation." Three interrelated aspects of calling, or vocation, bear upon the development of our personhood: *who* I am (that is, my self-identity); *how* I am to become who I am meant to be (that is, my vocational lifestyle); and *what* I am to do for God and creation in the process of my becoming (that is, my mission or ministry). Over the course of a lifetime, those three aspects of calling – together with our consciousness of them and our response to them – evolve. The actualization of our vocational *who, how* and *what* facilitates movement toward the fullness of our self hidden with Christ in God.

God brings us into being-becoming through the co-creative activity of our biological parents. God's loving us into existence as unique selves makes us children of God, children of our parents, children of the universe – all in the same instant. Moreover, God so loves us as to call us to share in the fullness of the divine life. Our destiny, or God's plan for us (Eph 1:3-14), is that we become God by participation – that is, transformed in God by God, sanctified, deified, divinized.[4]

Attainment of that goal marks the consummation of the creation of our hidden self. It is that destiny which instills in our hearts such restless yearning for the "I-don't-know-what."[5] Our entire human journey from our initial coming into being up to our personal death/resurrection is taken up into the process of transformation in God by participation.

Complete experience and understanding of transformation in God elude us in this life. What we are to be in the resurrection has not yet been fully revealed (1 John 3:1-2). No eye has seen, no ear heard, it has not even entered into our wildest imagination (1 Cor 2:9) what that destiny holds for us. Yet, we are already God's children and we participate now to some degree in transforming union with God. That experience sheds some light on our ultimate

---

[3] See *Called by God*, 1-4, 37-69.
[4] See *Contemplation*, 16-18; *Spiritual Direction*, 20-23; *Spiritual Journey*, 39-52.
[5] St. John of the Cross, *The Spiritual Canticle*, poem, stanza 7.

destiny, together with that of all creation.

Consummate transformation in God means that I have arrived at becoming completely who I have always been destined to be. It means that I now abide consistently in the utter simplicity of my unique personhood. It means that I am henceforth fully human and that I relate to myself, to God and to the entirety of creation uniquely out of that fullness.

The one who becomes God by participation is the completely individuated person, interconnected with all creation in God. That quality of self-actualization is the ultimate fruition of communion in love with the indwelling Father, Son and Spirit. In that intimate union the living flame of love – the Holy Spirit – transforms the person in God. In fact, according to St. John of the Cross, we become so God-like that we seem more divine than human.[6] We come into the fullness of our self hidden with Christ in God only by undergoing death. We have to lose our life in order to become our transformed self in God (Matt 10:39).

God's ongoing work within creation affects our self-actualization. Conversely, God's continuing transformation of each person affects the whole of creation. The destinies of all creatures are intertwined:

> The whole creation is waiting eagerly
>   for the children of God to be revealed...
> From the beginning till now, the entirety of creation
>   has been groaning
>   as in one great act of giving birth...
> And we too who have the firstfruits of the Spirit,
>   we are also groaning inwardly, waiting to be set
>   free (Rom 8:19-23).

D. Certain Concepts Related to Discovery of the Hidden Self

Our life hidden with Christ in God is beyond our grasp. Thus, we remain a mystery even unto ourselves. Yet, the mystery that we are reveals something of itself to us through our experience. We clarify now three terms related to transcendent self-experience as

---

[6]   *"El alma más parece Dios que alma, y aun es Dios par participación."* Ascent of Mount Carmel, II, 5, 7. See *Contemplation*, 16-18.

we employ them in this study:

- personality,
- self-identity,
- self-actualization.

(1) Personality

In popular parlance the word "personality" refers ordinarily to descriptive models of human character. The Myers-Briggs Personality Profile and the Enneagram are two such readily recognizable models.

Our personality designates a complex style of adaptation to the world around us. It describes our mode of relating, leading, behaving, interacting, etc. It denotes our manner of coping with pleasure and pain. Personality refers to what is knowable and observable about us. It pertains primarily to the tangible aspects of our being-becoming. Any personality style has both a light and a shadow side, giftedness and poverty, strengths and weaknesses.

We are more than our personality. Our life hidden with Christ in God transcends our preferred style of functioning in the world. Our personality is to our transcendent self like air to sunlight filtering through it. Our hidden self radiates through our personality, but always transcends it.

(2) Self-identity

The phrase "self-identity" infers being consciously in touch with the transcendent depths of our personhood. It implies some awareness of our hidden self and some ability to relate that insight to the world around us.

A sense of self-identity becomes evident when we speak with our own voice and see with our own eyes. It is manifest in the recognition and the valuing of our thoughts and feelings. A sense of identity enables us to establish a fitting balance of closeness and separateness in relationships. It empowers us to interact within a variety of circumstances and situations, without becoming either fused with other people or withdrawn from them.

(3) Self-actualization

Self-actualization denotes the labor of becoming fully the
self that God calls us to be. It is the way or the road that unites our
beginning with our end. It is the process of formation which our
hidden self undergoes in order to reach its full potential. Self-
actualization refers to the assertion of our inmost self ever more
undeniably and irresistibly upon our consciousness, attitudes, values,
choices and actions. Self-actualization suggests a certain integration
of our inner and outer world. It implies consistency and harmony
between who we are, how we live and what we do.

E. The Wisdom of the Hidden Self

Although our transcendent self eludes our grasp, it
influences profoundly our knowing, seeing and feeling; our choices
and commitments; our desires, attractions and aspirations. The
relentless imperatives of our hidden self wisely shape day after day
our loving, living and choosing.

On rare occasion it is the wisdom of the hidden self pure and
simple which motivates us to fly like a straight arrow in the
appropriate direction. A specific choice or commitment corresponds
exactly to our deepest desire and to God's will for us.

However, many issues require of us prolonged discernment
in order to sift through a myriad of leanings and to judge which
direction most accords with who we really are. When we do arrive
at a decision, we implement it in faith. We cannot know with
foolproof certitude that we are following the right way. We sort out
the various influences with the light that we receive, make the best
decision possible under the circumstances, and move forward with
our choice. We trust that God will make any necessary corrections
as we proceed.

The wisdom of our hidden self holds steadfast in the
actualization of our decisions, even when we change our reasoning
along the way. For example, our experience of living out over time a
specific choice may affirm that we made the correct decision at the
outset. Nonetheless, we realize that reasons, principles or values
quite other than those which now sustain us motivated our initial
option. We find ourselves interiorly and exteriorly where we need to
be on our journey, but only because of a twist of circumstances that
we could never have foreseen.

Closure on most discernments arises out of an intermingling of our wisdom and our waywardness. Although we proceed with good intentions, we see with consternation certain negative influences at work in our relating and decision-making; for instance: unresolved hurts, family dysfunctionality, failures of one kind or another; defense mechanisms inappropriate to the event at hand. The unknown realm surrounding a decision can trigger agonizing self-doubt and second-guessing in the implementation of a discernment: "Why did I really make that choice?" "What was my true motivation?"   Our woundedness, immaturity, confusion and insincerity do not in the long run obstruct our spiritual direction. By some happy chance we stumble our way somehow into our vocational who, how and what.

Beyond both the positive and negative, the conscious and unconscious motivations for our choices, something deeper, broader, freer and wiser persists in its work. That something is the depth of ourselves where our hidden life resides, where Christ makes his home in us. That hidden self innocently asserts itself and wisely pursues it own course, in the midst of and at times despite what is happening on the observable level of our identity and our world.

In living out our spiritual direction, we catch occasional glimpses of the ground at the bottom of the abyss. The light, wisdom and love which we receive from that source impel us to look down into those dark depths of ourselves, our personal history, our world, all held within a more collective and cosmic history. There we behold the mystery of our hidden life in God.

CHAPTER 4

God as Mystery

Human experience contains within itself a depth that opens out to the infinite. Encounter with our unique personhood and with creation all around us gives us access to a realm of the numinous. There we behold God as mystery.

To reflect upon human encounter with divine numinosity, we highlight in this chapter the following themes:

- mystery as the ground of experience;
- God as mystery;
- the issue of naming God;
- communion with God in mystery.

A. Mystery as the Ground of Experience

In the above chapters we explored human experience within the context of an evolutionary worldview. We reflected on: (1) the cosmos as one interconnected entity, (2) each creature as making a specific contribution to the whole, and (3) humankind as representing creation having become conscious of itself. Now, using that discussion as our basis, we summarize certain aspects of human experience which nurture our innate orientation toward mystery.

Those qualities of experience are:

- process,
- relationality,
- union,
- diversity,
- active collaboration,

- joy,
- suffering.

(1) Process

As we employ the term in this study, process has three connotations.

First, process refers to the functioning of the basic energies which characterize the human person: loving, desiring, knowing, imagining, remembering, etc. Each of those activities, when we follow its course to the end, thrusts us toward encounter with the immanent transcendence of God.

Secondly, process refers to the experience of becoming ourselves over the course of our life span. We discover ourselves to be an ongoing work of creation, the initiative for which comes from a Presence within us and all around us, but beyond us.

Thirdly, process refers to the historical movement in which we find ourselves immersed. That movement is a stream which ripples down through the centuries into our present and flows forward to a future yet unknown. That élan opens out to transcendence. Oriented toward mystery by our very nature, we recognize God's presence in history; God's purpose encompassing history; God's saving, redeeming, liberating and transforming activity throughout history; God's Word-made-flesh in history.

(2) Relationality

Relationality within an evolutionary worldview denotes the interdependency and the interconnectedness of all creatures. In the human sphere it designates a stance of love, care and compassion toward each creature and toward the universe as a whole.

Within the context of relationality the human heart encounters the infinite. Interacting with a beautiful landscape, for example, we find ourselves being drawn through it to something numinous at its core. That ineffable core element in turn trails off into ultimate mystery.

The depth dimension of each creature is itself inexhaustible. Especially in the case of love for another person, the beloved does not merely fascinate us for a moment, but rather draws us into ever more qualitative interpersonal communion. The loved one's hidden self undergoes further development even as we behold him/her in wonder.

(3) Union

The experience of the interconnectedness of all creation, all peoples and all history gives rise to a sense of unity. However, that oneness opens us out to "an-I-don't-know-what"[1] – a Presence who is the source of all unity and with whom we are one, a Presence whom we can never totally fathom or grasp.

(4) Diversity

In an evolving world union differentiates. Thus, we become aware of that union generating immense diversity. Each creature has its own shape, color, movement, space, time and history. A truly perceptive person recognizes that the grandeur and the beauty of this diversity could come only from the divine. Thus, diversity bespeaks transcendence as its ground. It witnesses to the immanent transcendence of God.

(5) Active Collaboration

Not only are we recipients in the evolutionary process, but also we collaborate with God's creative work. We develop a vigorous personhood, and we contribute by our activity to the becoming of the whole. We undertake tasks that promote justice and peace in our world. Our choice of specific works arises from the interaction of our talents, education and interests with the needs of our time.

(6) Joy

As participants in the cosmic dance, we experience personal joy and we share in the joy of creation as a whole. Personal joy denotes a sense of well-being and harmony both within oneself and with one's surroundings. The joy of all creation designates a universal sense of well-being and harmony, together with celebration of life, innocence and play. All joy is a participation in the delight

---

[1] St. John of the Cross, *The Spiritual Canticle*, poem, stanza 7.

that God – within us but beyond us – takes in creating, animating, sustaining and beholding the cosmic dance.

(7) Suffering

Suffering – particularly as epitomized in death – may appear from a surface perspective to be not an opening to transcendent experience and thus not a source of encounter with God. However, the truth is that we encounter God's immanent transcendence in a most privileged way in, through and beyond pain and death.[2]

Pain is integral to the evolutionary process itself – the pain of stretching forward, of making mistakes, of letting go. In the course of development each creature naturally suffers. Each one commits some faults. Each must leave something behind in advancing.

Moreover, since God is directing evolution toward a point of ultimate consummation, humankind – together with the entirety of creation – is moving from chaos to order, from imperfection to perfection, from immaturity to maturity, from scatteredness to wholeness.

> From the beginning till now all creation
>   has been groaning
>   as in one great act of giving birth (Rom 8:22).

That thrust toward fullness of being entails relentless struggle, consistent effort and enormous energy. Every advance costs something.

The laws of statistical necessity latent within evolution postulate pain and death. The universe contains a multitude of agents pursuing individual and collective progress. We can expect that those agents will at times not only cross paths, but also be at cross purposes. What is food for the coyote is death for the rabbit.

In addition to the suffering inherent in the act of becoming (developing, growing, maturing, evolving), creation suffers from violence inflicted upon it. For example, the ecosystems of planet earth suffer from humankind's devastation of forests and improper disposal of toxic wastes. In the global community a few nations control the world's riches and resources, while many other countries

---

[2] See *O Blessed Night*, 141-153.

drown in poverty. Everywhere the voices of oppressed peoples cry out for compassion and liberation. Each person in the course of life suffers diminishments of numerous kinds. From within us, emotional, spiritual and moral weaknesses assail us. From the outside, loss of loved ones, failures in undertakings, hurts inflicted by others befall us.

Yet, personal and cosmic suffering contains within itself depths transparent with the mystery of a suffering God, a God of compassion, a crucified Christ, a God suffering within us and with us as we undergo pain. God's caring for us works on our behalf in three general ways as we endure suffering.

The *first way* is after the manner of Job. In our loss or defeat we perceive God diverting our energies toward more propitious endeavors, but on the same level of means and ends. For instance, a business burns to the ground. The owner rebuilds a more efficient plant and becomes even more successful than before the fire.

The *second way* occurs when God uses a setback, failure or fall to direct our energies to more spiritual pursuits. In this case a misfortune becomes the catalyst that directs us to more qualitative levels of activity and receptivity. For example, a serious illness forces us to take stock of our true priorities and needs.

In both those ways we have some awareness of God's transformative presence with us and within the situation. We see specific gains from our suffering. We perceive in faith that our suffering bears good fruit.

However, the *third way* of God responding to us in our suffering leaves us completely in the dark. God's presence completely eludes us. We suffer without seeing any gain on any perceptible level: a drive-by shooting that leaves an innocent child mortally wounded, a fatal plane crash due to wind sheer. God's design remains utterly incomprehensible to us.

This third mode of God's working with suffering is the most trying to our faith. Yet, it is also the most fraught with potential for encounter and communion with God in mystery. In this form of suffering our predicament is most like that of the dying Jesus. We are gradually stripped of our material possessions, our health, our strength, our loved ones, and, yes, eventually even our biological life. At some point we have no hope of reversal of the circumstances that bear down upon us. We question what good can possibly come to us through our cross.

However, because Christ Crucified has already risen, a

mysterious hope permeates our passover in him. It is a hope in God and for God. It is a hope for transformed life in the fullness of God, a hope for "a new heaven and a new earth" (Rev 21:1). We believe that the presence of the Risen Jesus is at work in us as we undergo the dying process. We experience ourselves communing with him as we undergo suffering and death. Our faith enables us to perceive that our suffering in this life is nothing compared to the glory awaiting us. Moreover, that faith assures us that all creation will share in the glory that is ours as children of God in the Risen Jesus (Rom 8:17-25).

B. The Mystery of God

Human experience of creation orients us to mystery. God uses qualities of that experience such as process, relationality, union, diversity, active collaboration, joy and suffering to draw us into encounter with God as mystery.

God is the Mystery who contains all mysteries, from whom all mysteries flow, and to whom all mysteries redound.

God is the Mystery in whom all creatures exist and become, act and interact, die and rise.

God is the Mystery whom we see with our eyes, hear with our ears, touch with our hands, feel with our hearts, taste with our souls.

God is the Mystery with whom we interact through our loving, perceive through our thinking and intuit through our imaging.

God is the Mystery whom we undergo, cherish and celebrate.

God as Mystery is the passion of our being, the truth of our becoming, the meaning of our pursuits.

God as Mystery is the source of existence, the ground of being-becoming, the way to fullness of life.

God as Mystery is the One whom we seek, the One to whom we give ourselves from our deepest recesses, the One whose depths are without end, the One whom we adore.

God as Mystery is the Word made flesh, Christ Jesus.

God as Mystery is wise ineffability and ineffable wisdom; lucid unfathomability and unfathomable lucidity; incomprehensible truth and truthful incomprehensibility; dark light and luminous darkness; indefinable but all-defining; All in all, with all, over all; the source, the center and the matrix of the one great cosmic dance.

God as Mystery is consoler of the poor, bestower of justice, liberator of the oppressed, transformer of the liberated.

God as Mystery is our ecstatic joy, our abiding peace, our eternal love.

C. The Naming of God

The living God, the true God, God in God's own self infinitely transcends all that we feel, think, say or imagine God to be. Nonetheless, in our multifaceted experience of God immanent and transcendent we try to name God in some meaningful way. From encounter with God as mystery arises a plethora of names for God.

The Jewish and Christian scriptures are replete with a wide variety of names or descriptions for God. The Hebrew Scriptures draw nomenclatures for the divine from every aspect of life: from human relationships such as *mother* (Isa 66:13), *father* (Ps 89:26), *lover* (Cant 1-8), *friend* (Exod 33:11), *spouse* (Isa 54:5-6); from political offices such as *king* (Num 23:21), *warrior* (Judg 4:14), *judge* (Gen 18:25). God's activity in history is depicted in images like *potter* (Jer 18:1-6), *shepherd* (Ps 23:1), *artist* (Gen 2:7), *healer* (Hos 14:5). These scriptures employ also cosmic images to describe God's presence or influence; for example: *rock* (Ps 18:2), *gentle breeze* (1 Kgs 19:12), *fire* (Exod 3:2), *cloud* (Exod 13:21-22), *light* (Ps 27:1), *water* (Isa 35:7). Borrowing comparisons from the animal kingdom the Bible forges images of God as a hovering mother *bird* (Gen 1:2), a roaring *lion* (Job 10:16), a lurking *bear* (Hos 13:8). Biblical Wisdom literature applies the word *sophia* (wisdom) to God (Wis 7:24-26). Jesus reveals God in terms of trinitarian relatedness: *Father, Son* and *Spirit* (Matt 28:19).

Jesus spoke of God as Father, Son and Spirit abiding within us, making their home in us. In our own time some segments of the Christian community find it meaningful and necessary to complement that naming of God with other metaphors. For instance, drawing upon the *sophia* (wisdom) theme in Greek biblical literature and upon the experience of women, many people find the names, Spirit-*Sophia*, Jesus-*Sophia* and Mother-*Sophia*, an especially significant metaphor for the mystery of God's trinitarian relatedness.[3]

No one name or even the totality of divine names or

---

[3]   See Elizabeth A. Johnson, *She Who Is: The Mystery of God in Feminist Theological Discourse* (New York, NY: The Crossroads Publishing Company, 1992), 124-187.

descriptions exhausts the mystery of who God is. Naming is a way by which Judaeo-Christian faith expresses some glimpse of God transparent in creation. Yet, that glimpse is such that it points to deeper experience of God as mystery. Faith seeks understanding and understanding leads to deeper faith.

What we say of God is by way of analogy. Analogy highlights certain resemblances between things that are otherwise unlike each other. An analogy contains greater dissimilitude than similitude. When a name is used analogically of God – and all names are analogies – it declares something about God through a threefold sequence of affirmation, negation and eminence.[4]

Take, for example, love. *Affirmation*: We believe that "God is love" (1 John 4:16). From our human experience of loving we have some insight into the meaning of love as a divine name, since our loving is a participation in God's own love. *Negation*: Yet, at the same time we know that God is not love merely as we experience it. *Eminence*: Thus, the affirmation and the negation of God as love converge to open us to a third awareness: that of beholding the mystery of God as love, beyond our experience and understanding, while proceeding from them.

Analogical language about God moves our minds and hearts from *light* to *darkness* to *luminous darkness*. The negation does not deny the truth of the original affirmation. Rather, it serves to thrust the statement's truth beyond all limits into the mysterious. A divine name thus reveals a way of beholding God, of directing oneself to God, while not literally representing all God's mystery.

Naming God as mystery has become a common ground for dialogue between world religions. All religious traditions have their origin in the same incomprehensible mystery. Dialogical encounter between world religions begins with the shared experience of God as numinous. That approach requires no common doctrinal presuppositions and expects no resolution of doctrinal differences. Such communication entails listening to one another and allowing the experience of one religious tradition to enlighten the other, as each participant in the dialogue becomes strengthened in his/her own

---

[4] See Johnson, *She Who Is...* 113-117.

faith tradition.[5]

D. Communion with God in Mystery

In the Christian tradition prayer is a pivotal response on the part of a person who encounters God as mystery.

Christian community embraces a variety of prayer forms: the celebration of Mass and the sacraments; the Liturgy of the Hours; groups formed on the basis of an interest in a specific way of communing with God, such as charismatic, Ignatian or centering prayer.

In addition to participation in communal prayer, those who have come to experience God as mystery are ordinarily drawn to solitary prayer. This personal prayer is, broadly speaking, of two kinds: meditation and contemplation.[6]

In meditation, as in all other forms of discursive prayer, we commune with God through some means; for instance, a word, a symbol, an image. Through that activity we experience something of God's love and light. In contemplation, which for most people is preceded by a lengthy time practicing meditation, God draws us to commune *immediately* (i.e., not through a medium of words, symbols, specific trains of thought or feeling, etc.) and *directly* (presence to presence or face to face, so to speak). Contemplation is wordless, imageless, loving communion wherein we simply behold the One who is beholding us.

Our prayer response to God as mystery is not, however, confined to a specific time or place. Prayer – in the sense of obedient submission to God's initiative, loving receptivity to God's activity and unconditional openness to God's love – becomes an attitude that increasingly pervades every aspect of daily life. Prayer in that broad sense consists of the joyful welcoming of the Risen Christ who is becoming all in all.

---

[5] See Heinrich Ott, "Does the Notion of 'Mystery' – As Another Name for God – Provide a Basis for a Dialogical Encounter Between the Religions?" in *God: The Contemporary Discussion*, eds. Frederick Sontag and M. Darrol Bryant (New York, NY: The Rose of Sharon Press, 1982), 5-17; Ewert H. Cousins, *Christ of the 21st Century* (Rockport, MA: Element, Inc., 1992), 105-131.

[6] See *Contemplation*, 21-43; *Spiritual Journey*, 75-124, 231; *Exploring the Catechism*, 147-154.

CHAPTER 5

Transcendent Encounter as Creative

Ongoing encounter between creatures energizes the cosmic dance. Dynamic interaction within creation undulates with mystery.

Encounter affords us intimacy with our immanent transcendent God, as well as with creation in God. Encounter constitutes a matrix for the growth of our hidden self. The relational nature of encounter invites the exercise of both divine and human creativity.

In this chapter we examine the following themes which have bearing upon transcendent encounter as creative of us:

- listening presence as integral to encounter;
- God's love as transforming, purifying and enlightening;
- human influence upon God's creative activity.

A. Listening Presence

The word "encounter" is derived from two Latin prepositions: *in* (in) and *contra* (against). Originally, it denoted meeting with an adversary or engaging in a conflict. As the word evolved, the element of hostile opposition gave way to a more serendipitous connotation. Thus, its focus became that of relating to someone face to face or finding oneself unexpectedly involved in some event.

To encounter means to engage in, to become involved with, to connect, to interact. It designates entrance into a relationship with another person, event or thing. Encounter suggests mutuality. It occurs between at least two subjects who exert some influence upon one another.

Whether we meet with a person, thing or event, encounter entails presence-to-presence in a stance of listening. Encounter involves listening to the other with attentiveness, vigilance, expectancy.[1] Especially in interpersonal relationships listening enables us to step out of our world of experience and to participate in another's experience. While maintaining our own identity, we perceive, see, feel, think to some extent as the other does. Listening necessitates receptivity not only to what the other person says or does, but also to the other's inner self. Listening elicits in us intensity of being, heightened consciousness, some measure of commitment. In listening to another, we enter an unknown realm. We do not know exactly how the exchange will unfold.

Any encounter has the potential to open out to the realm of the transcendent. Ultimately, encounter involves our presence interacting with Presence in and through another presence. That is, we experience God's mysterious presence emanating from within our presence to ourselves, from within the presence of those people who touch our lives, and from within the presence of all creation. In the Christian tradition God's indwelling presence is revealed as trinitarian relatedness. In male terms God is Father, Son, Spirit. In a metaphor with female imagery God is Spirit-*Sophia*, Jesus-*Sophia*, Mother-*Sophia*.

B. Effects of God's Communion with Us

With respect to the activity of encountering, the word "creative" denotes engendering life in some manner. Interacting presences give birth to something new. A configuration emerges which has both continuity and discontinuity with the original form.

What occurs in our encounter with God's immanent transcendence to make that relationality creative of us? The response to that question depends to some extent on whether our communion with God is mediate or immediate.

In *mediate* encounter we experience God through a created means; for instance, through a loved one. In some way we intuit the uniqueness of that creature – perhaps by seeing the beloved's strength, perhaps by recognizing his/her vulnerability, perhaps by witnessing the interplay of those opposites. That particularity moves

---

[1] See *Spiritual Direction*, 56-66.

us, evoking intensity of feeling. The uniqueness of the beloved opens up to us a singular manifestation of God.

In *immediate* encounter we commune with God face to face, so to speak, without any medium of exchange. Contemplation is an example of this manner of communion. God reveals God's self directly from within us. We meet the indwelling Trinity in sheer faith, hope and love. Frequently in contemplation we experience God's mysterious presence as apparent absence. God is nothing (*nada*) that we can see, hear, feel, think or imagine. Yet, that emptiness contains the All (*todo*) for whom our heart yearns. In contemplation God becomes for us "*nada y todo.*"

Whether our encounter with God is mediate or immediate, we undergo in that communion life-engendering processes of transformation, purification and enlightenment.

(1) Transformation

God's mysterious presence within us not only influences us, but also transforms us. Transformation goes beyond change occurring on the same level of existence. It involves a metamorphosis wherein one thing actually becomes something new, but with a link to its previous state. For example, water boiled to a certain degree vaporizes; a caterpillar goes into a cocoon and emerges as a butterfly. In the spiritual realm transformation means that we are becoming God by participation in God, while simultaneously moving toward maximum personal individuation.

Christian tradition attributes the activity of transformation primarily to the Holy Spirit:

> All of us, who with unveiled faces contemplate
> > the glory of the Lord,
> > are being transformed into the same image,
> > going from glory to glory.
> This is the work of the Lord who is Spirit
> > (2 Cor 3:18).

Our entire life, from the instant when we come into being-becoming up to our passover into death-resurrection, is in effect one ever-intensifying encounter with God. Throughout our earthly sojourn the Spirit continuously transforms us into God's image and likeness. This divine activity affects every facet of our existence.

Not only our personhood, but also our relationships, lifestyle and work undergo profound change. Along the way our responses reflect fidelity and infidelity, love and selfishness. We experience successes and failures, forward leaps and abrupt halts. Yet, God works with us in each instance, incorporating everything into the process of our transformation. God remains faithful, even when we are unfaithful.

(2) Purification

God's incomparable love causes not only transformation, but also purification. The Spirit's re-creation of us in the divine image requires of us these forms of active collaboration that have a kenotic (or self-emptying) dimension:

- We surrender ourselves from ever greater depths to God whose depth is without end. This joyous abandonment to our Creator and Beloved causes death to self. We lose ourselves in order to find ourselves in God.
- We let go all that nurtures us at any given moment, so that we can continue to move forward toward consummate self-actualization.
- We undergo God's work of gradually and systematically emptying us of all that is un-God-like in us: egocentrism, sinfulness, immaturity, etc.

We die to ourselves in the process of the Spirit's work of raising us up as a new creation in Christ Jesus. As we die, our hidden self – Christ in us – grows ever stronger.

(3) Enlightenment

A third creative effect of transcendent encounter is illumination. As the Spirit transforms and purifies us, we grow in wisdom. We see, perceive, judge and value in a renewed way. We determine the meaningfulness of possible choices and directions increasingly in light of our growing commitment to Jesus in faith, hope and love.

The enlightenment which we receive as we encounter God consists above all in a quickened sense of mystery. That consciousness of the numinous emerges primarily through a process of unknowing. As we learn who we are not, who God is not, what life is not, we intuit something of who we really are, who God truly is, what life actually is. We grow in the conviction that God remains utterly transcendent, even as we attain heightening awareness of God's immanence in every creature.

Transformation, purification and enlightenment occur within us simultaneously. However, we tend experientially to focus our attention on one dynamic at a time.

C. Our Influence upon God's Creative Activity

An encounter involves at least two interacting presences. Our encounter with God is creative of us. But do we in some way affect God?

Certain currents of Christian tradition assert that our interaction with God does indeed affect God. The Bible affords ample testimony that we draw forth from God creative activity on our behalf. Yet, the renewing effects of encounter with God, which we have termed transformation, purification and enlightenment, pertain to us. It seems incorrect to speak of God as transformed, purified or enlightened by encounter with us, at least in the way those terms apply to human experience. But does God's communion with us do something for God?

Since God remains mystery, we do not know exactly how God's encounter with creation affects God. Yet, the following points suggest a sense in which encounter with us does influence God:[2]

- God is receptive to us. God listens to us. God first loves us, and desires our love in return. God wills mutual intimacy. The Father loved the world so much that he sent his Son to share with us their divine life. If God so longs for our love, then our loving response has to be of immense significance to God.
- God's activity of creating is ongoing. We are like clay in the potter's hands. How we turn out at any moment influences what stroke or line will come forth next in the Spirit's work of forming us.
- God's interaction with us has an aspect of relativity. God permits us to respond to the divine initiative with yes, no or maybe. If we say yes, God moves us forward. If we say no,

---

[2] See *Called by God*, 9-35.

God works toward our conversion. If we say maybe, God urges us toward decision.

- God responds to our response. We work with God, but God works also with us. God remains mysteriously engaged with us and active in our lives, when we are faithful and when we are unfaithful.
- The scriptures speak of "God becoming all in all" (1 Cor 15:28) and of Christ "who fills all in all" (Eph 1:23). Complementary to those phrases are sayings pertaining to the gathering up of all creation in God or in Christ (e.g., Eph 1:10; John 12:32). Both sets of images indicate that we, together with all creation, contribute to the increase of God's reign.

Human encounter with God is grounded in mutual faith, hope and love. First, God believes in us, hopes for us and loves us. That initiative elicits our response of believing in God, hoping in God and loving God. Our experience of being sought out by God opens us to the Spirit's creative work of transforming, purifying and illuminating us. In turn, we affect God in some manner. Our loving response, or lack of it, calls forth God's creativity. Transcendent encounter with God draws us to become co-workers with God in God's activity of becoming all in all.

CHAPTER 6

An Evolving Sense of Mystery

The phrase, "sense of mystery," bespeaks awareness of the transcendent in that which is intimately close to us. Sense of mystery denotes consciousness of God's indwelling presence, offered to us as free gift, enveloping us in benevolent love, interconnecting all persons and things, drawing all creation toward fullness in Christ.

In this chapter we explore our developmental awareness of God's immanent transcendence. The experience of mystery and the sense of mystery unfold for most people gradually through the following stages:

- mystery as primal unity – the prenatal months and early infancy;
- mystery as magic and wonder – childhood;
- mystery as idealism, possibility, confusion – adolescence;
- mystery as knowledge and achievement – early adulthood;
- mystery as unknowing – mid-life;
- mystery as wisdom and freedom – the elder years;
- mystery as transforming union – the final years.

We have indicated above the chronological phases of human life that optimally parallel the various stages in the development of our sense of mystery. Although those stages evolve sequentially in most people's lives, at any point on the human journey something of all those faces of mystery is present. It is a question of accent in our experience and awareness when we highlight a specific one. Moreover, each stage takes up in itself all the aspects of mystery evident in the preceding stages and carries them forward into the new experience.

A. Mystery as Primal Unity – the Prenatal Months and Early Infancy

We begin our human journey in the mysterious world of primal unity. Our first prenatal human experience is that of pristine oneness with all creation. When we come into being-becoming, our world consists of undifferentiated wholeness. As we perceive it, nothing or no one has distinct form or individual existence. I move and my whole world moves. My body and my mother's body operate in unison. Feeling, moving and acting constitute one entity for me. That world of undifferentiated unity is the arena of sensory-motor activity. While that original oneness is pre-conscious and pre-reflective, it is nonetheless experiential.

Our coming into being-becoming in a world of primal unity is also our spiritual beginning. Our initial experience of ourselves and of our world is eminently a contemplative experience, because all our activity consists in receiving our individual existence from God. God brings each of us into being-becoming as a unique person who by virtue of that creation is already participating in God's life and interconnected with the entire cosmos. We cannot do other than to receive the gift of self and of life.

From a spiritual perspective that experience of original oneness is the seed from which consummate transforming union with God springs in due time and in proper season.

B. Mystery as Magic and Wonder – Childhood

Soon after our birth, from the unformed and undifferentiated whole of original unity emerge our first acts of separateness: crawling, standing, walking, speaking, etc. We begin to realize that we are distinct from mother, father, the people around us, and the environment. We move beyond our body experience of oneness with all into an experience of embodiment that is the dream-like and magical world of childhood.[1]

With the dawning of consciousness the process of our differentiation and individuation begins in earnest. Personal awareness triggers a new relationship to ourselves and to the world

---

[1] With respect to evolving bodily realities throughout the chronological phases of human life, see Charles M. Johnston, *The Creative Imperative: A Four-Dimensional Theory of Human Growth and Planetary Evolution* (Berkeley, CA: Celestial Arts, 1984), 117-120.

around us. Moving out of the undifferentiated whole, we stand in a fresh stance toward our origins. During our childhood years a world of mystery bubbles up through our actions and sparkles in our interactions. That mystery embodies itself in imagination, magic, make-believe and play.

Childhood experience of mystery contains not only benevolent, but also sinister dimensions. There are not only tooth fairies, but also monsters. The frightening side of mystery manifests itself particularly in the context of actual or threatened loss. It is in childhood that most persons encounter for the first time death and dying. That experience can range from the demise of a beloved kitten or puppy to the loss of a family member or close friend.

As children we tend to form a concept of God based on our rapport with our parents. We transfer our parents' benevolence or harshness onto God. Moreover, especially as the childhood years progress, we tend to see God as bound by absolute standards of right and wrong. The content of our Christian faith relies heavily on mythic representations in story form of our families and communities. Praying consists in formal prayers like the *Our Father* and in spontaneous prayers arising out of a specific situation, such as giving thanks to God for having made a new friend. The contemplative dimension of this phase of life – that is, openness and receptivity to God – manifests itself in a sense of wonder as we discover and explore our world. In the case of children raised practicing the religion of their parents, the accent for them falls on finding a place in the established Christian order.[2] This direction is enriching in the sense of receiving the faith and learning basic spiritual practices. It is limiting to the extent that prejudices and poor theology infiltrate the educative process.

C. Mystery as Conflict and Confusion – Adolescence

Adolescence marks the transition between childhood and adulthood. The special strengths of this phase are expanded capacity to sustain a variety of friendships and increased ability to engage in abstract thought.

During adolescence we find ourselves pulled in opposite directions, both within ourselves and in our relationships. Our body experience moves from the magical to the visceral/muscular. We

---

[2] See *Called by God*, 102-104.

perceive our changing body as both friend and enemy.   In relationships we swing back and forth between dependence and independence. In our behavior we vacillate between impulsiveness and responsibility.

Spiritually, we become capable of relating to God as our special friend.[3] Our burgeoning skill in abstract thinking enables us to practice a more meditative type of prayer. Our primary sense of mystery takes the form of experiencing ourselves torn between bipolar realities such as dependency and independence, impulsiveness and responsibility, rebelliousness and accountability. Our sense of mystery becomes connected with chaos, ambiguity, confusion, rootlessness, absence of direction.   With childhood innocence lost and with the world of magical play behind us, we tend as adolescents to associate mystery somewhat with darkness and evil. Yet, our fidelity to friends, our knowledge of right and wrong, and our perseverance in undertakings reveal to us positive aspects of mystery.

From one perspective the beginning of adolescence seems to mark a diminishment of a sense of mystery. That observation contains some truth. Adolescent development of self-identity and empathy for others coincides with a propensity to silence or to control the more receptive and playful dimensions of personhood. However, from another perspective what appears as loss is a temporary shift of focus. The direction of consciousness toward the world of light and clearly distinguishable forms prepares us for an enriched experience of mystery later in our life.

D. Mystery as Light – Early Adulthood

Mystery experienced primarily as conflict and ambivalence gives way eventually to the perception of mystery as knowledge, light and form. Whether we attain understanding through religion, science or the arts, insight itself becomes numinous to us. Consideration of certain systems as wholes or discovery of the convergence of several disciplines upon one truth, for example, can be a numinous event.

Spiritually, our understanding of our identity, life history, needs and hurts, together with our intimate knowledge of significant persons, bespeaks mystery to us. The sense of calling which has

---

[3] See *Spiritual Journey*, 55-95; *Called by God*, 104-108.

emerged over the years in vocational discernment of our lifestyle and ministry, together with our faithfulness in actualizing that direction, embodies mystery for us.[4]

Early adulthood is the developmental period that parallels optimally the experience of mystery as light. During those years we tend to think we know exactly who God is, who we are, what constitutes fidelity, what we desire to achieve in life, etc. We feel some certitude about our present. A sense of security in the world that we have constructed for ourselves pervades. We assume that our future will merely perpetuate our present way of life. Ordinarily, we have a sense of being in control, gaining mastery, achieving goals. Competence and personal authority in our relationships and in our chosen work or profession are on the increase. We may tend to view our body as somewhat separate from ourselves, as something like an efficient machine to help us attain fulfillment of our desires.

Many factors can detract throughout early adulthood from our sense of mystery as light; for instance: considering our knowledge as an object of our attainment, as a possession or as the fullness of truth; clinging to what we perceive as light; slipping into an excessive materialism wherein we expend our time and energy on the pursuit of wealth, pleasure and status.

E. Mystery as Unknowing – Mid-life

No sooner do we become accustomed to light than another shift occurs. Our experience of ourselves and of our world begins to change radically. Darkness starts to descend upon us. The chronological phase of life that optimally parallels this crossroads is mid-life.

One characteristic of the middle years is confrontation with limits. On the level of bodily being, for instance, we notice signs of aging: graying hair, some wrinkles, decreased energy level, less stamina, certain health problems. Yet, by a strange reversal our heightened awareness of limitations disposes us toward increased depth in living. St. Paul describes the paradox this way:

> As the outer person is falling into decay,
>   the inner person is being renewed day by day
>   (2 Cor 4:16).

---

[4] See *Called by God*, 108-110.

Previously on the spiritual journey, our primary task had been developing ourselves and our world for the sake of Jesus. Now we move forward by dying to self and to our world for Christ. In losing ourselves, we become more truly our self hidden with Christ in God. This reversal is a dark night wherein we come to encounter ourselves, God and creation by way of letting go. As we move in this direction, a renewed sense of mystery takes shape in our kenosis.[5]

In relation to our unique self, we undergo a reevaluation of personal identity. Self-knowledge and life achievements take on a certain relativity. We begin to know by unknowing. On the one hand, we see starkly that there is far more to us than we have come to grasp. On the other hand, we sense that much about ourselves is illusory.

In relation to creation, we undertake a reassessment of our commitments and values. We encounter our loved ones in greater depth by going beyond limiting concepts of them. We begin knowing them by unknowing our images of them, thereby letting the mystery of their identity assert itself more forcefully upon our awareness. Values such as presence, listening, freedom of spirit and simplicity gain ascendancy.

That reassessment can result in cessation of a relationship, lifestyle or work. However, for many people the outcome is renewed commitment and enhanced quality of loving encounter.

In relation to God, a radical change occurs. The Spirit guides us beyond meditation to contemplation.[6] We learn to let go our previous form of activity in solitary prayer and abide in silent loving presence. We unknow our concepts of God as we encounter God immediately and directly. In unknowing, we commune with God in sheer mystery.

F. Mystery as Wisdom and Freedom – the Elder Years

In a sense, we complete the remainder of our earthly sojourn by way of unknowing. Yet, as we learn to peacefully acquiesce to God along ways that are uncharted and unfamiliar, new experiences and perceptions occur. Thus, our sense of mystery as unknowing gives way to a sense of mystery as wisdom and freedom.

---

[5] See *Contemplation*, 60-71; *Spiritual Journey*, 99-113, 163-198.
[6] See *Contemplation*, 27-59; *Spiritual Journey*, 114-124.

Wisdom is loving knowledge. It is a general awareness that is the fruit of intimate communion with God becoming all in all. While certain insights and feelings can arise out of this general loving knowledge, wisdom itself cannot be reduced to any specific concept, affection or image.[7]

Wisdom draws us to affective being-becoming, intimate presence, connectedness with all creatures in God. Wisdom enables us to know by unknowing, to find fullness in emptiness, to feel security in darkness. It empowers us to experience night as light and light as night. It reveals to us the truth of paradox and the paradox of truth. Wisdom invites us to behold God as mystery.

Freedom is the condition in which we discover ourselves as we let go our ways, concepts, knowledge and judgments. It is the vibrant way of being which results from healing of our woundedness, forgiveness in our failures, liberation from our addictions, release from our attachments. Freedom creates within us and our world space for trust and spontaneity, wonder and awe, joy and enjoyment. Freedom elicits ever more expansive and intensive loving, communing, surrendering.

Wisdom and freedom together reshape our sense of mystery. In the human life cycle, mystery as wisdom and freedom is ordinarily most operative after mid-life, particularly in the elder years. From the perspective of the spiritual journey, this experience of mystery pervades what mystical writers term Spiritual Betrothal and Spiritual Marriage.[8] Mystery as wisdom and freedom is the fruit of a contemplation that is passionate communion in love with God indwelling all.

G. Mystery as Transforming Union – the Final Years

Transforming union denotes sharing in God's life and holiness in such a way that we become God by participation. That unity is such that God remains God and we attain the pinnacle of our personal individuation.

By virtue of God's bringing us into being-becoming, God initiates in us the process of transforming union. In creating us, God sets us in a direction toward full participation in divine life. We participate in transforming union with God for many years before the

---

[7] See *Spiritual Direction*, 95-107.
[8] See *Spiritual Journey*, 201-226.

reality of it dawns upon our consciousness. Awareness of transforming union begins to assert itself acutely when we embark upon the contemplative way of unknowing. That realization becomes especially intensified throughout the experience of mystery as wisdom and freedom. Eventually, transforming union itself constitutes our sense of mystery. For most people that experience comes at the end of life's journey when personal death/resurrection beckons on the horizon.

The mystery of transforming union, particularly as we perceive it when death becomes imminent, differs qualitatively from the primal unity of the first phase of human existence. We do not return to exactly the same place and mode of being that marked our beginning.

Our primal experience of unity is like a seed containing the potential for our complete development in God's image and likeness. Transforming union is like the plant at its peak and in full blossom. The primal experience of unity sets us on our course. However, like ourselves, that oneness is unformed, undefined, unshaped, undifferentiated. At the summit of transforming union we abide in God in the fullness of our personal identity, which has been enriched by a lifetime of loving, believing, and hoping and enhanced by a consummated work of service for God and for God's world. We have then the unrestricted freedom of spirit and the loving wisdom necessary for our final surrender to God as mystery. In the complete abandonment of ourselves to God, we become in God present anew to the entirety of creation. We become God's cosmic dance.

Transforming union opens to us unforeseen depths of God's immanent transcendence. Yet, that encounter with the divine recapitulates all the other encounters with mystery that have come our way previously. Mystery as transforming union encompasses and stretches beyond our experiences of mystery as primal unity, as magic and wonder, as confusion, as light, as unknowing, as wisdom and freedom.

> Anyone in Christ is a new creation.
> The old things have passed away;
>> behold all things have become new
>> (2 Cor 5:17).

CHAPTER 7

Creative Expression of Transcendence

Communion with God as mystery is both matrix and catalyst for the actualization of our hidden self. Transcendent encounter is itself creative of us, for in it God transforms, purifies and enlightens us. It is creative also in that it impels us to express ourselves in some fashion in the world around us. Thus, transcendent encounter empowers us to become collaborators with God in God's continuing work of creation.

Creative expression has bearing on the *who, how* and *what* of God's calling of us. It is an essential activity in ongoing discernment and actualization of our identity, lifestyle and mission/ministry. By means of our creative expression we manifest something of our hidden self and contribute to the building up of the Body of Christ.

Creative expression helps us harmonize our daily life with our experience of transcendence. It puts flesh on our pivotal choices. It affects the work that we do, the manner in which we dress, the decor that we choose for our environment. It embodies our affection and care for other creatures. It is a response to pain as well as to joy.

In this chapter we consider in relation to creative expression of transcendence the following points:

- divine *perichóresis*: a metaphor for God's creative activity;
- divine wisdom: another metaphor for God's creative activity;
- the human person as a co-creator with God in ongoing creation;
- two expressions of transcendent experience.

A. Divine *Perichóresis*

The Judaeo-Christian scriptures proclaim God as Creator. In the beginning of the Book of Genesis, for example, the Priestly account of creation describes God forming by word and spirit the world and every creature in it. The Yahwistic account in Chapter 2 of the Book of Genesis portrays God bringing forth creatures from the dust of the earth.

Moreover, the Judaeo-Christian scriptures proclaim that God's work of creation continues throughout history. For instance, in the Book of Isaiah we find this word of Yahweh:

> Behold, I create a new heavens
> and a new earth (Isa 65:17).

The Gospel according to John contains a saying of Jesus that epitomizes his teaching on God's creative activity:

> My Father goes on working,
> and so do I (John 5:17).

Early Christian writers explored the theme of creation through a variety of images. One appealing metaphor is that of *perichóresis*.[1]

In classical Greek *perichóresis* denotes a cyclical movement, a revolving action like the turning of a wheel. In reference to the Christian revelation of God as trinitarian, the term *perichóresis* refers to the three persons indwelling each other, while remaining distinct. The word designates the dynamic presence of each person to the other two. It describes divine love and life joyfully flowing among the Father, the Son and the Spirit so that there is a coincidence of the three persons or an encircling of each one around the other two as in a dance. That intimate relatedness within God cannot contain itself. The energy of love and life circulating among the divine persons bursts outward freely and exuberantly. Thus, that energy brings creation into being and sustains it in its becoming. At the same time that energy swirls back again into God, drawing all

---

[1] See, for example, G. Lampe, *A Patristic Greek Lexicon* (Oxford, England: Claredon Press, 1961), 1077-1078; Brian Hebblethwaite, *The Incarnation: Collected Essays in Christology* (Cambridge, England: Cambridge University Press, 1987), 11-20.

creation to share in the divine dance and each creature in its own measure to participate in the trinitarian life. That continuously circling energy of love and life is divine creativity.

B. Divine Wisdom

The biblical notion of wisdom (Hebrew: *hakmáh*; Greek: *sophía*) is intricately related to God's creativity.[2]

Sapiential literature describes wisdom as the cosmic creative principle in God. She was with the Lord in forming the world, delighting God the Creator and ever at play in God's presence (Prov 8:30). The people of Israel came to personify wisdom (Sir 24:3) and described her many qualities. She is intelligent, holy, unique, discerning, invulnerable, benevolent, shrewd, irresistible, beneficent, steadfast, reliable, peaceful, powerful. She is swifter than any motion and permeates all things. As breath of God, she reflects God's power and goodness (Wis 7:22-26). God alone knows the way to wisdom. Creation cannot contain her (Job 28:12-23). God is the origin of wisdom. In the measure that God desires, she abides with those who love the Lord (Sir 1:9-10).

Israel believed itself to be uniquely privileged among all nations with regard to divine wisdom, for God had sent wisdom to abide in the midst of that people (Sir 24:23-24), especially in the Torah. Yet, the prophets of Israel recognized wisdom manifest in all creation and thus accessible to all nations. They saw wisdom's influence operative in every aspect of people's lives, ranging from skill and dexterity in daily tasks to knowledge and discernment of God's purpose in intricate circumstances.

The personification of wisdom reaches its apex in the person and the mission of the Word-made-flesh (John 1:14). The Synoptic Gospel writers portray Jesus as the Wisdom of God when they proclaim his fulfillment and transcendence of the Law (e.g., Luke 4:21; Matt 5:17-18). The Pauline Corpus speaks of each person of the Trinity as wisdom: the Father (Rom 16:27), Jesus (1 Cor 1:24, 30; 2:7), the Spirit (Eph 1:17). The infinite treasures of God's hidden wisdom are visible in Christ Jesus (Col 2:3).

In one sense then, wisdom is God. In another sense, it is a gift of God to us, causing us to participate in divine life. Wisdom is an aspect of God's mysterious energizing presence within us and

---

[2] See *Spiritual Direction*, 95-107.

within the world. In God's wisdom God engages in the activity of creating a new heavens and a new earth and of enabling us to be co-creators in that process.

C. Co-creators with God

When we "create" something, we tap into the flow of divine love and life emanating from the community of Father, Son and Spirit, circulating through creation and redounding back to God. Human creativity manifests in a specific space and time something of God's own creativity and God's generative love for the cosmos. Human creativity witnesses to divine wisdom at play posing new questions, forging new relationships between familiar things, presenting the known in fresh ways, and pointing to unexplored horizons.

Strictly speaking, we do not observe creativity in itself any more than we behold wisdom as such.   We see expressions of creativity and acts of wisdom.   Creativity is an effect of encounter with an energizing Presence (God), either directly face to face or indirectly through another presence.   That creative force activates us, eliciting our free response to its stirrings and causing us to give birth to a new form of life.

In creative activity we do have some awareness of wisdom at play within and through us. As an interior energy extending into action, creativity conjures up a myriad of images:

- Creativity is like the enkindling of fire. Something ignites in us, smolders, spurts, sizzles, blazes and becomes a living flame, purifying and transforming into itself whatever it touches.
- Creativity is like good soil nurturing seed into a ripe harvest. Day and night, when the farmer is awake or asleep, the seed sprouts and grows, yielding first the shoot, then the ear, then the full grain. How? The farmer does not know.
- Creativity is like the wind blowing wherever it pleases, without our knowing where it comes from or where it is going. Wind assumes various forms: a hurricane, a tornado, a blizzard, a gust, a squall, a gale, a gentle refreshing breeze. Wind is one of nature's ways of pruning and renewing.
- Creativity is like the ebb and flow of the ocean. It tosses and churns, swells, rises and falls. It billows and heaves, undulates and rests. It broods and seethes.

• Creativity is like a river carving out its path. As it moves downstream, it gushes, gurgles and babbles; spurts, cascades and spills; foams and froths. It forms tranquil pools and forceful currents, as it pleases.

Our human capacity for creativity carries with it responsibility. Having tapped into this energizing power, we have the choice of using it for good or evil, for love or selfishness, for service to God and creation or for self-interest.

D. Expression of Transcendent Experience

The need for self-expression usually asserts itself in one of these scenarios: (1) We desire to share with other persons something that we have come to see or to know in a fresh way and that people seem not to have noticed. Or (2) we desire to explore the meaning of some experience, to place that meaning before ourselves and possibly other persons, and to do so by means of word, movement, sound or image.

In the first scenario we have a certain inner clarity which is the fruit of having already processed a significant event. In the second scenario what initially moved us may be unclear even to us. The activity of self-expression itself becomes an inquiry into the original experience. In the process of producing the word, movement, sound or image we strive to discover our question, to identify glimmers of light, to let the whole take shape and reveal its meaning.

Both the above scenarios for self-expression involve in most instances some communication and communion with another person or group. Most works of self-expression are incomplete without the participation of at least one beholder. On the one hand, a beholder's presence and feedback in relation to a specific form of self-expression may reveal further to the artist the mystery and the meaning of the original experience. On the other hand, a person's work of self-expression can dispose the beholder to consider his/her personal experience of transcendent encounter.

Two examples – one from the linguistic sphere, the other from a visual perspective – illustrate the interaction of artist, work and feedback from other people. They are: (1) a biblical text: 1 John 1:1-4, and (2) painting in the Zen tradition.

(1) 1 John 1:1-4

In the opening verses of the First Letter of John, its author expresses the purpose of the letter:

> That which existed from the beginning,
>> which we have heard,
>> which we have seen with our own eyes,
>> which we have beheld
>> and which we have touched with our own hands –
> This we proclaim to you:
>> the Word of Life.
> This life was revealed;
>> we have seen it.
> We bear witness and proclaim to you
>> the eternal life which was with the Father
>> and was manifested to us.
> We announce what we have seen and heard
>> so that you may have communion with us.
> And our own communion is with the Father
>> and with his Son, Jesus Christ.
> We write this to you
>> so that our joy may be complete.

That text expresses transcendent experience. The author actually heard, physically saw, corporeally touched eternal life revealed in Jesus, Son of God. The author writes about that experience in order to bear witness to God's immanent transcendence. His hope is that through his written word others may enter into the same encounter with God. Moreover, the participation of other persons in that communion will enrich the writer's own experience by intensifying his joy.

(2) Painting in the Zen Tradition

The impetus for self-expression in the Zen tradition is usually an experience of being moved profoundly by someone or something. A moment of enlightenment comes our way – enlightenment that can take the form of a question, a riddle, an insight, a feeling, an intuition. That illumination opens to us a transformed way of seeing our ordinary world. In Zen practice enlightenment, creativity and artistic expression interrelate.

As an example of the Zen approach to self-expression, let us suppose that I am enthralled by a flower and wish to paint it.

The art of Zen painting presupposes that I first behold the flower in solitude and quietness. I focus my spiritual energy on penetrating into its inner being, its nature. I harmonize my spirit with the flower's spirit to the point that the flower and I become one. Then, I am able to render the flower in such a way that it moves alive on my paper or canvas in harmony with the pulsating rhythm of my own spirit.

With respect to the finished painting, three points are of significance:

- The painted flower is an immediate expression of the rhythm of my spirit which has harmonized itself with the life-rhythm of the flower. The painting is thus a landscape of my spirit, a pictorial self-expression of my hidden being. The painting is, in other words, the externalization of the internal me.
- However, because I have grasped the inner reality of the flower, the painting is also through my brush a self-expression of the external world itself. Therefore, nature externalizes its own interior through my artistic activity.
- Thus, the creative process entails in a single act a double externalization of the interior. My act of expressing my interior life is in itself also the act of nature expressing its own interior; that is, its inner rhythm of life which pervades the universe and which courses through creation.[3]

In the Zen tradition three key dynamics apply to the creative process of expressing enlightenment in a specific form such as a painting or a poem. These dynamics are contained in the Japanese words: *ki-in*, *myo* and *yugen*.

- *Ki-in*: This word means spiritual rhythm. It is vibrating pulsating life. It is movement.
- *Myo*: This word denotes a sense of the mysteriousness of life. It indicates that which transcends human thought. It depicts an attitude emanating from one's inmost self. It describes an

---

[3] See Toshihiko Izutsu, *The Interior and Exterior in Zen Buddhism* (Dallas, TX: Spring Publications, 1975), 18-36.

activity immediate and direct, beyond every conceptual framework. It is the creativity of the unborn, the unconscious, the realm of possibility. *Myo* is that area of freedom where the mind follows its own course like water flowing downstream or wind blowing where it pleases.

- *Yugen*: This word denotes a glimpse of the Unfathomable, of Mystery and Transcendence within the world of constant change.

Thus, personal enlightenment expressed in word, image, sound or movement vibrates with spiritual rhythm, revealing the mysterious or offering a glimpse into the Unfathomable.[4]

In the act of creating – a painting, a poem, a book, etc. – the person draws out the meaning of an experience. The fresh form reveals meaning to its creator. Moreover, it becomes an invitation to other persons to participate in the original experience, to apply its meaning to their lives or to recognize similar experiences in their lives. For the beholder the created form offers access to transcendence.

---

[4] See Daisetz T. Suzuki, *Zen and Japanese Culture* (Princeton, NJ: Princeton University Press, 1970), 218-226.

CHAPTER 8

Creative Expression: Psychological Dynamics

From a spiritual perspective human creativity is a participation in and an extension of God's own creativity. In the Judaeo-Christian tradition wisdom is integral to God's activity as creator. Wisdom is at play also in our creative expression. Wisdom awakens the inspiration or insight that we seek to express in word, image, sound or movement.

In this chapter we focus on the psychological dynamics of creative expression. Specifically, we address these issues:

- the successive stages in a creative process;
- the significance of form in expressing ourselves;
- the choice of a specific form of self-expression;
- future direction in the study of creativity.

A. The Stages of the Creative Process

Indications that human creativity is indeed a process reach far back into antiquity. Most people are familiar, for example, with the story of Archimedes in the bathtub, pondering the question of how to determine the proportions of silver and gold in the king's crown. Suddenly, he shouted: "Eureka!" ("I have found it!"). However, it took time and effort to arrive at that moment of resolution.

It was not until the late nineteenth century that people began to consider the creative process in terms of successive stages. Herman Helmholtz, a German physiologist and physicist, described his scientific discoveries as unfolding in three stages. The first stage, that of research, he termed saturation. The second stage, the pondering of the information, he described as incubation. The third stage, the sudden insight, he called illumination.

With the onset of the twentieth century Henri Poincaré, a French mathematician, pointed out a fourth stage to the process: that of verification. This designation underscored the work of putting the insight or solution into specific form, while scrutinizing it for error and practicality.

In the early 1960's Jacob Getzels, an American psychologist, made another modification in the schema by referring to a stage of problem finding or formulating. He situated this before Helmholtz's saturation stage. Getzels' refinement came to be referred to as first insight.

Thus, the creative process came to be described in terms of these five sequential stages: first insight, saturation, incubation, illumination (that is, the "ah-ha!" or "Eureka!" moment) and verification.[1]

The amount of time required for passage through each stage is unpredictable and can be quite extensive. Only the stage of illumination tends to be instantaneous, like a flash of lightning.

In his book, *The Courage to Create*, Rollo May delves at length into the dynamics of the stage designated "illumination."[2] What happens, he asks, at the moment of breakthrough? Reflecting upon his personal experience, May notes the following characteristics of the moment of insight:

- The insight tends to surface to our conscious mind against rational thought. The unconscious breaks through in opposition to the conscious beliefs to which we cling. Thus, breakthrough involves feelings of guilt and anxiety over letting go preconceptions, together with joy at the emerging vision.
- The moment of breakthrough carries with it heightened sensory experience in relation to every aspect of the immediate environment.
- The insight does not come in a hit-and-miss fashion. Rather, it emerges according to a pattern, one essential element of which is commitment. Thus, insight is born from unconscious levels into the areas in which we are intensively and consciously searching.

---

[1] See Betty Edwards, *Drawing on the Artist Within* (New York, NY: Simon & Schuster, 1987), 2-5.
[2] See Rollo May, *The Courage to Create* (New York, NY: Bantam Books, 1976), 61-72.

- The insight tends to surface at a moment of transition between work and relaxation. It seems as though concentrated work on the problem sets the process in motion and sustains it, while some yet unforeseen segment of pattern struggles to be born. That birth cannot occur, however, until we relax our conscious application. Thus, breakthrough from our unconscious requires the alternation of intense work and periods of relaxation, with illumination often occurring in a moment of shift.

But, we may ask, why does this specific insight or awareness, and not another, emerge into consciousness? What is the principle of selection in the creative process? Could it be empirical accuracy? Practicality? Logical conclusion? To some degree those principles come into play. However, Rollo May contends that the decisive principles of selection are aesthetic; for example: the harmony of an internal form, the inner consistency of a hypothesis and the quality of beauty that touches our sensibilities.[3]

B. The Significance of Form

Creative expression takes many forms: word, image, sound, movement. It can consist of a photograph, a song, a poem, a book, a musical score, a painting, a dance, a carving, a rearrangement of our immediate living environment, etc.

Spontaneity expresses itself in a specific shape. Form or embodiment arises from the freedom of the creative process. Yet, form puts spiritual, psychological and physical limits to that process. Embodiment requires that we contain a way of seeing within certain boundaries. The limits which form imposes on creativity facilitate the birthing of a particular thing and no other. Form helps name, clarify, delineate, synthesize, simplify to the core, the creation taking shape.[4]

The aliveness of form emerges from our presence interacting with another presence, or in spiritual terms: our presence encountering God's presence transparent in us or in another creature. Form can express an insight, an inspiration or a feeling. Shaping a form can be a way of identifying a question or resolving a conflict.

In creating form – whether a poem, an essay, a song, etc. –

[3] See Rollo May, *The Courage to Create*, 73-74.
[4] See Rollo May, *The Courage to Create*, 133-169.

we work out meaning. Finished form expresses meaning. It makes complete what is incomplete. It rounds off the whole. Beautiful form is the embodiment of meaning.

Self-expression through a specific form entails working out meaning interiorly, as well as shaping a fresh reality exteriorly. It is not an entirely subjective process for two reasons: (1) We carry within ourselves a cosmic history and a collective unconscious.[5] (2) We give birth to a new entity that has a life of its own.

Form bespeaks our identity. The forms that we create reveal us to ourselves as well as to other people, thereby nurturing our self-actualization. In form we try to express something of the mystery that has moved us.

Creatively bringing form to completion requires qualities such as courage, risk-taking, experimentation, decisiveness, persistence, endurance and commitment. It necessitates our confrontation with any tendencies in us toward scatteredness, impatience, laziness, irresponsibility, fear or mediocrity.

C. The Choice of A Specific Form

More questions arise: Why does the creative imperative within us in a specific instance lead to the selection of one form and not another? Why am I drawn at a certain moment to express myself in dance rather than in sculpture? Why is one person a painter, another a poet, a third a combination of potter and writer?

Numerous factors undoubtedly come into play; for example: genetic makeup, environment, culture, education, personality, talents. However, of special interest in regard to choice of a specific form is the issue of human intelligence.

Until recently most people understood human intelligence as a single general capacity of the mind. According to that view, each individual is born with a certain amount of intelligence that can be measured once and for all by standardized verbal tests.

Within recent decades another concept of human intelligence has been gaining acceptance. Psychologist Howard Gardner has

---

[5] Carl Jung described the collective unconscious as a psychic substratum in each person that contains the whole spiritual heritage of humankind's evolution. It appears to consist of mythological motifs or primordial images. It can be studied in mythology and in the psychoanalysis of an individual. See Carl Jung, "The Structure of the Psyche," in *The Collected Works of C. G. Jung*, trans., R.F.C. Hull (Princeton, NJ: Princeton University Press, 1969), 8:139-158.

reignited interest in the theory of multiple intelligences or frames of mind.[6] This theory posits the existence in each person of several relatively autonomous human cognitive competencies. The precise number of those intelligences has not yet been determined, nor have exact boundaries been set for all of them. Yet, research affirms the existence of intelligences that are relatively independent of each other and which individuals or cultures can shape and combine in multiple adaptive ways.

Using a biological and a cross-cultural perspective, Gardner initially identified and described seven forms of cognition:

- linguistic intelligence,
- musical intelligence,
- logical-mathematical intelligence,
- spatial intelligence,
- body-kinesthetic intelligence,
- two personal intelligences (one of which pertains to accessing one's feeling life; the other which consists of the ability to listen well to people).

In later research, Gardner designated an eighth form of intelligence: naturalist.[7]

The idea of multiple intelligences has implications for the way in which a person's creative process is fleshed out. The theory of frames of mind sheds light also on the particularity of personal preference and on the choice of specific forms for self-expression. If intelligence is pluralistic, so too is creativity. Thus, in related research Gardner applied the idea of multiple intelligences to the study of creative people.[8] Gardner found that each person whom he selected for his study approached life from a dominant intelligence or a dominant combination of intelligences. Moreover, each person tended to exercise creativity according to that perspective. For example, Pablo Picasso's strengths lay in spatial, personal and kinesthetic intelligences, while scholastic intelligence was his primary weakness. Albert Einstein excelled in logical-spatial

[6] See Howard Gardner, *Frames of Mind: The Theory of Multiple Intelligences* (New York, NY: Basic Books, 1983), especially 73-298.
[7] See Howard Gardner, *Intelligence Reframed: Multiple Intelligences for the 21st Century* (New York, NY: Basic Books, 1999), 48-52.
[8] See Howard Gardner, *Creating Minds: An Anatomy of Creativity Seen Through the Lives of Freud, Einstein, Picasso, Stravinsky, Eliot, Graham, and Ghandi* (New York, NY: Basic Books, 1993).

intelligences, while being undeveloped in the personal intelligences.

D. Continuing Study of the Creative Process

In the field of psychology, study of the creative process continues from a number of perspectives, among which are the following:[9]

- *The psychometric approach*: This method relies on testing to assess creative ability.
- *Cognitive approaches*: Two examples of these methods of investigation are: (1) computer-based investigation of full-scale scientific problem-solving, a process necessitating creative thought for attainment of an original solution; and (2) focus on unambiguous instances of creative processes, as embodied in the behavior and thinking of productive artists, scientists and other workers.
- *Personality and motivational approaches*: For example, in the psychoanalytic vein Sigmund Freud held that creative persons tend to sublimate much of their sexual energy into secondary pursuits such as writing, drawing, composing or investigating scientific puzzles. Freud noted the parallels between child-play, adult-daydreaming and creative activity of the artist. B. F. Skinner, who took a behaviorist perspective, believed that people engage in creative activity because of previous experience of reward or positive reinforcements. Teresa Amabile, a social psychologist, has drawn attention to the significance of intrinsic motivation in creative activity. Her findings indicate that creative solution to problems occur more often when people engage in an activity for its sheer pleasure than when they do so for possible external rewards.
- The *historimetric approach*: This perspective, a methodology for investigation, is associated with the psychologist Dean Keith Simonton. He formulates as clearly as possible classical questions concerning creativity. He then seeks quantitative data that can help resolve those issues.

Academic study of creativity in the future will probably move in an interdisciplinary direction, involving neurobiology,

---

[9] See Howard Gardner, *Creating Minds*, 19-27.

psychology, philosophy and sociology.   As this study proceeds, humankind will attain further understanding and appreciation of the creative process.   Thus, we will learn more effective ways to encourage people to be creative from their earliest years.

However, because the creative impulse is a spark of God's own creativity, complete understanding of the creative process will always elude us.   The activity of creative self-expression is ultimately grounded in the mystery of God and our life in God as mystery.

CHAPTER 9

Transcendence, Self-actualization,
Creative Expression

Transcendence refers to a reality that is beyond us. It denotes that which is within our reach, but outside our grasp. It pertains to the depth dimension of life. In the Christian tradition transcendence refers to God infinitely beyond us, yet so close as to abide within us and within each monad of the cosmos. Hence, God's transcendence is also immanent in that it permeates our being-becoming, together with that of all creation. For those persons who with faith, hope and love behold creation, the immanent transcendence of God shines through each creature.

Self-actualization refers to the process by which we attain the fullness of our unique personhood. While inclusive of all aspects of human growth – physical, emotional, cognitive, psychosexual, etc. – self-actualization, in the sense in which we have used it in this study, accentuates the spiritual dimension of development. Self-actualization begins when we come into existence, and it extends to our personal death wherein we become fully who God has called us to be. Yet, self-actualization means more than moving toward fullness, maturity or wholeness. From a Christian perspective it designates our transformation in God – that is, our becoming God by participation, even as we attain the pinnacle of our personal individuation.

In the process of becoming ourselves through encounter with God indwelling creation, a desire awakens in us to express in word, image, sound or movement something of that experience. Thus, *creative expression* stands in relation to transcendence and self-actualization.

A. Three Interconnected Realities

Our experience of transcendence, our process of self-actualization and our impulse toward creative self-expression are ultimately three aspects of one dynamic: our encounter in faith, hope and love with God as mystery.

On an existential level, transcendent encounter, self-actualization and creativity operate simultaneously. Moreover, each one continuously interacts with and influences the other two. We might envision the three realities as inter-penetrating globes of dynamic energy.

On the level of cognitive awareness, we cannot begin to grasp fully the complex interworkings of those three realities. At best, we but catch glimpses of the whole dynamic. In some situations we sense the coincidence of all three as they work together. In many instances we have the impression of moving sequentially from one to another. The possible directions of this movement are myriad. To cite a few examples: The path may proceed from encounter with transcendence to awareness of an unforeseen dimension of our personhood to a form of self-expression. Or the course could follow the reverse direction. A creative expression may serve as a catalyst for new self-understanding, which in turn opens us to unexpected encounter with God's immanent transcendence. Again, the way may begin with a gain in self-development that leads to encounter with the mystery of God and then to the need for creative expression of our experience.

Transcendence, self-actualization and creative expression constitute some of the components of authentic prayer, whether meditative or contemplative. We can therefore use the example of praying to see possible ways in which those three realities interact.

With respect to meditation, several combinations are conceivable; for instance:

- Having gained some insight into ourselves in relation to God by praying with a biblical text, we then express that experience in painting, dancing or singing.
- We sense God's presence to us in the process of expressing ourselves in an activity wherein we employ words, images or movements.
- A creative expression of ourselves in relation to God gives way to silent acquiescing to the divine presence.

Also with respect to contemplative prayer, the interplay between transcendence, self-actualization and creative expression can take several forms; for example:

- Our silence and wordlessness, full of loving presence, is itself an authentic form of creative expression of the encounter of our hidden self with the mystery of God.
- At the end of a time of silent loving attentiveness to God, we feel drawn to express the personal meaning of that prayer in some form: by writing in a journal, composing a poem, drawing a mandala, engaging in a dance, etc.
- We may have an intuition of immediate direct communion with God indwelling us as we engage in an activity such as doing a flower arrangement or a calligraphic painting.

In the above examples we have taken prayer as a point of reference. However, other scenarios are possible. One such scenario is involvement in artistic expression without any intent, at least at the outset, to do so for spiritual purposes. "Art for the sake of art" is a widespread attitude. Artistic endeavor can exist in its own right. Yet, even when no intended reference to the spiritual is present, any art that taps into the depths of life is capable of becoming a catalyst for meditation or contemplation. Such creative expression by its very nature opens the artist and the beholder to increasing consciousness of personal identity and transcendence.

B. Two Witnesses: Thomas Merton and Georgia O'Keeffe

We have explored in the preceding chapters the interplay of transcendence, self-actualization and creative expression. We move on now to flesh out that interrelationship in the lives and the works of Thomas Merton and Georgia O'Keeffe.

Several factors converge upon the choice of those two persons for this segment of our study:

(1) The two individuals are contemporaneous. Thomas Merton was born in Prades, France, on January 31, 1915. He died in Bangkok, Thailand, on December 10, 1968, after living twenty-seven years as a monk at Our Lady of Gethsemani Cistercian Abbey in Kentucky. Georgia O'Keeffe was born in Sun Prairie, Wisconsin, on November 15, 1887. She died on March 6, 1986, in

Albuquerque, New Mexico, having dedicated most of her life to the art of painting.

(2) Merton and O'Keeffe are also contemporary. They not only lived in approximately the same time frame, but also they did so in recent history. Their lives were situated within the broad historical currents of the twentieth century in which we ourselves have our roots.

(3) Although Thomas Merton and Georgia O'Keeffe are contemporaneous and contemporary, no correspondence passed between them. Moreover, no evidence exists of a significant influence of one upon the other. However, they did meet on at least one occasion.

From May 16-20, 1968, Merton was a guest at the Monastery of Christ in the Desert, Abiquiu, New Mexico. On May 18th he wrote in his journal that he had driven with a companion around the plaza in Abiquiu and had seen the adobe walls of O'Keeffe's house, together with her garden full of vegetation.[1] In another journal entry dated May 19th Merton mentioned that Georgia O'Keeffe had not come to the monastery for lunch that day, since she had to wait at her house in Abiquiu for a framer.[2] Those two journal entries suggest that a meeting with O'Keeffe eluded Merton during his May 1968 sojourn in Abiquiu.

Merton returned to New Mexico from September 11-16, 1968. In a letter dated September 17, 1968, to Brother Patrick Hart, Merton noted that while in Abiquiu he had stopped at the house of Georgia O'Keeffe.[3]

Quite possibly the visit with O'Keeffe came about in this manner: It was O'Keeffe's custom to invite to her home once a year the monks from the Monastery of Christ in the Desert. That year the monks arranged for the annual dinner to take place during Merton's visit, probably on September 11 or 12. Most likely, O'Keeffe had not heard of Thomas Merton prior to that occasion. Story has it that during the meal she turned several times to him and said: "Now, Father, what did you say your name is?"[4]

For his part, Merton did not leave any detailed account of his visit with Georgia O'Keeffe. However, in a journal entry dated

---

[1] See *The Other Side*, 106. See also, Thomas Merton, *Woods, Shore, Desert* (Santa Fe, NM: Museum of New Mexico Press, 1982), 30.

[2] See *The Other Side*, 107. See also, Thomas Merton, *Woods, Shore, Desert*, 36.

[3] See *Merton in Alaska*, 39.

[4] Brother Patrick Hart, OCSO, provided this information.

September 12, 1968, he recorded in a stream-of-consciousness style his impressions of the artist:

> Georgia O'Keeffe – a woman of extraordinary quality, [a]live, full of resiliency, awareness, quietness. One of the few people one ever finds (in this country at least) who quietly does everything right. Perfection of her house and patio on ghost ranch, low, hidden in desert rocks & vegetation, but with an extraordinary view of the mountains – especially the great majestic mesa, Pedernal.[5]

Merton seems to have been very eager to meet Georgia O'Keeffe. Why? Merton himself does not reveal his intent. Robert E. Daggy has offered this theory: Merton may have wanted to talk with O'Keeffe, at least in part, about his father, Owen Merton, who had been a painter. From approximately 1966 up to his death Merton had been trying to gather information about his father and to locate any of his father's surviving paintings. Owen had known Alfred Stieglitz, O'Keeffe's husband, and had most likely met Georgia. In 1920 Stieglitz had exhibited at his "291 Gallery" in New York City some of Owen's watercolors. Since Owen Merton often dragged his young son around with him, it is conceivable that Thomas Merton had a vague memory of having met O'Keeffe in his early years. Most likely, O'Keeffe did not know of or remember meeting Owen. Had Merton received from her any information about his father, he would have certainly recorded it.[6]

Another probable motivation behind Merton's desire to meet O'Keeffe was some sense of affinity with her. From his early years at Gethsemani Merton had an attraction to the solitary life. In fact, from 1965-1968 he lived as a hermit. O'Keeffe's solitary living and simplicity of lifestyle centered around her painting in the desert of New Mexico must have struck resonant chords in Merton. They held other values in common as well. For example, each of them was an artist. Each one found inspiration in the Zen approach to life. Each one had a special love of nature.

(4) A fourth reason for the choice of Thomas Merton and

---

[5] Thomas Merton, *The Other Side*, 174. See also *Woods, Shore, Desert*, 57. In a letter to Br. Patrick Hart, dated September 17, 1968, Merton asked that copies of *Conjectures, Chuang Tzu* and *Monks Pond* be sent to O'Keeffe (see *Merton in Alaska*, 39; also *The Other Side*, 173).
[6] Dr. Robert E. Daggy provided this information.

Georgia O'Keeffe is the fact that one is a man and the other a woman. That gender difference adds an element of richness to our study, especially as we look at the self-actualization of each of them.

(5) Another factor in the choice of Merton and O'Keeffe pertains to differences in their modes of creative expression. Thomas Merton's primary artistic involvements included being a writer, an essayist, a journalist, a poet.   Yet, he did some photography and at one point in his life a series of calligraphic abstract paintings that went on exhibit.   Georgia O'Keeffe was primarily a painter.   However, she did write a few short articles, a brief reflection on some of her drawings, a book about some of her paintings, and letters to significant people in her life.

With reference to the theory of multiple intelligences, we could say that both Merton and O'Keeffe show evidence of considerable linguistic intelligence and spatial intelligence.   Yet, judging by the work each produced over the course of a lifetime, linguistic intelligence dominated Merton's modes of expression, while spatial intelligence was the primary influence on O'Keeffe's choice of expressive media.

Linguistic communication occurs in the form of statements, questions, exclamations, commands.   Visual intelligence forms or presents a visual proposition.   Where verbal language is organized upon rules of grammar, visual thinking works from a set of perceptual strategies (e.g., ability to view an object from different angles; capacity to imagine movement or internal displacement among the components of a configuration; ability to think about those spatial relations in which the body position of the observer is an integral aspect of the question).   Vocabulary is essential to the exercise of linguistic intelligence, whereas with visual intelligence the working tool is an open-ended set of evolving visual forms that have a general meaning, yet are infinitely variable in nuance and application.

While grammar and syntax are pivotal in linguistic thinking, relationship and properties such as color and texture are key elements in visual process.   While linguistic intelligence relies on words, visual intelligence uses optical images.   Where linguistics incorporates context, visualization integrates negative spaces. Where linguistic thinking draws upon concepts and logic, visual intelligence looks to the interrelationship of light and shadow.[7]

(6) A sixth factor in the choice of Thomas Merton and Georgia O'Keeffe is their different paths to transcendence.

For the most part Merton's spiritual development transpired in the context of an organized religion – Roman Catholicism – and a specific religious order – the Cistercians of the Strict Observance, or the Trappists. Within that milieu came forth Merton's outpouring of books, poems, essays, letters and journals.

As for O'Keeffe, the paternal side of her family was Irish Catholic, while the maternal line was Episcopalian. O'Keeffe herself had a leaning toward Roman Catholicism, at least during certain phases of her life. However, she was never a practicing member of any organized religion or any religious institution. Although O'Keeffe was without official religious affiliation, her art indicates in-depth spiritual experience and creative expression of transcendence.

In a sense, Thomas Merton represents the contemplative as artist, while Georgia O'Keeffe embodies the artist as contemplative.

C. Perimeters of This Study

Before moving into a reflection upon the lives and the works of Thomas Merton and Georgia O'Keeffe, it is appropriate to state the principal boundaries of this study.

First, we focus on a specific theme: the interrelationship of transcendence, self-actualization and creative expression over the course of each one's life. Although we draw upon biographical data in presenting that theme, this study is not intended as a biography of either Merton or O'Keeffe.

Second, we look upon both Thomas Merton and Georgia O'Keeffe as unique individuals. Our study of each one stands on its own. Thus, our intent in this work is not to do a comparison of the two persons, although some obvious similarities and basic differences will surface in the course of our considerations.

Third, both Merton and O'Keeffe exhibited throughout their lives a remarkable degree of personal integrity. Yet, our purpose in studying them is not to imitate their lifestyles or choices. Rather,

---

[7] See Howard Gardner, *Frames of Mind: The Theory of Multiple Intelligences* (New York, NY: Basic Books, 1983), 73-98, 170-204; Betty Edwards, *Drawing on the Artist Within* (New York, NY: A Fireside Book, Simon & Schuster, Inc., 1987), 11-13.

pondering their fidelity to their spiritual journeys will encourage us to be true to our unique personhood and our specific path through life.

Fourth, our interest lies in creative expression as process, together with the relationship of creative expression to transcendence and self-actualization. Consequently, this study prescinds from undertaking a comprehensive critical evaluation of the works produced by either Thomas Merton or Georgia O'Keeffe.

Part II:

Thomas Merton

(1915-1968)

CHAPTER 10

Transcendent Experience

The themes of transcendence, self-actualization and creative process echo throughout the writings of Thomas Merton. To set the stage for our study of the interrelationship of those motifs in his personal life (chapters 13-18), we begin with a synthesis of his mature insight on each theme (chapters 10-12).

In this chapter we take up Merton's understanding of transcendence. We focus on the following points:

- the meaning of transcendent experience in general;
- the self in encounter with the numinous;
- the specifically Christian dimension of transcendent experience;
- the relationship of transcendent experience to contemplation.

A. The Meaning of the Phrase, "Transcendent Experience"

In a brief but significant essay entitled, "Transcendent Experience,"[1] Thomas Merton stressed these characteristics of encounter with the numinous:

- A person undergoes simultaneously a metaphysical or a mystical self-transcending and a meeting with the Transcendent – the Absolute Ground of Being or God – not so much as object but as Subject.
- The accent in that meeting is on interiority. From within God

---

[1] See "Transcendent Experience," in *ZBA*, 71-78.

and from within him/herself, the person encounters in some way the Absolute Ground of Being and the Godhead as infinite uncircumscribed freedom.

- Consequently, a radical change occurs in the person. S/he experiences both a loss of self and the emergence of a "self that is no-self."
- The "self that is no-self" is the transcendent self. It is metaphysically distinct from the "Self" of God, while yet being so identified with God by love and freedom that there appears to be but one Self.
- Encounter with the "self that is no-self" is an illumination of wisdom.
- Integral to transcendent experience are these personal awarenesses: realization of connectedness with all that exists; formulation of a sense of meaningfulness in life; discovery of a unique place in the whole of reality; ability to relate with all creation on the basis of love and identity.

To guard against any misinterpretation of those dimensions of transcendent experience, Merton proceeded in the same essay to name some things which encounter with the numinous is not. It is not synonymous with a peak experience. It is not a regressive immersion in nature, the cosmos or pure being, wherein a person basks in narcissistic tranquility or loss of identity. It is not identifiable with erotic experience. It goes beyond both aesthetic transcendence and moral transcendence, although it can combine with either of them.

Merton noted also that transcendent experience exceeds the ordinary level of authentic religious or spiritual experience in which the human mind and heart receive insight into the meaning of revelation, existence or life. In that situation the person not only remains to some degree aware of him/herself as subject, but also undergoes intensification and purification of subjective consciousness.

B. The Self in Transcendent Experience

In the essay, "Transcendent Experience," Thomas Merton addressed certain issues pertaining to the person in encounter with the numinous. In that respect, he took up the question: Who is it that engages in this experience? Or more precisely, what levels of personhood are most operative in it?

According to Merton, many people assume the ego-self to be the subject and the beneficiary of encounter with the numinous. Although the ego-self is capable of transcending itself, ego-transcendence is not equivalent to self-transcendence. In fact, ego-transcendence expands and intensifies ego-consciousness. Mimicking Descartes' saying, "I think, therefore I am," Merton described the ego-self coming to the conclusion, "I have experiences, therefore I am." Rather humorously, he illustrated that judgment by means of the image of an ego with sufficient elasticity stretching itself almost to vanishing point and then coming back to chalk up another experience on its score card.

Zen, Sufism and Christian mysticism share in common a radical and unconditional questioning of the ego that appears to be the subject of transcendent experience. Moreover, those traditions challenge the notion of experience itself as "experience." In that respect Merton highlighted these questions:

- Can we legitimately speak of experience when the subject is not a limited, well-defined, empirical self?
- Is it accurate to speak of consciousness when the subject is no longer aware of oneself as separate and unique?
- If the empirical ego has any degree of consciousness, is it not aware of itself as transcended, left behind, irrelevant, illusory and as the source of all ignorance?

In an earlier work Merton had pondered the same enigma. Referring to our union with God indwelling us, he wrote:

> Would you call this experience? I think you might say that this only becomes an experience in ... memory. Otherwise it seems wrong even to speak of it as something that happens. Because things that happen have to happen to some subject, and experiences have to be experienced by someone. But here the subject of any divided or limited or creature experience seems to have vanished. You are not you, you are fruition. If you like, you do not have an experience, you become Experience.[2]

---

[2] *New Seeds*, 283.

C. Christian Transcendent Experience

Having described transcendent experience in general,
Thomas Merton proceeded in the essay, "Transcendent Experience,"
to accentuate the specifically Christian dimension of encounter with
the numinous.

Authentic transcendent experience in all religious traditions
is a matter of superconsciousness rather than a regression into a
preconscious or an unconscious state. In the Christian tradition that
transcendent consciousness consists of putting on the mind of Christ
who emptied himself and who became obedient unto death (see Phil
2:5-11). The subject of Christian transcendent experience is never
solely the empirical ego. Still less is it the neurotic or the narcissistic
self. Rather, it is the person as found and actualized in Jesus. The
Christian mystic identifies with Jesus. S/he takes on the identity of
Christ to the point of oneness:

> I live now, no longer I,
>   but Christ lives in me" (Gal 2:20).

In Merton's view, the processes of self-emptying and self-
transcendence are for Christians a participation in the life, death and
resurrection of Jesus. The processes of dying to self and rising in
Jesus define the specifically Christian dimension of transformation
of consciousness.   As the Christian undergoes that kenotic
transformation, every dimension of his/her personhood eventually
becomes transparent with the light and love of God.

In a complementary vein Merton described Christian
transcendent experience as a knowing and a seeing in the Spirit.
Drawing upon Pauline theology, he referred to the Spirit as one who
fathoms everything, even the abyss of God and as one who
understands the thoughts of God (see 1 Cor 2). Merton portrayed the
Spirit given to us in Jesus as a transcendent superconsciousness of
God and of the Father.

Merton acknowledged a definite place for an I-Thou
relationship between the Christian and God.   For instance, by
practicing moral discipline and by participating in liturgical worship,
a beginner on the spiritual journey finds personal identity,
encouragement and direction. However, Merton insisted that those
who desire to progress spiritually have to relax their grip on their

notions of what constitutes the goal of the spiritual life and who it is
that will attain it.

D. Christian Contemplation

Ordinarily, Thomas Merton spoke of Christian transcendent
experience as contemplation. Throughout his writings we find
innumerable descriptions of contemplation. For example: It consists
of an experiential awareness of the transcendent and inexpressible
God. It awakens us to the Real within all reality. In contemplation
we become fully alive to our existential depths which open out into
the mystery of God. Contemplation connects us with the infinite
Being who is the root and the ground of our being. It enables us to
be an "I am" in God the I AM.[3]

Merton identified three possible beginnings of
contemplation:[4]

(1) Some people experience the inception of contemplation
in the form of a sudden unexpected emptying of the soul in which
images, concepts, words vanish. Freedom and clarity permeate these
persons, as they embrace the wonder, depth, obviousness, yet
emptiness and incomprehensibility of God.

(2) Other people pass through over a considerable period of
time a desert of aridity, wherein they see, feel, understand nothing
and suffer interior pain and anxiety. Nonetheless, these persons find
that the dryness and darkness hold for them increasing peace,
stability and intuition of the divine presence.

(3) Still other people find their will resting in a profound,
luminous and absorbing experience of love, while their imagination,
intellect and senses remain empty. God seems mysteriously hidden
in a cloud, yet so close as to be within them, outside them and all
around them.

Although Merton referred to those beginnings of
contemplation primarily in terms of experiences of three groups of
people, he recognized that any one person could experience at the
inception of contemplation something of all three approaches.
Moreover, he noted that in all those beginnings of transcendent
experience, we are still far from full participation in divine life. Our
sense of being a separate self and our awareness of distance from

---

[3] See *New Seeds*, 2-13.
[4] See *New Seeds*, 275-289.

God are two indications that we have a long way to go. The manner in which we actually move forward astonishes us. We do not go anywhere, yet we find ourselves one day there. The separate entity that we were seems to have vanished. God's love and our love become one love loving in freedom. All that appears to remain is God living in God.[5] However, on an ontological level the creature remains distinct from the Creator, and retains individual identity.

Paradoxically, our transcendent self is hidden in what we judge to be nothingness and void. We perceive our free and personal reality only by entering into a darkness that conceals both the mystery of our identity and the mystery of God. The discovery in contemplation of our transcendent self and of God within us entails a process of letting go the familiar and launching into the unknown. The unfolding of our contemplative path brings forth purgation and dread,[6] as well as joy and peace.

Plumbing those depths of our transcendent self which open out into the infinite mystery of God requires solitude of heart, together with a measure of external aloneness suitable to our vocational way of life. It requires wrestling with our poverty of spirit. Divine light illuminates our way. Yet, according to our perception that light itself is a dark night. As God gradually strips us of our false self, we rise up a new creature, a transformed person in Christ Jesus. Then it becomes normal and natural for us:

> to see ... without seeing, to possess clarity in darkness, to have pure certitude without any shred of discursive evidence, to be filled with an experience that transcends experience and to enter with serene confidence into depths that leave us utterly inarticulate.[7]

In Thomas Merton's view, contemplation can indeed be one prayer form among other ways of praying. As such, it constitutes the summit of a Christian life of prayer. However, contemplation, or transcendent experience, is more than a way of encountering God during a period of time specifically designated for solitary prayer. Contemplation is integral to life and inseparable from daily

---

[5] See *New Seeds*, 282-285.
[6] See, for example, *Contemplative Prayer*, 96-102; *New Seeds*, 233-238.
[7] *New Seeds*, 226-227.

activities. It is ultimately the fullness of a thoroughly integrated life.[8]   Thus, the invitation to contemplation, or transcendent experience, is integral to the calling to be Christian.

---

[8] See "Poetry and Contemplation: A Reappraisal," in *Literary Essays*, 338-339.

CHAPTER 11

The Secret of Identity

Who am I? Who am I to become? What gives meaning to my existence? Those questions both blessed and plagued Thomas Merton for almost his entire life.

Merton came to see that the secret of his identity lay hidden in God's merciful love. He found his quest for self-identity to be a doorway to the transcendent. He discovered his work of self-actualization to be an opening to encounter with God. In turn, his communion with God in mystery helped intensify his self-development.

That interrelatedness of transcendent experience and self-actualization is evident in a poignant prayer of Merton. He began that prayer with recognition that God loving him in God's own self had led God to call him forth out of God's self. Merton went on to confess that to him God's "infinite light is darkness" and God's "immensity is as the void." Moreover, Merton acknowledged that if God did not continue "to hold him to [God's self] in the Heart of [the] only begotten Son," Merton would be "lost in this darkness" and "would fall away ... into this void."[1]

Elsewhere, Merton related his identity and his purpose in life to God's word:

> What am I? I am myself a word spoken by God.
> Can God speak a word that does not have any meaning?[2]

---

[1] See *Thoughts in Solitude*, 69. See also *New Seeds*, 29-46.
[2] *Contemplative Prayer,* 68.

But how does God call forth by love a human being out of God's own self? In what sense can a person be a word uttered by God? In this chapter we explore Merton's mature thought on the subject of self-actualization. We focus on these aspects of the issue:

- person as a new spiritual creation;
- self-realization in the Spirit;
- the inner self and the outer self;
- nothingness as a passageway into God.

A. The Human Person: A New Spiritual Creation

On the question of humankind's original relationship with God, Thomas Merton subscribed to the prevailing theological opinion of his day. According to that perspective, God and humankind existed in an initial state of harmonious unity. The human person did not experience in the beginning inner division, self-alienation or disconnectedness from either God or creation. However, in the course of history humankind rejected God. That turning away from God constituted the Fall from Grace or from Original Justification. Yet, God, being infinitely merciful, offered humans the possibility of recovery of that original union by means of redemption in Christ Jesus.[3]

For Merton, it is especially the Spirit who effects our rebirth in Christ. The Spirit unites our hearts with God's own heart, thereby penetrating our inmost depths. The Spirit indwells us, seeking to call forth from within us a new world and a new spiritual creation. With our collaboration, the Spirit creates for us a transformed identity by becoming our identity.[4]

In Merton's thought, spiritual regeneration is not a single event but a continuous process of interior renewal. As the Spirit's mysterious presence becomes increasingly active within us, we grow in our identity as a new spiritual creation. That developmental process implies for us gradual purification and transformation, ongoing death and resurrection. That inner revolution requires

---

[3] I personally subscribe to a different theology of the relationship between God and creation, particularly in regard to the issue referred to as "original justification" and "original sin." In *Part I* of this study, I proceeded from a relational and evolutionary perspective with regard to the covenant between God and creation.

[4] See, for example, "Theology of Creativity," in *Literary Essays*, 368; "Rebirth and the New Man in Christianity," in *Love and Living*, 192-202.

ultimately transcendence of cultural norms and attitudes, of familiar religious practices, of even our very self.

The Spirit who makes us a new creation is the Spirit of Christ. Thus, in some contexts Merton described the identity that we receive through spiritual rebirth as a participation in the identity of Jesus. Through our spiritual regeneration Christ himself becomes our transformed and hidden self. He who is other than us identifies himself so perfectly with us that we attain in him the fullness of our unique personhood.[5]

Merton believed that the call to spiritual rebirth and transformed identity is irresistible. The Spirit's desire to rebirth us in Christ coincides with "the obscure but insistent demand" of our human nature "to transcend itself in the freedom of a fully integrated, autonomous, personal identity."[6] A yearning for newness, renewal and liberation of creative power is innate to our humanity. We desire to activate within us an interior energy that will revolutionize our lives. Yet, we realize intuitively that this transformation which we seek is a recovery of what is deepest, most original, most unique in our personhood.[7]

Merton identified love as the creative energy or force capable of effecting that interior change. God is love. God's love calls forth a person into existence out of God's own self. Thus, God creates humankind in the divine image. Love becomes our identity, the reason for our existence and the source of our creativity. Merton gave personal testimony to that experience in this passage:

> To say that I am made in the image of God is to say that love is the reason for my existence, for God is love.... Love is my true identity. Selflessness is my true self. Love is my true character. Love is my name.[8]

B. Creative Self-realization in the Spirit

Thomas Merton's understanding of the Christian concept of personhood implies full recovery of our likeness to God in Christ by the activity of his Spirit. We dispose ourselves to receive that

---

[5] See, for example, *Honorable Reader*, 98; *Bread in the Wilderness*, 76.

[6] "Rebirth and the New Man in Christianity," in *Love and Living*, 194.

[7] See "Rebirth and the New Man in Christianity," in *Love and Living*, 196.

[8] *New Seeds*, 60.

renewed identity by openness to the divine life residing within us, by faith in Jesus and by love for him. That activity on our part prepares the way for the Spirit to seize and to transform our humanity.[9]

We work together with God in the process of our spiritual rebirth. We bring to the endeavor a delicate balance of receptivity to God's initiative and active collaboration with the Spirit's work. We labor with God in the creation of our identity, life and destiny.[10] We cannot know beforehand the precise way or the specific outcome of this endeavor. The process entails for us hope, joy, celebration, together with sacrifice, anguish, risk. It demands of us continuous attentiveness to reality and great fidelity to God's elusive presence in each new situation. It calls for commitment to a lifetime work of self-discovery, self-development and self-actualization in the Spirit.[11]

Furthermore, our personal collaboration with God interconnects with the creative activity of other people around us who are also questing for fullness of life in God. Together we form a community of love, and participate in the creative work of living in our world. We assist each other in actualizing our individual destinies and in generating a new world for those who come after us. That activity is a prolongation of God's own creative work.[12]

C. The Inner Self and the Outer Self

In describing the process of Christian self-actualization, Thomas Merton contrasted two aspects of the human person: the inner self and the outer self.

Merton once likened recovery of the inner self to plumbing the depths of the sea in order to draw up from the bottom a precious jewel out of the nondescript, trivial, sordid and ephemeral.[13]

Throughout his writings Merton used a variety of expressions which are synonymous with the phrase, "inner self"; for example: the inmost center of our spirit; the real self, the deep self, the hidden person, the true self, the true identity, the true personality, the transcendent self. Similarly, he employed numerous equivalent

---

[9] See "The Good News of the Nativity," in *Love and Living*, 226.
[10] See *New Seeds*, 33.
[11] See "Christian Humanism," in *Love and Living*, 140-141; also *Dancing in the Water*, 67, 334.
[12] See "The Universe as Epiphany," in *Love and Living*, 177-179.
[13] See *New Seeds*, 38.

phrases to denote the outer self; for instance: the superficial self, the external self, the mask, the exterior self, the routine self, the outward and false self, the imaginary self, the illusory self, the finite self, the empty self.

However, Merton's discussion in *New Seeds of Contemplation* of the terms *person* and *ego* conveys perhaps best his basic understanding of those two aspects of human identity.[14] He designated *person* as the spiritual and hidden self that is united to God. He described the *ego* as the exterior, empirical self, the psychological individuality that forms a kind of mask for the inner hidden self. In his explanation Merton noted these points:

- The outward self's biography and its existence end in death. The inmost self has neither a biography nor an end.
- The outer self is not identical with the body, nor is the inner self identical with the soul. The inner self is not merely a part of us. It is our whole reality. The outward self is a self-constructed illusion.
- Both body and soul subsist in our real self, the person that we are. Our ego has at its disposal our body and part of our soul, because as a consequence of the Fall from original justification the ego has taken over certain functions of the inner self.

In interjecting the notion of Fall, Merton connected the concepts of person and ego to the theme of Paradise Lost and Paradise to be Regained. Returning to God and to our true identity requires that we begin from where we actually are; that is, in the alienated condition of our ego-self.

Merton's overall view of the relationship of the outer self to God is threefold.

(1) At times he designated the exterior self as the sinful aspect of ourselves. It is our condition of disobedience to God.

(2) In other contexts Merton viewed the outward self in a somewhat neutral fashion. He saw it as a mode of being which is necessary for functioning in our world as it is. Christ blesses the outer self in that sense with merciful love. God respects the ego-self, and allows it to carry out the function which the inner self cannot yet assume on its own. However, Merton offered a word of caution. While we must act from our outer self in daily life, we need to

---

[14] See *New Seeds*, 279-280.

remember that we are not entirely what we appear to be. Moreover, the self that we seem to be will vanish eventually into nothingness.

(3) From yet another perspective Merton recognized the outward self as a transparent medium in which God's presence manifests itself in our world. The mask that we wear thus becomes a disguise not only for our inner self, but also for God wandering as a pilgrim in our midst. By virtue of the Incarnation the face of Christ shines mysteriously through each and every person.[15]

D. Passing Through Our Center of Nothingness into God

According to Thomas Merton, our true self is hidden in obscurity and nothingness at the center of our being where we remain in direct dependence upon God's merciful love.[16] At that depth God and the self are one, yet distinct. We recover our true self by dwindling down to a vanishing point and becoming absorbed in God through that center of nothingness.[17] That point of nothingness Merton named *le point vierge*.[18] There the divine presence indwells us, like a pure diamond ablaze with heavenly light.

Merton emphasized that letting go the external self is not only an interior movement, but also an external going forth. We can interiorly pass through the center of our nothingness into God only by simultaneously passing out of ourselves in selfless love of other people.[19] Thus, practicing love of God, people, creation and self is the milieu wherein we die to the false self and rise anew in Christ Jesus who becomes our true identity.

It is in the events and relationships of our daily life that we pass through the center of our nothingness and recover our inner self in God. Yet, dying to self is no easy matter. It involves compunction: that is, accepting responsibility for our failures to love and repenting our infidelity. It means undergoing dread: that profound, confused, metaphysical realization of basic antagonism between the self and God.[20] The process of abandoning attachment to our external self and surrendering to Christ is a purification, a

---

[15] See *New Seeds*, 295-296.
[16] See *Contemplative Prayer*, 70.
[17] See *New Seeds*, 182.
[18] See *Conjectures*, 131, 151, 158.
[19] See, for example, *New Seeds*, 64.
[20] See *Contemplative Prayer*, 97.

crucifixion, a dark night, but one filled with the hope of resurrection and transforming union with God. Recovery of the inner self is a participation in the Paschal Mystery of Jesus. We die to ourselves as we rise transformed in God. The outer self passes away as the inner self is renewed in the Spirit.

The passage through ourselves into God indwelling us is necessary whether we view the external self as the sinful aspect of our personhood, as a mode of adaptation to our environment or as an instrument of God's transparency in the world. In the case of the sinful dimension of ourselves, attachment to the false self impedes our growth. When the external self is understood in the sense of effective coping in daily life, that world as we know it is passing away and so too is the self which encounters it. From the perspective of God transparent in us, our outer observable self does not and cannot contain the fullness of God. God remains more and beyond. Therefore, we have to keep straining forward to the One who is still to come. On that pilgrimage we must penetrate ever more deeply the unknown in our own personhood and the unknown in God.

CHAPTER 12

Liberation of Creative Power

Thomas Merton identified the source of creativity as a divine love too great for us to perceive or to understand. God's love creates us and our world. As we increasingly abandon ourselves to the creative power of love, we in turn become empowered to be creative. According to Merton, therefore, human creativity means more than original and spontaneous self-expression. It exceeds exposition of the hidden dynamism of historical events. It surpasses mere productivity. It differs from an artist's fashioning of works as a monument to him/herself. Human creativity is a participation in and an extension of God's own creativity.[1]

In this chapter we focus on Merton's insight into the creative process. We address these two areas:

- Merton's view of the specifically Christian dimension of creativity;
- certain qualities which converged to form for Merton a climate of creative love.

A. The Creativity of the Christian

In Thomas Merton's theological framework, the main exercise of human creativity before the Fall consisted in letting God live and act with perfect freedom within each person. By disobedience to God we lost touch with our true identity and our full creative potential. Restoration of our creativity is then an aspect of the recovery of our likeness to God in Christ through rebirth by the

---

[1] See "Theology of Creativity," in *Literary Essays*, 358-368; also *Dancing in the Water*, 41.

Spirit.[2]

Merton related the specifically Christian dimension of human creativity to our participation in the Passover of Jesus. The Spirit of Jesus reforms us in his likeness, raising us from death to life in Jesus. The Spirit accomplishes that work by unleashing the creative energy of God's love within us and by enflaming us with generative love in response. Our creativity contributes to God's work of recapitulating all creation in Jesus (Eph 1:9-10) and of reconciling all in Christ (Col 1:9-29). The creativity of the Christian has an eschatological dimension in that it reaches out to the ends of time and the limits of the cosmos.

Merton insisted that the creative Christian is not an elite disciple of Jesus. Rather, creative work is integral to the calling of every Christian. Each person needs to discern in the light of his/her vocation how to contribute to the restoration of all creation in Christ. Each one exercises creativity both in the development of his/her unique personhood and in the building up of the Body of Christ in this world. Moreover, that creative collaboration with God is the responsibility not only of each individual Christian, but also of the Church as a whole.

B. The Climate of Creative Love

Liberation of the creative power of love within us is a gift of the Spirit. Yet, certain qualities, attitudes or actions on our part enable us to be receptive to divine creativity and to co-create with God.

We synthesize now eight primary factors that converged to constitute for Thomas Merton a climate conducive to the exercise of creative love.[3] They are:

- experience,
- personal crisis,
- freedom of spirit,
- spontaneity,
- symbol,
- silence,

---

[2] The principal source for the material in this section, unless otherwise indicated, is "Theology of Creativity," in *Literary Essays*, 368-370.

[3] On the importance of living in a climate of creative love, see "The Climate of Mercy," in *Love and Living*, 203-219.

- faith,
- interactiveness.

We ponder Merton's insight on those themes only as they relate to the issue of creative process.

(1) Experience

Over the years Thomas Merton developed a trust in profound direct experience as the best foundation for self-expression.[4]

Merton once advised a young man that writing should follow upon thorough learning of what one desires to say. Moreover, Merton cautioned the youth against writing with the intent of meeting other people's expectations. He counseled the young man to express what was deepest in his heart and what he knew by instinct to be also deepest in the hearts of his prospective readers. He thus encouraged this youth to attempt in his writing to shed light on pressing issues that touched the lives of ordinary people.[5]

In his own work Merton tried to be faithful to those basic principles. He experienced God as mystery and perceived the transcendent depths of all creation. He knew the immanent transcendent God as one who had so loved us as to become flesh in Christ Jesus. As Merton responded with love for God and creation, a need arose within him to express and to share something of his experience. Thus, his contemplation became the wellspring of his creative process. His autobiographical writings represent reflections upon his faith journey. His books and essays sprang from whatever aspect of Christian life captivated his attention at a given time. His best writing flowed from conscientious study and careful faith reflection brought to bear upon lived experience.

Particularly in his comments on poetry we catch glimpses of how central experience was in Merton's creative process. He declared himself and other poets to be children of the Unknown.[6] He asserted that poets have a responsibility to plumb the intimate, ontological sources of life which the human mind cannot apprehend clearly by way of concepts, but which it can penetrate by means of

---

[4] See, for example, *Road to Joy*, 338.
[5] See *Road to Joy*, 336.
[6] See "Message to Poets," in *Literary Essays*, 374.

intuition.[7] He declared the inner experience that a poem expresses to be more important to him than the poem itself.[8] His poetic experience was grounded in identification with a person or a thing. He believed that the poet becomes the conscious expression of the creature who moves him/her. In that vein he described the poet as feeling for, singing for, being aware for the subject of inspiration.[9]

Approximately a year and a half before his death, Merton described himself as having been summoned to explore a desert region of the human heart beyond the reach of all explanations. In that solitary place he had learned anew that only experience counts.[10]

(2) Personal Crisis

In the context of his relationship with God, Thomas Merton struggled during certain periods of his life to reconcile what appeared to him as dichotomies; for example: being a monk and a writer; detachment from the world and compassion for the world; contemplating God and composing poetry; living in community and desiring a solitary life.

In a journal entry Merton reflected upon the dynamics of conflict resolution.[11] He noted that personal crisis occurs when we become aware of seemingly irreconcilable opposites within us. When the tension between the polarities reaches sufficient intensity, we feel that we cannot hold ourselves together and will fall apart. Merton identified two possible avenues of resolution for that predicament. On the one hand, we could opt for various pathological resolutions. For example, we could identify with one component of the opposites and project upon the world or other people what we consider the unacceptable quality. On the other hand, we can choose the direction of accepting the inner conflict and of working toward an integration of the two opposites into a higher unity. With the latter approach, a personal crisis becomes a formidable source of creative and salutary energy, enabling an individual to become a more developed and integrated person. Merton himself tried to follow that course in resolving his apparently irreconcilable

---

[7] See "The True Legendary Sound: The Poetry and Criticism of Edwin Muir," *Literary Essays*, 30.
[8] See *Road to Joy*, 90.
[9] See *MZM*, 246.
[10] See *Hidden Ground of Love*, 156.
[11] See *Conjectures*, 208-209, and *Dancing in the Water*, 78-79.

opposites. In so doing, both his experience of conflicts and his effort
to resolve them became powerful catalysts for untold creative energy
and diverse forms of creative expression.

(3) Freedom of Spirit

Thomas Merton believed that inner freedom is essential for
the functioning of the creative process.[12]
Responding in 1965 to questions from readers of a certain
magazine, Merton noted that in the society of his time the artist had
inherited the combined functions of hermit, pilgrim, prophet, priest,
shaman, sorcerer, soothsayer, alchemist and bonze. He warned
artists to avoid falling into the trap of identifying with any role
which society has set in advance for them. To drive home his point,
Merton shared a personal anecdote. He had noticed how for almost
twenty years some readers had been insisting that he conform to the
idea of him that they concocted on reading his autobiography, *The
Seven Storey Mountain.* Yet, the same people who demanded that he
remain forever the superficially pious, rather rigid, and somewhat
narrow-minded monk of the 1940's were simultaneously circulating
a rumor that he had left his monastery. Instead of paying attention to
those demands and rumors, Merton had chosen to pursue his own
course over the years. He had simply lived his contemplative life at
Gethsemani and developed in his own way, without consulting the
public about it.

In Merton's thought authentic artistic freedom differs from
sheer willfulness or arbitrary posturing. Freedom pertains to the
choice of work and not to the choice of playing a role determined by
other people for their own reasons. It manifests itself in the artist's
perception of veritable possibilities that s/he explores with courage
and actualizes with perseverance. Yet, the question remains: How
does an artist know whether a creation has come forth from true
freedom or whether it panders to societal expectations? Merton's
response is that the work itself bears witness to the spirit of the artist.
The process of self-expression enables the artist to develop personal
freedom and to form artistic conscience. The artist can discern
whether the work was done freely by beholding the final outcome.

---

[12] The source for material in this sub-section is "Answers on Art and Freedom," in *Literary
Essays,* 378-380; see also *New Seeds,* 191-213.

(4) Spontaneity

In Thomas Merton's understanding, spontaneity accentuates immediacy of our response to an encounter. We honor that response, no matter how unconscious, irrational, foolish or unacceptable it appears at first glance. Merton distinguished spontaneity from both haste and knee-jerk reactiveness. Desire for quick results, speed in trying to attain them and inability to take the time necessary to complete a work squelch spontaneity.

Merton insisted that establishing an intellectual point and then devising a form to embody it kills creative expression. Form, he believed, should emerge spontaneously out of a person's experience. While he recognized writing disciplined prose or qualitative poetry as worthwhile, Merton valued that activity as a secondary concern in comparison to the duty of first writing nonsense. He advocated learning the knack of free association. He encouraged artists to let what is hidden in their depths burst out. He emphasized the importance of expanding imaginative thought over condensing it prematurely. He spoke of the need to release the face sweating under the mask and to let it sweat out in the open on occasion, without expecting to win a prize for beauty or meaning. He taught that from the spontaneity of that activity writers could accumulate fresh material which might itself suggest new forms. While that process might require considerable rewriting and the discarding of much initial writing, in the end it offered the possibility of original work, free of ego obsessions and imitation of other people.[13]

Merton's advice to other artists reflected his personal experience of creativity. Describing to friends how he composed poetry, for instance, he wrote of just getting an idea, putting it down, adding to it, deleting what seems useless, and trying to end up with a poem.[14] He observed in a journal entry how hopeless it was for him to do prose writing without being fired up by the heat of some new ideas.[15] Nonetheless, once Merton got down on paper his initial expression, he sought accuracy and clarity by means of extensive revision, rewriting and editing.

On one occasion Merton compared the development of

---

[13] See "Why Alienation Is for Everybody," in *Literary Essays*, 382-383; *Dancing in the Water*, 64.
[14] See *Road to Joy*, 90.
[15] See *Entering the Silence*, 278-279, and *Sign of Jonas*, 157.

poetic logic (which is the logic of language or experience itself) to the growth of a living organism. Each spreads out toward what it loves, and is heliotropic. Specifically, he likened the crafting of a creative expression to a tree growing out into a unique organic shape. Both forms are free rather than ideal, individual instead of typical.[16] With those analogies Merton advocated letting go the effort to control the outcome and going with the inner flow of the creative process.

Merton's preference for spontaneity is evident also in his attraction to Zen. He wrote certain poems in Zen style. During the 1960's he did a series of Zen calligraphic drawings. Experience and artistic expression are one in Zen. Experience consists of an emptiness, an original suchness, an intuition of existence that is beyond the reach of the false and illusory self. The work of a Zen artist springs out of this emptiness and with a few brush strokes appears on paper.[17]

(5) Symbol

According to Thomas Merton, the fundamental task of artists is not photographic realism, material representation or literal portrayal. Rather, it is expression of personal experience in a fresh and new light. It is intimation of hidden spiritual realities. Consequently, symbolism has a prominent role in creative expression.[18]

Merton understood symbol as a manifestation of union between God, humankind and creation in a vibrant and sacred synthesis. A symbol contains an innate structure that in some way calls forth in the beholder heightened awareness of the meaning of life and reality. Merton believed that the human person as a sacred being has an inherent need for symbols. Our capacity to perceive the known and the unknown, the visible and the invisible as a meaningful unity is conditional upon the creative vitality of our symbols.

Merton saw the responsibility of artists as twofold:

---

[16] See *Secular Journal*, 24.
[17] See "Theology of Creativity," in *Literary Essays*, 362-365; *MZM*, 3-44; 215-288.
[18] The primary sources for this section, unless otherwise indicated, are "Symbolism: Communication or Communion?" in *Love and Living*, 54-79; "Poetry, Symbolism and Typology," in *Literary Essays*, 327-337; "Sacred Art and the Spiritual Life" and "Absurdity in Sacred Decoration," in *Disputed Questions*, 151-164, 264-273; *Contemplative Prayer*, 83-86.

(a) plumbing primarily by means of intuition the intimate or
ontological sources of life; and (b) enabling other people access to
those depths through symbolic and imaginative celebration of
them.[19] By drawing us into encounter with the mysterious origin of
energy, meaning, creativity, love and truth, a symbol intensifies and
enhances our life.

Yet, symbols have a double power. When they are vibrant
and generative, they direct human action toward goodness and
beauty. When they are pathogenic and depraved, they lead in the
direction of evil and destruction. Merton lamented the loss of the
sense of symbol in the world of his time. He interpreted that loss as
symptomatic of spiritual decay. He identified contemplatives and
artists as those most aware of that disastrous situation.

(6) Silence

For Thomas Merton silence is a mediator between
transcendent experience and creative expression.

Merton described God's speech as so silent that we judge it
to be no-speech and God's listening as so quiet that we conclude it to
be no-hearing. Yet, in God's silence all words are spoken and heard
in the one Word, Christ Jesus. That one Word, the Father's utterance
of love, remains the ground of all being and all history. We listen to
that Word in the quietness and solitude of an open heart. Words rise
up sometimes out of our encounter with God in silence. The truth
embodied in language then serves to plunge us deeper into God's
silence.[20]

Merton taught that silence itself is creative. It helps us
gather up the dissipated energies of a broken existence. It enables us
to discover a sense of purpose, which arises from a coincidence of
our deepest longings and God's cherished desire for us. Silence
reveals to us the mystery of God abiding within the numinous depths
of our personhood as well as within all creation. It opens to us those
solitary interior depths wherein we find ourselves united to all
creation in Christ Jesus.[21]

In Merton's view, the rhythm of life takes shape in silence.
That rhythm surfaces when expression necessitates it, then flows

---

[19] See "The True Legendary Sound: The Poetry and Criticism of Edwin Muir," in *Literary Essays*, 30.
[20] See "Love and Solitude," in *Love and Living*, 18-21; *Thoughts in Solitude*, 84.
[21] See "Creative Silence," in *Love and Living*, 38-45; *Thoughts in Solitude,* 67-70, 86.

back into more profound silence, only to reappear in a finished form, after which it then fades away into the silence of eternity.[22]

Merton made frequent reference to the relationship between silence and words. He described silence as the mother of human speech.[23] We experience reality directly (face to face) and immediately (without any medium) in silence. Out of the silence emerge words to express that encounter. Yet, Merton recognized an interplay between silence and language. We would be incapable of experience in silence if language had not brought us to the brink of it.[24] Poets in particular embodied for Merton the relationship between silence and words. He referred to them as "ministers of silence."[25]

(7) Faith

In Thomas Merton's view, Christian faith is more than belief in a set of doctrines or a system of truths. Above all, it means believing in the person of Jesus.

Faith puts us in touch with our inmost spiritual depths. It opens up to us the Unknown who is God indwelling us, together with our unknown transcendent self that is one with God. Moreover, faith renders depth to our experience and perception by incorporating the unknown and the unconscious into our everyday life. Faith awakens our consciousness to the interpenetration of the unknown and the known, as it integrates them into a living whole.[26]

Faith lets us see that which we seek to express creatively in form. Faith sheds the light that we labor to embody in word, image, sound and movement.

(8) Interactiveness

Creative process entails four basic constituents of interaction on the part of the artist. They are: (a) the subject of inspiration, (b) the expression taking shape, (c) other persons who behold the finished form, (d) the society of which the artist is a member.

Encounter between the artist and a subject of inspiration

---

[22] See *No Man Is an Island*, 261.
[23] See *No Man Is an Island*, 258.
[24] See *Thoughts in Solitude*, 110-111.
[25] See "Message to Poets," in *Literary Essays*, 374.
[26] See *New Seeds*, 135-139.

constitutes experience. As we have seen above, Thomas Merton situated experience at the heart of creative process.

Interactiveness between the artist and the artistic creation is evident in Merton's creative endeavors. For instance, he observed that the purpose of a poem eludes the poet until the poem exists, just as the meaning of an event is discovered only in the actual living of it.[27] In other words, the poem that emerges out of the poet's silence becomes for him/her a symbol of the original experience, while at the same time drawing the poet into new depths of that encounter. Merton interacted with his own written word also by means of his constant revision. He sought to improve his composition and to clarify his message by finding a more precise term, exact phrase or clear image, frequently even after publication.[28]

Merton's interaction with readers of his works affected his creative process. A poet's or a writer's renewed way of seeing and hearing gives birth to a new sound, music and structure expressed in living line and generative association. The written word then communicates to perceptive readers a novel start and a new creation. Therein they discover for themselves a fresh beginning in hope, life, imagination.[29] Yet, the response of readers can creatively renew the artist. To a college student who liked his poetry, Merton expressed how grateful he was for having readers who were attuned to his message. He observed that he did not write in a void and that he delighted in reaching the hearts of readers.[30] His poem, *The Originators*,[31] describes the mutual influence of author and readers upon each other. Merton had a profound sense of spiritual bondedness with many readers. He recognized that the same Spirit indwelling both him and them enabled him to speak to those people with the voice of their own inmost self.[32]

Finally, Merton had definite ideas on the interaction of artists and their society. He situated artists in a marginal position vis-à-vis their society. From that vantage point they intuitively key into cultural shifts and transmutations. There they fulfill their prophetic responsibility of seeing reality and of voicing their awarenesses. They protest against destruction and violence in

---

[27] See "Message to Poets," in *Literary Essays*, 371.

[28] See the introduction by Robert E. Daggy to *Honorable Reader*, 3-6.

[29] See "Louis Zukofsky – The Paradise Ear," in *Literary Essays*, 128.

[30] See *Road to Joy*, 361.

[31] See *Collected Poems*, 613.

[32] See, for example, "Preface to the Japanese Edition of *The Seven Storey Mountain*, August 1963," in *Honorable Reader*, 67.

society, while simultaneously proclaiming the possibility for rebirth in the moment at hand. They accomplish that task not by setting out to be didactic, but rather by operating in fidelity to their experience. Merton insisted that artists are not to be in bondage to established political systems and cultural structures. In the exercise of creativity within society they must depend instead upon their innate child-like innocence.[33] Merton personally lived by those convictions. From his marginal stance as a monk he provided prophetic leadership in addressing the burning issues of his time, especially with regard to spiritual growth, monastic renewal, justice, peace and ecumenism.

---

[33] See "Message to Poets," in *Literary Essays*, 371-374.

CHAPTER 13

Born Under the Sign of the Water Bearer

Our Passover with Jesus to the Father consists of both a geographical journey and an inner pilgrimage. The path that we carve out in time and space as we walk through life comprises our geographical journey. The way that we traverse to God indwelling us constitutes our interior pilgrimage. Thomas Merton once described the geographical journey as the symbolic enactment of the inner pilgrimage and the inner pilgrimage as the interpolation of the meanings and signs of the outer journey.[1] The inner and outer dimensions of a person's passover are inseparably connected. The interior pilgrimage and the exterior journey are two faces of one reality: life hidden with Christ in God. Each way opens out into transcendence. Each path confronts us with the mystery of God and of our identity in God, together with the calling to collaborate creatively in God's work.

Having reviewed Merton's mature understanding of transcendence, self-actualization and creative expression, we turn our attention now to the interrelationship of those realities in his personal life. To flesh out our study, we draw primarily upon those writings of Merton which are autobiographical in nature.

During childhood and adolescence Merton had only sporadic, rather superficial exposure to institutional religion. Throughout that period he showed virtually no interest in committing himself to spiritual practices. Nonetheless, those years are integral to his pilgrimage to God. They form the foundation upon which his adult transcendent experience, self-actualization and creative expression take shape. Thus, we begin by highlighting three aspects

---

[1] See *MZM*, 92.

of Merton's childhood and adolescent years.[2] We use these themes as signposts along the way:

- Thomas Merton's family of origin;
- the educational institutions which he attended in various countries;
- his visit to Rome in 1933.

A. The Early Years

On January 31, 1915 – under the astrological sign of the Water Bearer – Thomas Merton came to birth in Prades, France. He was the eldest of two sons born to Owen Merton, a New Zealander, and Ruth Jenkins, an American. His parents were both artists who had met and married in England. Shortly after birth, he was baptized in the Church of England and given the name "Tom." We do not know exactly when he began signing his name "Thomas Merton," but he was doing so as a student at Columbia University (1935-1940). Approximately a year after Tom's birth, in order to relieve their financial difficulties and to escape the war then raging in Europe, the Mertons moved from France to Long Island, New York.

In 1919 Owen's mother and sister came from New Zealand to visit the Merton family, then living in Flushing, New York. It was this grandmother who taught Tom the *Our Father*. Although he went years without praying it, the boy never forgot it.

At the age of six, Tom received a letter from his mother who was in the hospital, informing him that she would never see him again. She died shortly afterwards of stomach cancer. He remembered her mostly as thin, pale, worried and rather severe. In reaction to her perfectionism Merton began from his earliest years to form an image of himself as a child who could not measure up to her expectations. Possibly, he internalized that parental voice, which would somewhat account for his struggle with self-doubt in his adult years. He rarely measured up to his own expectations of himself. According to his standards, he never seemed to be perfect enough as a monk or good enough as a writer. His lack of satisfaction with himself and his work derived for the most part from a positive force: a constant straining forward toward new horizons, a stretching out to

---

[2] Unless otherwise indicated, the principal source for this chapter is *Seven Storey Mountain*, 3-130.

the fullness of his identity, a restlessness that could find rest only in more of God. Yet, to some degree the drive which powered his endeavors seems to have been an attempt to compensate for some sense of personal deficiency.

Merton's mother did not give much import to formal religion and weekly church attendance. Her hope may have been that left to himself her son would grow up to be an unassuming believer in some sort of deity, free of attachment to any organized religion and unperverted by superstition.

Merton claimed to have inherited from his mother versatility and dissatisfaction with the world. He believed that he had received from his father his way of seeing things and some of his integrity. Merton ascribed to his father's outlook qualities of sanity and balance, together with respect for structure, for relationships between things and for the circumstances that impress a unique identity upon each creature. In a word, he judged his father's way of seeing as religious and clean.

Owen Merton had grown up with a well-developed faith as presented in the doctrines of the Church of England. The baptism of his son Tom was probably at his behest. As an adult, however, Owen was not a regular churchgoer – unless he was hired to play the organ at Sunday services. Looking back on his childhood, Merton observed that the only really valuable moral training he received had been from the example of his father in the course of ordinary living. Merton's general description of his father gives evidence of considerable idealization. In fact, Owen Merton was mostly an absent father.

With the death of Ruth Merton an immense grief, loneliness, rootlessness set into young Tom's soul. While his mother's illness and death were beyond her control, the boy most likely perceived her passing as if she had abandoned him. With her demise Merton became in effect an orphan. He once described his early life precisely that way, pointing out to a correspondent that he knew firsthand how inhuman and frustrating it is to be passed around from family to family as a ward or an object of charitable concern.[3] On another occasion he referred to his childhood as a "desperate, despairing time."[4]

Ruth Merton's death meant that her husband no longer had

---

[3] See *Hidden Ground of Love*, 605.
[4] *Learning to Love*, 11.

ties to one place. He was free to go wherever he desired to paint. Life for young Tom thus began to alternate between traveling with his father and being left for lengthy periods mainly with his maternal grandparents. He saw his little brother, John Paul, who lived uninterruptedly with those grandparents, only on his intermittent so-journs at their home. Merton narrated how on one occasion his father came back to get his drawing boards and himself in order to head off to Bermuda. His mentioning of the drawing boards first in the sequence gives the impression of a boy feeling second to art in terms of his father's priorities. As for Bermuda, it was the scene of a horrendous experience for the boy.[5] There Merton's father entered into an intimate and stormy relationship with a woman. Young Tom detested her on two counts. On the one hand, he perceived her presence as an effort to replace the mother whose loss he was still grieving. On the other hand, she meted out severe punishment to him for slight misbehaviors, sometimes for no apparent reason at all.

By the age of nine Merton found himself strongly adverse to the thought of any religion. Moreover, he had picked up from his maternal grandfather by way of osmosis an attitude of hatred and suspicion toward Catholics.

B. France

When Tom was ten years old, Owen returned to the United States one day from a successful exhibition of his paintings in London. To the young boy's astonishment Owen announced that they were going to live in France. Tom was reluctant at the time to leave his relatively stable life with his grandparents and younger brother. Later in life he surmised that perhaps ultimately his Christian vocation went all the way back to the three years that he spent in France.

Thomas Merton identified in his autobiography several probable spiritual influences during those years in France. For one thing, his father introduced him to the story of St. Joan of Arc, patroness of France. Secondly, he and his father lived for a while in St. Antonin where every street pointed more or less inward to the center of the town, which was the church. Merton noted that the

---

[5] See Arthur Callard, "Father of the Man: An Investigation into the Roots of Thomas Merton," in *The Merton Seasonal of Bellarmine College* (Spring/Summer 1986): 5-8; Robert E. Daggy, "Birthday Theology: A Reflection on Thomas Merton and the Bermuda Menage," in *The Kentucky Review*, 7 (Summer 1987): 62-89.

layout of the town forced a person to be at least a virtual contemplative, since in moving around the town a person kept looking toward the center.   Thirdly, young Tom was constantly visiting old churches, as he tagged along with his father who painted scenes from the French countryside.   On their outings the boy was continually visiting the ruins of ancient chapels and monasteries. Fourthly, he and his father used in 1926 some Christmas gift money to purchase a three-volume work entitled, *Le Pays de France* (*The Country of France*).   Young Tom was fascinated with it, especially the photographs of cathedrals, ancient abbeys, castles, towns and cultural monuments.   Looking at pictures of the ancient Grande Chartreuse, the boy experienced a longing to breathe the air of that solitary valley and to listen to its silence.   Fifthly, Merton cherished the summer of 1927, which he spent with the Privat family in Murat, France.   He was profoundly touched by the affection those people lavished upon him, a love which he reciprocated.

When Tom was eleven and a half years old, his father sent him to the Lycée Ingres, a boarding school in Montauban, France. Tom found that school to be a place of desolation, abandonment and bitterness.   After a rocky start the boy adjusted somewhat.   By the middle of his first year there, he and a small group of students were engaged in furiously writing novels.   Thus began Thomas Merton's first sustained attempt at creative self-expression.   He wrote two novels while at Montauban and another in St. Antonin before going to the lycée.   None of those novels is extant.

Since Merton was not a Catholic, he did not attend Mass on the Sundays when he remained at the lycée.   Instead, he and some boys gathered with a Protestant minister for religious instruction.   In retrospect, Merton did not associate anything significantly spiritual with that teaching.   Nonetheless, he was grateful for having received at least that much religion at a time when he badly needed it.   It had been years since he had even been inside a church for any purpose other than to look at stained glass windows or Gothic vaulting.

One bright sunny morning in May 1928 Owen Merton arrived at the Lycée Ingres.   He immediately told his son to pack his bags.   The Mertons were leaving France to live in England.   Young Tom felt like a man who had chains struck from his hands.   At last, escape from the dreadful lycée!   The boy's one regret was never having lived in the house that his father had been gradually building during their sojourn in France.

C. England

England for Thomas Merton meant going to his Aunt Maud's and Uncle Ben's house in Ealing, near London. It was in a conversation with that aunt that he first expressed the desire to be a writer. While residing in England, he continued his education at two boarding schools: first, Ripley Court in Surrey and then Oakham Public School in Oakham.

(1) Ripley Court

Thomas Merton was received at Ripley Court like an orphan or a stray who needed both pity and attention. Being the son of an artist, having just come from two years in a French school, and not knowing Latin added up to everything Mrs. Pearce, the head mistress at Ripley Court, abhorred. In fact, she exhorted Merton to consider looking to a career in business in order to make a living for himself and not become a dilettante like his father. Nonetheless, Merton experienced Ripley Court as a pleasant and happy place compared to the French lycée.

The years 1928-1929, when he was thirteen to fourteen years of age, Merton later designated as his religious phase. According to his assessment, he was almost sincerely religious at that time. He found many occasions for praying and for lifting up his mind to God. For the first time in his life he saw people kneeling publicly by their beds before getting into them and sitting down to meals after saying grace. Years later Merton did not see anything deeply spiritual about this religious phase. Yet, he believed that in some obscure and uncertain way God had been working in him.

Toward the end of the 1929 summer school term at Ripley Court, Tom learned that his father had become ill and was staying at Aunt Maud's home. Tom went to visit him. When he asked his father what was wrong, Owen Merton responded that no one seemed to know. By mid-August Owen had recovered enough to go with Tom for a period of recuperation at the home of a friend who lived in Insch, Aberdeenshire, Scotland. However, while there Owen's condition quickly deteriorated. He requested that Tom remain with his friend's family for the duration of the vacation. Owen meanwhile returned to London and entered Middlesex Hospital. As the August vacation wore on, Tom reverted more and more into sadness and isolation. At times he tried to break out of his sense of alienation by seeking out solitary places where he read novels or by bicycling into the country to look at the huge ancient stone circles where druids had gathered to offer human sacrifice to the rising sun.

Then one day when he was alone at his host's home, Tom received a strange telegram from his father still hospitalized in London, informing the boy of his entrance into New York harbor and reporting that all was well. The bottom fell out of young Tom's world. He later described his desperation this way:

> I sat there in the dark, unhappy room, unable to think, unable to move, with all the innumerable elements of my isolation crowding in upon me from every side: without a home, without a family, without a country, without a father, apparently without any friends, without any interior peace or confidence or light or understanding of my own – without God too, without God, without heaven, without grace, without anything.[6]

On Tom's return to Ealing, his Uncle Ben informed him that Owen Merton had a malignant tumor on the brain.

(2) Oakham Public School

In the autumn of 1929 shortly after learning of his father's diagnosis, Thomas Merton began studies at Oakham Public School. There he continued his education until December 1932.

The year 1930, after Tom had turned fifteen, marked a significant point in his development. He attained a sudden clear awareness of his independence and individuality. While that realization is in itself a healthy development during adolescence, it took in Merton's life an egotistical turn. As he described it, he bared his teeth and fought back against the humiliation of giving in to people. He formed a hard core of resistance to whatever displeased him. In short, he thought what he wanted, he did what he wanted, and he went his own way.

Two factors provided Merton the means to proceed in that manner. His maternal grandfather gave him financial security and emancipation by making available to him over a number of years

---

[6] *Seven Storey Mountain*, 71-72.

what would have been his inheritance. His godfather, Doctor Tom Bennett, invited him to stay at his flat when in London, giving him freedom to do as he wanted and introducing him to sophisticated society. Bennett encouraged Merton also to prepare for the English diplomatic or consular service. He exerted every possible effort to see that the young man advanced toward that goal.

A visit to the hospital in the summer of 1930 left Merton crushed by the sorrow of his father's overwhelming helplessness. He visited Owen regularly that summer. On one occasion he found his father's bed covered with little sheets of blue notepaper on which he had drawn pictures of small irate Byzantine-looking saints.

Owen Merton died on January 18, 1931. Tom anguished for a few months afterwards in a state of sadness and depression. When those feelings waned, he discovered himself stripped of all constraints on his will to do as he pleased. He thought himself to be utterly free. Moreover, he discarded from his life any remaining traces of religion and set about becoming what he later designated as the complete twentieth century man.

Merton excelled in his academic studies at Oakham. In the autumn of 1931 he became editor of the school journal. He was also an active member of the debating society. Yet, throughout those years his resistance to organized religion intensified. He told the story of how, on the occasion of the students reciting the *Apostle's Creed* in their chapel, he deliberately stood with lips tightly sealed – his way of declaring that he believed in nothing.

Despite himself, however, Merton's propensity for silence and solitude was a source of spiritual nourishment during his years at Oakham. A favorite haunt of his was Brooke Hill near the school. He liked to go off there alone. For hours he would walk, sit, read, think, draw or just drink in the beautiful landscape.

By the time of his graduation from Oakham Public School Merton was ready for a change. It was not that he disliked the school, but rather that he longed for emancipation. Then almost eighteen years of age, he imagined himself a grown-up. He thought that he could reach out and take from the world whatever he wanted.

D. Rome, Italy

On February 1, 1933, the day after his eighteenth birthday, Tom Merton set out for Italy. He underwent in the city of Rome a significant spiritual experience. He had gone to Rome as a tourist.

Once there, without planning it, he became a pilgrim confronted with the transcendent.

A *first* dimension of Merton's spiritual experience in Rome pertains to sacred art. He became fascinated with Byzantine mosaics of the fifth to the seventh centuries. He haunted the Roman churches which housed those mosaics. It may have been that the mysterious small drawings which he had found spread out on his father's bed sparked his interest in that medium of expression. As Merton beheld those mosaics, he began to discover something of who this person is that people call Christ. By Merton's own testimony it was in Rome that he first encountered Christ and formed his basic concept of him. The Christ whom he discovered was the Christ of the Apocalypse, the Christ of the Martyrs, the Christ of the Fathers, the Christ of St. John, St. Paul, St. Augustine and St. Jerome. It was Christ God, Christ the King.

A *second* aspect of the spiritual impact of the visit to Rome relates to conversion. One night, alone in his room, he had a vivid, real and startling sense of his father's presence with him. Together with that awareness of presence, Merton had a profound insight into his own sinfulness and misery. He was horrified at the sight of himself. As he described it later, his whole being revolted at seeing his condition, and he urgently desired escape, liberation, freedom. It was then for the first time in his life that he began to pray – not some intellectual prayer, but a prayer springing out of the roots of his being and his life to God whom he had never known. It was prayer beseeching God to free him from himself.

The morning following that experience Merton went to the Church of Santa Sabina for no other reason than to kneel down in prayer to God. This act seems to have been Merton's way of celebrating in ritual his moment of conversion. In retrospect, Merton could never be sure to what extent the event originated in his own feelings or imagination and to what measure it was directly from God. However, he remained morally certain that the experience was truly a great grace in his life.[7]

A *third* dimension of the spiritual experience in Rome for

---

[7] What Merton actually experienced on that night in 1933 is difficult to determine. The above account of the event follows *Seven Storey Mountain*. That account is from the perspective of Merton as a young Trappist monk around 1946. In an unpublished work, *The Labyrinth* (1940), Merton gave another account of the incident, making no mention of his sense of his father's presence and describing how in the middle of a great depression he saw himself as an unbearable person.

Merton was his visit to the Trappist monastery of Tre Fontaine. There the thought came to him that he might like to become a Trappist monk.

E. Clare College, Cambridge

Alas! Thomas Merton did not follow through at that time on the grace of those experiences in Rome.

From October 1933 to May 1934 Merton was a student at Clare College, Cambridge, England. Whereas Rome had been a spiritual high, his time at Clare College became his descent into hell. Spiritually, morally, academically, Merton hit rock bottom. Pleasure-seeking, especially in the forms of heavy drinking and womanizing, became the goal of his existence. All indications are that during that period Merton fathered a child outside marriage. Evidence suggests as well that Merton at one point engaged in a wild night party at which he may have volunteered to be the main character in a mock crucifixion.[8]

Merton's behavior at Clare College led to estrangement from his godfather, friend and guardian, Tom Bennett. During a 1934 summer visit to New York, he received a letter from Bennett curtly advising him to remain permanently in the United States. It took less than five minutes for Merton to come to agree with him.

Later in life Merton was able to reassess the meaning of the Cambridge episode. Through the lens of his Christian faith he interpreted it this way:

> God in His mercy was permitting me to fly as far as
> I could from His love but at the same time preparing
> to confront me, at the end of it all, and in the bottom
> of the abyss, when I thought I had gone farthest
> away from Him.[9]

---

[8] For details of Merton's Cambridge experience, see William H. Shannon, *Silent Lamp: The Thomas Merton Story* (New York, NY: The Crossroad Publishing Company, 1992), 65-77; Michael Mott, *The Seven Mountains of Thomas Merton* (Boston, MA: Houghton Mifflin Company, 1984), 74-85.
[9] *Seven Storey Mountain*, 123.

CHAPTER 14

The Wise Incomparable Weavings of Providence

By the age of twenty Thomas Merton had fled as far as he could from God's love. Yet, in that desolate place he discovered God awaiting him. At the bottom of the abyss the divine presence confronted him. God's providence was there to turn everything around, weaving both the joyful and the painful events of Merton's past into a pilgrimage toward new possibility and unforeseen hope.

One catalyst for that conversion was self-knowledge. By the grace of God, Merton recognized his immense misery and admitted that it resulted from his own doing. However, in addition to the salutary effect of acknowledging his condition, a further series of experiences – some conducive to his growth, others seemingly causing diminishment – prepared Merton's heart for radical conversion to God.

In this chapter we focus on Merton's geographical journey and interior pilgrimage from the beginning of his permanent residence in the United States (December 1934) up to his entry into the Cistercian Abbey near Louisville, Kentucky (December 1941).[1] We organize our study primarily by reference to the institutions central to Merton's life during those years, namely:

- Columbia University,
- St. Bonaventure University,
- The Cistercian Abbey of Our Lady of Gethsemani

We consider certain key events and institutions inasmuch as

---

[1] Unless otherwise indicated, the principal sources for this chapter are *Seven Storey Mountain*, 131-423; *Run to the Mountain*; *Secular Journal*.

they reveal something of the interrelationship of transcendence, self-actualization and creative process in Merton's life.

A. Columbia University

From January 1935 to the spring of 1940, Thomas Merton studied at Columbia University in New York City.   Merton expressed during the 1960's his gratitude to that institution for turning him loose in all its rich resources of library, faculty, curriculum and student body. He felt the university had let him be himself and let him make of the situation what he liked.   He compared his response to the ambiance at Columbia to being turned on like a pinball machine.[2]   At Columbia he came into his own. There he flourished as a person, a student and a prospective writer. Columbia was a providential instrument in his encounter with the immanent transcendence of God, in his process of self-actualization and in the burgeoning of his creativity.

Among the catalysts for his spiritual genesis during those years are the following:

- the formation of close friendships, some of which would endure for a lifetime;
- professors, including Mark Van Doren and Daniel Walsh, whom Merton looked upon as spiritual mentors;
- the deaths of his beloved maternal grandparents;
- the book, *The Spirit of Medieval Philosophy*, by Etienne Gilson, in which Merton discovered the idea of the aseity of God; that is, God really exists and is not simply a projection of the human imagination;
- the book, *Ends and Means,* by Aldous Huxley, which led Merton to delve into the meaning of detachment and to discover the possibility of experiential mystical encounter with God;
- meeting with Bramachari, a Hindu monk from India, who witnessed to a life of discipline and meditation and who directed Merton toward spiritual writings of the West such as St. Augustine's *Confessions* and Thomas à Kempis' *The Imitation of Christ*;
- the art of William Blake. Merton chose Blake's work as the subject of his thesis for the degree of Master of Arts in the

---

[2] See "Learning to Live," in *Love and Living*, 12-13.

Columbia University Department of English and Comparative
Literature. In his thesis, "Nature and Art in William Blake: An
Essay in Interpretation" (1939), Merton attempted to understand
Blake through the lens of Thomistic aesthetics as interpreted by
Jacques Maritain.

During his years at Columbia University Merton was
increasingly attracted to Roman Catholicism. He began attending
Mass and reading Catholic writers such as Gerard Manley Hopkins,
James Joyce and Richard Crashaw. Yet, he remained hesitant to
commit himself to God according to that religious tradition. Finally,
his moment of decision came.

It was late September 1938. Merton had just returned to his
room in a house behind the library of Columbia University. Rain
was gently falling outside. He picked up a book on Gerard Manley
Hopkins which he had borrowed that morning from the library. He
was reading a chapter that told of Hopkins expressing to John Henry
Newman his desire to become a Catholic. Suddenly, Merton
experienced something stirring within him. It was like a voice
questioning him about what he was waiting for and why he was still
hesitant. It confronted him with the fact that he knew what he had to
do. It urged him to act.

Merton moved in his chair, lit up a cigarette, gazed out his
window at the rain, trying to silence the voice. He told himself that
these thoughts were crazy, irrational, impulsive. Yet, they persisted
until he could no longer bear the inner struggle. He got up, laid
down the book, put on his raincoat, went out. Off he went to see
Father Ford at the Church of Corpus Christi. Seated together in a
parlor, Merton told the priest that he wanted to become a Catholic.

On November 16, 1938, at Corpus Christi Church in New
York City after several months of preparation, Merton was received
into the Roman Catholic Church. According to the practices of the
time, reception into the Roman Catholic Church of a person baptized
in the Church of England consisted of conditional Baptism,
Confession, Mass and Communion. Recalling that pivotal event
later, Merton expressed its meaning in terms of God having called
out to him with intimate love from God's own immense depths –
God, the center who is everywhere and whose circumference is
nowhere. Merton experienced himself found and loved by God
through the Spirit of love incorporating him in Christ. Indeed,
Merton believed that the door to vast realms of mystery opened to

him that day.

Nonetheless, Merton swam in the waters of contradiction. His reception into the church set him on a decisive spiritual course. He did reading in spirituality, although he did not read spiritually. He attended Sunday Mass and on occasion Mass during the week. He prayed. He received the sacraments frequently. Yet, he found himself full of dissipating and useless desires. Still there were parties, drinking and hangovers with which to contend. He became preoccupied with becoming a published author. Reputation and success as a writer became his utmost concern.

Before his reception into the church, Merton had attempted composing verse, but found it difficult. After he became a Roman Catholic, he discovered in himself a gift for writing poetry. He would get an idea. Then he would walk around the streets in New York City, among the warehouses, toward a poultry market, and on to a chicken dock where he would sit in the sun. There he would try to work out several lines of verse in his head. Eventually, after taking in the surrounding scenery, he would write the poem down on a scrap of paper, go home and type it out. It was his common practice to mail it off to a magazine. His poems were returned, but he did manage to have a few book reviews accepted for publication.

Amidst his literary pursuits, Merton's inner questioning persisted: What was he doing with his life? Why was he so procrastinating, so confused? Why this uncertainty and insecurity?

After completing his Master of Arts in English and deciding to commence studies for a Doctor of Philosophy degree at Columbia, Merton spent the summer of 1939 with two close friends at a cottage in the hills overlooking the town of Olean. There they engaged in a contest to see who could be first to complete a novel. Much of Merton's unpublished novel, *The Labyrinth*, was probably composed during that time.

The threat of war in Europe loomed over that entire summer. In early September 1939 with the German bombing of Warsaw, Poland, World War II erupted. A profound sense of guilt crept upon Merton. He concluded that his personal sin had contributed to this condition within the world. Although his guilt contained some exaggeration of the effects of his past behavior, it nonetheless indicated an emerging sense of social responsibility. He was seeing that the action of one person does, for better or for worse, affect the whole.

In that local and global framework Merton continued

discerning his Christian vocation. One afternoon in New York City as he sat on the floor in his room with two friends eating breakfast, the thought came to him that he would like to become a priest. He described the realization as an insistent attraction that suddenly made itself felt. It constituted a clear sense of the direction which he ought to pursue. It was a question of conscience. Out of the blue, he proceeded to casually remark to his companions that he was thinking of entering a monastery and becoming a priest.

While Merton had thus come to accept the religious life and the priesthood as a possible calling, it remained for him to make a decision. Still ruminating on the idea of becoming a priest, he went into a Catholic church that evening just as exposition of the Blessed Sacrament was ending. The congregation was singing the Latin hymn, *Tántum Érgo*. As Merton knelt in his pew, the question of whether he really wanted to be a priest confronted him. He knew that his whole life was at a crossroads. Once again, he stood on the edge of an abyss, but this time he named the abyss God. At that moment, in love, peace and joy he gave his yes to God's calling of him to the priesthood.

Some time later Merton sought out Daniel Walsh, his friend and advisor, for help in discerning where and how to pursue his vocation. Merton had already identified clearly one principle of discernment; that is, his need for solitude in order to attain breadth and depth as a person and in order to allow God's loving gaze to open him up, as a plant spreads out its leaves in the sun.

After considering various religious orders, Merton felt most attracted to the Franciscans. Around October 1939 he finalized arrangements to enter the Franciscan novitiate in August 1940. Initially he felt quite at peace with his plan. With that decision he had let God become more the center of his existence. He marveled at the change it made in his life.

In the interim Merton went to daily Mass and communion. He took up certain daily devotional practices like the Stations of the Cross. For one month he spent an hour each day doing the Spiritual Exercises of St. Ignatius. He taught a class in English composition at the Columbia University School of Business. He did a course on St. Thomas Aquinas.

Recovering from an appendectomy, Merton visited Cuba during Easter 1940. One peak moment during that trip occurred at a Mass where little children were proclaiming, "*Creo en Dios...*" ("I believe in God..."). He experienced heaven as being right there in front of him. That is, his intuition of the presence of God in those children opened out to the realization of God already transparent in all creation.

Despite that profound intuition, Merton's personal prayer remained mostly discursive. It was not systematic (that is, proceeding from point to point), but rather spontaneous affective meditation that sprang from time to time out of his reading. Considerable daydreaming about his future in the Franciscan novitiate intermingled with his prayer.

As August 1940 approached, Merton awoke one morning to find that the peace which had been with him for approximately six months had suddenly vanished. His Eden disappeared, and he found himself once more naked, alone, out in the cold. His desire to become a religious and a priest remained firm. However, he thought that his past behavior – most likely, the fact of having fathered a child outside marriage – might according to church law pose an impediment to his eventual priestly ordination. He came to the conclusion that none of the significant people with whom he had discussed his vocation knew who he really was.

Consequently, Merton sought out his Franciscan contact and revealed to him the story of his past. The following day that priest advised Merton to withdraw his application to enter the novitiate. In response, Merton could only hang his head and wordlessly behold the ruins of his vocation. It seemed to him that he was excluded from the priesthood forever. To make matters worse, he went to confession at a nearby church immediately after hearing the bad news. The Capuchin priest to whom he confessed took a harsh stance toward Merton's distraught emotional state. Merton came out of the confessional shattered to pieces. All that he knew, besides his immense misery, was that he must no longer consider a vocation to the religious life and to the priesthood.

That turn of events put Merton in a stance of openness to follow a way that surpassed his understanding and planning. It disposed him to pursue a path that transcended his own will. He pulled himself together eventually, and set out alone to climb back up from the depths of his misery to solid ground.

Although Merton was tempted to abandon his spiritual quest, his desire to remain intimate with God was unquenchable. He decided that if he could not live in a monastery, he would live in the world as if he were a monk. He believed that direction to be God's will for him in view of the circumstances. Thus, he purchased a set of breviaries to pray the Divine Office. Merton opted also to seek a teaching position in a Catholic college. He resolved to turn his back on the wild desires and excess of pleasure in which he still indulged.

During August 1940 Merton made his way to Olean to spend time with close friends and to check out the prospects of a job at St. Bonaventure University.

B. St. Bonaventure University

Father Thomas Plassman, then president of St. Bonaventure's, warmly welcomed Merton to an interview for a teaching position at the university. Plassman ended the meeting by offering him a job. Thus, in September 1940 Thomas Merton – now almost twenty-six years of age – took up residence at St. Bonaventure's in a small room on the second floor of a large red-brick building which served as both dormitory and monastery. With the United States on the brink of entering World War II, all students and secular professors at St. Bonaventure's had to register for the draft during November of that year. The registration reminded Merton that his now pleasant, safe and stable life was not his to enjoy forever.

February 1941 found Merton thinking about making a retreat at a monastery during Holy Week and Easter of that year. He had experienced over the preceding few months something opening out within him, which demanded at least a week in monastic silence, austerity and prayer. After examining his options, he elected to go to the Cistercian Abbey of Our Lady of Gethsemani in Kentucky. He had been working on another novel. But toward the beginning of Lent 1941 he shifted suddenly to writing poems. He would sometimes go several days at a time, writing a new poem each day. He enjoyed seeing some of those poems accepted for publication.

In early March 1941 Merton wrote the Trappists at Gethsemani, asking to make a reservation for Holy Week. His request was approved. Around the same time he received a letter from the Draft Board ordering him to enlist in the army. Merton decided to apply for status as a noncombatant conscientious objector. However, he did not pass the medical examination due to longstanding dental problems.

Merton made his retreat at Gethsemani from April 7-14, 1941. He was quite impressed by the monastic life. In a burst of idealistic exuberance he concluded that the monastery was the center of all the vitality in America and the reason for the nation's cohesion. That retreat reawakened in Merton awareness of his desire to be a religious and a priest. However, because of the devastating outcome of his plan to enter the Franciscan novitiate, he harbored a great fear of reopening the issue. Before leaving Gethsemani, he did take the step of praying for the grace of a Trappist vocation, if it were pleasing to God.

Back at St. Bonaventure University life went on. In June 1941 Merton began another novel entitled, *Journal of My Escape from the Nazis*. It was a thinly veiled autobiographical novel about a young man experiencing identity confusion who returns to Europe in the midst of the war. That summer Merton taught a course on bibliography and methods of research. He met Baroness Catherine de Hueck and worked for a while at her Friendship House in Harlem. When September came around, he reorganized his spiritual activities. He arose early each morning to pray the Little Hours of the Divine Office at dawn before going to Mass and Communion. He spent forty-five minutes daily in solitary prayer. He did spiritual reading, which included lives of certain saints and the writings of St. John of the Cross.

Intuitively, Merton knew that it was about time to move on from St. Bonaventure's. In November 1941 he agreed to a request from Baroness de Hueck that he begin living at Friendship House as of January 1942. No sooner was the decision made, however, than Merton's leaning toward monastic life and priesthood forcefully reasserted itself. One day a friend confronted him about why he had abandoned that direction just because of one person's opinion. His friend's words revived Merton's will to act. He began to discern anew his calling. Three days later he found himself with the powerful, irresistible and clear conviction that the time had come for him to become a Trappist monk. With anguished urgency he proceeded to consult a friar at St. Bonaventure's about the possible obstacle from his past life. The friar assured him that his past behavior posed no impediment to his entrance into religious life or to his ordination to the priesthood.

Merton then wrote Gethsemani, requesting to make a Christmas retreat and intimating that he would like to enter the Cistercian Order. A letter of acceptance from Gethsemani and a letter from the Draft Board arrived almost simultaneously. The Draft Board informed him that due to certain policy changes he would probably no longer be exempt from active duty in the armed services. In response, Merton requested from the board a month's deferral on the basis of intent to enter a monastery. On December 8, 1941, the day after the Japanese attack on Pearl Harbor, Merton received the board's permission for a one-month extension of exemption. He immediately began preparations to leave for Gethsemani. Merton was almost twenty-seven years old.

C. The Abbey of Our Lady of Gethsemani

Thomas Merton stepped off the train onto the station platform at Louisville, Kentucky, on December 10, 1941 – exactly twenty-seven years prior to the day of his death. Happy and exultant, he boarded the half-full Bardstown bus and sat in a dilapidated seat. On arrival in Bardstown, he got a local man to give him a car ride to the Cistercian Abbey. The driver dropped him at the gate and went on his way. Merton rang the bell and waited. A brother who recognized him from his previous visit let him in. The brother locked the gate behind him, and Merton found himself enclosed within what he described later as the four walls of his new freedom.[3]

On December 13, 1941, Dom Frederic Dunne, the abbot of Our Lady of Gethsemani, officially accepted Merton into the Cistercian Order as a postulant. Merton brought with him a basic sense of identity, intimacy with God and vocational direction. He felt that at Gethsemani he was entering a new world of freedom. Merton came there to live the contemplative life as a Trappist monk and priest, knowing full well that he was bringing with him the instincts of a writer.

Thus, God's loving mercy brought Thomas Merton on his geographical journey from Prades to Bermuda to St. Antonin to Oakham to London to Cambridge to Rome to New York to Columbia to St. Bonaventure's to the Abbey of Our Lady of Gethsemani. On Merton's dark and winding path to truth and intimacy, God had been with him, providing for him, leading him, calling out to him from the abyss. The wise incomprehensible weaving of God's providence had worked into the very fiber of his being and life the basic solution to his quest for identity, meaning and direction.

---

[3] See *Seven Storey Mountain*, 372.

CHAPTER 15

Enclosed in the Four Walls of New Freedom

During the 1940's the Abbey of Gethsemani had a program of initiation for men embarking upon the Trappist way of life. A man spent a short time at the outset as a postulant. That phase permitted the Order and the neophyte to look one another over firsthand. A two-year novitiate followed postulancy. The novice studied and practiced the basics of Trappist life, while continuing discernment of his vocation with his religious superiors. Profession of simple temporary vows for a three-year period marked the end of the novitiate. Cistercian monks made five vows: poverty, chastity, obedience, stability and conversion of manners. Those vows expressed the monk's desire to dedicate himself to God in faith, hope and love. They were means to lead him to the full maturity of life hidden with Christ in God. Completion of the three-year temporary profession marked yet another crossroads. The monk then considered two fundamental vocational options: either to leave the monastery or to dedicate himself to God as a member of that community for the rest of his life. A decision to remain was celebrated in solemn perpetual vows.[1]

From 1941-1947 Thomas Merton went through those stages of monastic life. His geographical pilgrimage and his inner journey unfolded within the daily rhythm of life at Gethsemani. His experience of God, self-development and writing took shape in the context of his basic formation as a Trappist monk. In this chapter we focus upon three pivotal concerns in Merton's life during that interval:

---

[1] With regard to the structure and the routine of Cistercian life at Gethsemani during the 1940's, see: *Entering the Silence*, 489; S*ign of Jonas*, 3-11; Thomas Merton, *The Silent Life* (New York, NY: Dell Publishing Co., Inc., 1959), 80-110.

- the nature of the contemplative life;
- his persistent desire for more solitude than possible in the ordinary routine of Trappist life;
- conflict between the contemplative and the artist within him.

We consider those issues in reference to the interrelationship of transcendence, self-actualization and creative process.[2]

A. The Nature of the Contemplative Life

Thomas Merton's description of his entry into Gethsemani is paradoxical. "Enclosed in the four walls of new freedom"[3] are not concepts that we ordinarily use in association. The notion of living in the same space with the same people for the remainder of one's life conjures up for most people images of restriction, narrowness, confinement, imprisonment, even claustrophobia.   Yet, Merton thought of that situation in terms of increasing liberation. How did he reconcile those apparently opposite concepts?

The Abbey of Our Lady of Gethsemani symbolized for Merton the wedding of his inner and outer paths.   From the perspective of his interior pilgrimage, the freedom that he had found within himself had an innate thrust toward increasing freedom of spirit. With regard to his geographical journey, the Abbey embodied a vocational lifestyle that Merton perceived as witnessing liberation. In his judgment, his spirit and that of Gethsemani not only connected, but also in some way mirrored each other. He believed that this community would nurture his growth and that he in turn would contribute positively to its well-being.

Thus, the "four walls" provided Merton a milieu in which to focus on the essential. Those boundaries enabled him to seek God single-heartedly. The enclosure of monastic life represented for him not a negative confinement but a deliberate narrowing down of his options to "the one thing necessary" (Luke 10:42). That point of convergence   enabled   Merton's   emergence   into   ever   more transcendent depths of God and of his identity in God, which in turn would unleash in him immense creativity.

Both conscious and unconscious motivations affected

---

[2]   The principal sources for this chapter, unless otherwise indicated, are *Seven Storey Mountain*, 372-423 and *Entering the Silence*, 1-153.
[3]   See *Seven Storey Mountain*, 372.

Merton's decision to become a Trappist. Some reasons were lofty, while others masked immaturity. Certain motives arose from human longings which, while being positive, are not in themselves indicative of a contemplative vocation; for example: needs to belong, to have roots, to be at home, to find acceptance and love. Other influences had a negative tinge; for instance: a measure of disdain toward the world, a bent toward extremism rather than balance, a certain withholding of himself in his romantic involvements with women.

Yet, Merton had a sense of vocation that outweighed all specific motivations, whether positive or negative. Deeper than all influences and permeating all aspirations was his experience of being called by God to live the contemplative life as a Trappist monk and priest. Merton had experienced the love of Jesus for him in such a way that it impelled him to proceed in the direction of the contemplative life. This vocational imperative welled up from within his inmost being. He found within himself an existential inability to be and to do otherwise.[4] As Merton experienced it, he had to go that path, although freely, in order to be true to himself, to God and to the world. It would be in Merton's fidelity to that vocation over the course of his life that God would fulfill his heart's desire. Integral to that process of fulfillment was God's pruning of Merton's excesses and God's mellowing of his harsh judgments into compassion.

When Merton entered Gethsemani, the thrust of his experience of transcendence was already well set. Basically his encounter with God was in darkness by way of faith, hope and love. He believed that nothing accessible or comprehensible to his senses, feelings or intellect could grasp God in God's own self. He considered God to be ultimately sheer mystery. His prayer was that of contemplation in the sense of wordless, imageless, loving communion with the indwelling Father, Son and Spirit.[5]

It did not take long for reality to begin tempering Merton's idealism toward Trappist life. For instance, just a few days after his arrival at Gethsemani as he awaited official word of his acceptance into the Cistercian Order, Merton found unsatisfying the explanation of contemplation that he read in the monastery's *Spiritual Director*. That document spoke of "the exercises of the contemplative life"

---

[4] In *Conjectures*, 266, Merton spoke of the primordial *yes* that is in our being, but not of us. See also *Called by God*, 65-120; *Discerning Vocations*, 109-179.
[5] See, for example, *Seven Storey Mountain*, 172-175; 397.

which occupy most of a Trappist's day; namely: the Mass, the Divine Office, prayer and pious reading. Merton had no language at that time to articulate his understanding of the contemplative life. Yet, the idea of the contemplative life as divided up into "exercises" seemed to him an inadequate concept.[6]

With respect to prayer itself, the *Spiritual Directory* left Merton with the impression that contemplation was not a top priority in a Trappist monastery. Moreover, he discovered in that document the advice that should a young monk have a desire for mystical contemplation he had better use caution in his expression of that inclination. Very soon Merton found himself drawn away from his contemplative practice of prayer and caught up in attempting to follow what he later described as a complex and absurd system of meditation.[7]

Over the years of formation Merton concluded that Cistercian monasteries nurture very few contemplatives. As he viewed it, too much activity militates against the formation of mature contemplatives. Merton quickly discovered at Gethsemani an attitude in some monks of almost exaggerated reverence for work and for penitential practices. That way of living, which Merton surmised to be common throughout Trappist communities, went by the nomenclature of "active contemplation." Merton once wryly noted that while the adjective "active" is well chosen, the noun "contemplation" is not without a touch of poetic license.

B. Merton's Intense Desire for Solitude

After becoming a monk, Thomas Merton had no desire to return to his former way of life. He claimed that it was easy for him to forget that world as soon as he left it. His struggle was of another nature. Although he discerned a calling to the monastic life, he often wondered in his early years at Gethsemani whether he should go to another type of monastic community.[8]

Even before his decision to enter Gethsemani, Merton had an attraction to a solitary rather than a cenobitic form of the contemplative life. The Carthusian Order with its eremitical orientation appealed to him. He admitted frankly that had the

---

[6] See *Seven Storey Mountain*, 374-375; *Sign of Jonas*, 44.
[7] See *Seven Storey Mountain*, 385.
[8] See *Seven Storey Mountain*, 383-384; *Sign of Jonas*, 13; *Entering the Silence*, 41.

opportunity existed he would have entered a Carthusian Charterhouse rather than a Trappist monastery. However, no Charterhouse existed in the United States and World War II made travel to Europe impossible. It may appear that for Merton the Cistercian Order was from the outset a second choice. Yet, he did not exhibit an attitude of choosing Gethsemani only because of the impracticality of his first preference. On the contrary, his faith perceived God at work in those historical circumstances, guiding him to Gethsemani.

During his novitiate Merton did entertain the thought of leaving the Trappists for the Carthusians. Yet, the idea remained on an academic and speculative level. It did not become a question of conscience or disturb his inner peace. But as Merton approached solemn vows, his attraction to a more solitary form of the contemplative life took on some urgency. In his journal entries for that period we see him vacillating between a desire to remain at Gethsemani and an inclination to go elsewhere.[9]

In the course of wrestling with the issue, Merton came to recognize within himself a repetitive cyclic pattern. Intense desire to leave Gethsemani would erupt. After a time it would pass. Then he would find himself content to be a Trappist. Yet, his longing to live a more solitary contemplative life elsewhere would soon be reactivated. In his wavering Merton decided to trust his religious superiors' assurance that his vocation was to remain at Gethsemani.[10] In following that course he came gradually to a discovery of interior solitude. He realized that whether alone or with his brother monks he could commune intimately with God present yet hidden within him and all around him.

The question of a possible calling to a more solitary life remained with Merton to his dying day. He forever longed for greater physical solitude than the circumstances of his Trappist vocation permitted him.

C. Creative Expression

Thomas Merton described writing as the one activity born in him. He acknowledged that the desire to write was in his blood. It was integral to his identity. Prior to joining the Trappists, he had

---

[9] See, for instance, *Sign of Jonas,* 19, 22, 25, 26, 30; *Entering the Silence*, 33-44.
[10] See *Sign of Jonas*, 25-26; *Entering the Silence*, 39.

written novels, book reviews and poetry, although very little of his work saw publication. When he entered Gethsemani, he brought with him all the instincts of a writer and he knew it. However, integration of his gift for writing with his contemplative vocation proved quite difficult for him. He felt as if he were going full speed in two irreconcilable directions. He had to find a way for the monk and the writer to live together in harmony. He sought to discover how those two dimensions of his life converged upon his deepest self and upon God's calling of him.

During the 1940's when a man became a Trappist novice, he was given a new name to signify his new identity in Christ. Merton received the name "Louis." When Brother (and after his ordination, Father) Louis wrote for publication, he used the pen name "Thomas Merton."   We could describe the young monk's challenge to harmonize his contemplative calling and his gift of writing in terms of integrating "Louis Merton" and "Thomas Merton" into a coherent sense of self.

We address this issue of integration during the years 1940-1947: first, by exploring Merton's creative process and, second, by examining the conflict itself.

(1) The Work

Thomas Merton had entered the Trappist community in early December 1941. Before the end of the Christmas season he had half-filled an old notebook with ideas that came swimming into his head as he participated in the Cistercian celebration of the liturgical feasts. He especially appreciated the early mornings of great feast days, between four and five-thirty. Saturated with peace and the richness of the liturgy after having spent two or three hours in prayer, he beheld outside the cold windows dawn breaking upon the landscape. When it was warm, the song of birds would be already welcoming the new day. Merton found that milieu a fruitful time for composing poetry. It seemed to him that in the silence and peace whole blocks of imagery would crystallize naturally and the poetry would almost write itself. Merton's account of that experience illustrates clearly transcendence, self-actualization and creative process interrelating in his life.

Merton's practice of composing verse in the early morning came to an abrupt halt, however, when the Father Master told him to cease writing at that time and to study Scripture as the Trappist Rule required. Merton claimed that he came to find more fulfillment in doing that study than in composing verse. He asserted that he lost all preference for any of his own writing when he began reading the great saints of early Christianity. Formation studies, the daily succession of the Hours of the Divine Office, the unfolding of liturgical feasts and seasons, the work of farming, he declared, filled his life with such satisfaction that ordinarily there was neither time nor desire to write.

Was the Father Master's advice the course most favorable to Merton's spiritual growth? Or does the incident indicate a system placing the observance of the regulations and the customs of Trappist life over the needs and the talents of a specific person? As for Merton's quick relinquishment of his self-expression, another question arises. What combination of motives was at work in him: beginner's overzealous religious fervor, genuine interest in the reading required of him, eagerness to explore the novelty of his new life, desire to conform to expectations of his superiors in order to gain acceptance, recognition that it was the appropriate time to give precedence to formation in monastic life over creative expression?

During Christmas 1943 Merton had a visit from Bob Lax, a close friend from the years at Columbia University. When Lax returned to New York City, he took with him a manuscript containing some of Merton's poetry. Half the poems, Merton had written during his novitiate. Most of the remaining poems, he had composed when he taught at St. Bonaventure's. It was the first time that Merton had reviewed the latter works since coming to Gethsemani. As he was putting together the manuscript for his friend, he felt as if he was editing the work of a stranger, a dead poet, someone forgotten. Through a former professor of Merton, that selection of poems came to be published under the title, *Thirty Poems*. A copy reached Merton near the end of November 1944. He relished seeing his work in print. He described going out near the cemetery on a cold overcast day which threatened snow and standing in the wind as he held the printed poems in hand.

When Bob Lax encouraged Merton to write more poetry, Merton did not argue with him. Yet, Merton did not believe that direction to be what God desired. Merton's confessor concurred with that discernment. Then, one day the Abbot, Dom Frederic Dunne, told Merton in the context of spiritual direction to go on writing poems. Thus, there appeared eventually two more books of Merton's poetry: *A Man in the Divided Sea* (1946) and *Figures for an*

Apocalypse (1948).

By the mid-1940s a retreat movement had sprung up at Gethsemani. Men came to spend time in prayer and to participate to some extent in the liturgical life of the monks. The coming of retreatants necessitated that the monastery make available some writing on the Trappist life, on prayer and on related spiritual themes. Since Merton had a flair for writing, his superiors assigned him considerable work in that regard. The Abbot had put Merton to work during Lent 1943 translating books and articles from French into English. He would quickly fill yellow sheets at a long table in the novitiate scriptorium, while another novice would immediately type the pages. By May 1946 Merton had completed the following Cistercian-related books: *Trappist Life* (a revised guide for postulants); *The Monks of the Golden Age* (a five hundred page volume of the lives of Cistercian saints); *Exile Ends in Glory* (a biography of Mother Mary Berchmans); *The Spirit of Simplicity; Cistercian Life; Life of St. Lutgarde.*

At the time that *Thirty Poems* hit the market, Merton may have already begun work on his autobiography, *The Seven Storey Mountain*. He completed it in 1946, and later added the epilogue which he composed on the feast of the Sacred Heart in 1947. That autobiography was first published in 1948 after considerable modification by order of Cistercian censors. For most of Merton's monastic life censorship would continue to be a significant factor modifying much of his creative expression. By virtue of his vow of obedience, he had to submit his work prior to publication to the duly appointed censors within the Trappist Order. They had the authority to demand specific revisions or deletions in a manuscript or even to deny permission for publication.

(2) The Conflict

The arrival of the book, *Thirty Poems,* triggered serious thinking in Thomas Merton about the relationship between his contemplative vocation and his gift of writing. In effect, Merton had set up a dichotomy between those two dimensions of his life. Three examples provide us glimpses of how Merton contended with that dilemma:

a.   The Writer as Shadow

A first example comes from Thomas Merton's autobiography, *The Seven Storey Mountain.* By the time that his first book of poetry appeared in print, Merton thought that he should have been free of any problems pertaining to his identity. According to his naive line of reasoning at the time, his profession of simple vows should have assured that liberation. Yet, in the cloister he kept running into a disconcerting part of himself: a shadow, a double, a writer whose name was Thomas rather than Louis. So ill at ease was he with this writer that he wondered whether the name "Thomas Merton" designated an enemy.

Merton the monk found this shadow whom he believed should have been dead stalking him at every turn. This shadow awaited him at the doorway of all his prayers, followed him into church, knelt with him behind the pillar. Moreover, this double chattered incessantly to him. This shadow was always full of ideas, concocting strange notions and devising new schemes. The core of Merton's conflict with this shadow centered upon the purpose of silence. Merton the monk believed that silence should be replete with the "infinitely productive darkness of contemplation," whereas Merton the writer used the silence to generate books. How were the two ever to live together in peace?

Merton found himself unable to rid himself of this shadow. His superiors were unwilling to kick him out. In fact, this double had their blessing. Merton persisted in the dichotomy of his own making, claiming that either he or the double had to die. Some days he felt that because of his writing there was nothing left of his contemplative vocation. Meanwhile, his superiors were calmly assuring him that writing was integral to his vocation.

b.   Indecisiveness

A second example of the split between the writer and the contemplative within Merton comes from *The Sign of Jonas.*[11]

From March to April 1947 Dom Dominique, the Abbot General of the Cistercian Order, came from France to Gethsemani for visitation. Dom Dominique assured Merton that it was good and even necessary for him to proceed with his writing. The Abbot

---

[11] See *Sign of Jonas*, 34-46; also *Entering the Silence*, 53-70.

General put that advice in the context of the Order's need for specialists – writers, liturgists, theologians, canonists. Since Merton had a gift for writing, he should therefore use that talent for the good of the Order.

In a journal entry dated April 16, 1947, Merton articulated his position after weighing Dom Dominique's words. While previously he had desired to cease writing, now he concluded that he must continue writing. Moreover, he resolved to let the unusual conditions imposed by Cistercian life modify his attempts to express himself. Those conditions included limitations on his choice of topics and on the amount of time available for writing, as well as submission of his work to the judgment of the Trappist censors.

The same journal entry indicates some movement toward reconciliation of the monk and the writer in Merton. He acknowledged that he could become a saint by doing his best at writing and by using that talent for the glory of God. He surmised that proceeding with that outlook would give him opportunity to deny himself and to temper his haste to get into print. He concluded that his typewriter was an essential aspect of his asceticism.

By May 1, 1947, however, Merton's thoughts had swung again in the opposite direction. That point in time found him with no less than twelve projects in various stages of completion. Questions and doubts hounded him. What was the purpose of all this writing? Did the fact that he was doing it out of obedience to his superiors really make it pleasing to God? Was it an act of virtue for him as a contemplative to let himself get snowed under by all these activities? He wanted clear answers, but they were not forthcoming.

c.   The Essay, "Poetry and the Contemplative Life"

A third illustration of the conflict that Thomas Merton had created within himself between contemplation and creative expression comes from an article published in a July 1947 edition of the periodical *Commonweal*.

In that article, entitled "Poetry and the Contemplative Life," Merton delved into the relationship between the task of the artist and the calling of the contemplative. His interest in the question sprang from the tension in his own life between writing and contemplation. Merton's reasoning proceeded according to the categories of the scholastic theology which he had studied during his years of formation. In that vein he opined that poetic art could lead a poet to "active" contemplation, possibly even to the threshold of "infused" contemplation. However, once a person had entered the realm of contemplation, poetry could obstruct the way to transcendent experience. Merton maintained that, standing on the brink of intimate encounter with God, the poet as artist would be tempted to begin expressing the experience rather than entering further into mystery. Merton insisted that in that situation only one course of action was fitting; namely, the poet must totally and ruthlessly sacrifice creative expression for the purpose of contemplation.[12]

While advocating that solution, Merton himself had already written at least nine books and was devising a number of new projects. On an intellectual level he may have sincerely believed that rejection of creative expression for the sake of contemplation was the correct path for him to follow. Yet, neither his instincts as a writer nor his contemplative bent would let him succumb to that simplistic reasoning. Very soon after publication of that article he started to revise his opinion on the matter. For example, in a letter dated March 30, 1948, he shared with a correspondent that he was beginning to see everything in a new light. No longer did he lean toward stating the problem in terms of being *either* a contemplative *or* a writer. Rather, he saw the essential issue as that of reaching a unique destiny and a personal fulfillment reserved by God for him alone. He stated the proper resolution of the relationship between poetry and contemplation consists of personal discernment of God's will and action in the immediate circumstances of the present moment.[13]

---

[12] For a similar view, see *Seeds of Contemplation* (Norfolk, CT: New Directions, 1949), 57.

[13] See *Road to Joy*, 22-23.

CHAPTER 16

In the Belly of a Paradox

The years 1948-1955 mark a period of radical transition for Thomas Merton. In that respect his life was a microcosm of the global reality. The nations of the world were in a time of reassessment, working to establish a new order after the devastation of World War II. Within the Roman Catholic Church winds of change were stirring. A renewed faith perspective had begun to take shape, and a fresh theological outlook was in the making. Many Christians were moving away from an attitude of detachment from the world to a perception of the world as a divine milieu. Those developments reached a critical point in 1959 with the announcement by Pope John XXIII of plans for the Second Vatican Council.

Significant landmarks on Merton's outer journey during the years 1948-1955 include completion of his formative program of theological studies; ordinations to the sub-diaconate, the diaconate and the priesthood; attainment of American citizenship. After his priestly ordination Merton served at Gethsemani first as Master of Scholastics and later as Master of Novices.

On his inner journey from 1948-1955 Merton underwent radical change. He moved away from a conformist approach to Roman Catholicism toward a questioning faith. The young monk who had sought holiness by adherence to the Trappist ideal became the adult monk who began exercising generative responsibility for monks in formation. The man who had felt such disdain toward the world when he entered the monastery began turning back to the world with compassionate love. The person determined to become a saint made significant headway in befriending his shadowy side.

Merton's conversion of heart came about in the furnace of

burning inner conflicts. He had construed certain apparent opposites as dichotomies; for example: a vocation to the contemplative life and the gift of writing; desire to remain a Trappist and longing to become a Carthusian; appreciation of the communal dimensions of his life at Gethsemani and irresistible attraction toward increased solitude. Those conflicts had been present during Merton's years in Trappist formation, but now they confronted him as full-blown crises. The scholastic thrust of his theological studies with categories such as nature/grace, natural/supernatural and secular/sacred, together with the institutional structures of Roman Catholicism during that period, compounded his difficulty in reconciling the seemingly divergent directions within himself.

The primary symbol which Merton used to describe this period of his life was Jonas the prophet. Merton believed that his life was especially sealed with the sign of Jonas, because like that prophet he was journeying to his destiny in the belly of a paradox. Jonas was fleeing to Tarsus, while God was insisting that he go to Nineveh. Merton was trying with all his might to go in one direction, while God was drawing him along another way.[1]

With respect to the years 1948-1955, we focus on these areas:

- Merton's growth in contemplation;
- his newfound self-knowledge;
- that insight as a fruit of his contemplation;
- his renewed attitude toward the world;
- his emerging attitude of compassion;
- his instinct for self-expression.

We consider those topics as they pertain to the interrelationship of transcendence, self-actualization and creative expression in his life and his works.[2]

A. Contemplation: A Dark Radiance

On December 13, 1948, approximately five months before his ordination to the priesthood, Thomas Merton made a frank

---

[1] See *Sign of Jonas*, 10-11; *Entering the Silence*, 469-470.
[2] Unless otherwise identified, the principal sources for this chapter are *Sign of Jonas*, 89-362; *Entering the Silence*, 153-488; *A Search for Solitude*, 1-41.

observation in his journal, *The Sign of Jonas.* He wrote of his conviction that his interior life had deepened over the years, but stated that he was at a loss to say exactly how.

From 1948 onward, Merton continued to nurture his spiritual life with a rich variety of prayer forms; for instance: daily Mass, the Rosary, the Divine Office. Yet, he especially valued his solitary prayer. Merton displayed at times in *The Sign of Jonas* a reticence to reveal his intimate experience of the numinous. However, certain entries give us glimpses of his communion with God.

For example, in an excerpt dated February 13, 1949, Merton wrote of his solitary prayer as oriented toward silence and darkness rather than speculation. He described that prayer as a waiting in darkness and a receiving of God's Word, Christ Jesus, in his wholeness rather than in fragmented shadows of feeling and insight.

At the beginning of his monastic life Merton had flung himself into practicing a complex system of meditation. Very quickly he ran up against the inadequacy of acts, thoughts, desires and words in prayer. In a May 15, 1949, entry in *The Sign of Jonas,* Merton shared that from his days as a novice his solitary prayer had unfolded along the dark path of contemplation. He wrote of how resting in God, reposing in God's silence and abiding in God's darkness had for the preceding seven years nourished his growth. He discerned that way of praying to be his vocation.

Shortly afterwards on June 4, 1949, Merton described his contemplation as a dark radiance filling the depths of his soul and burning in the silence of his imageless faith.

As Merton progressed on his journey, he entered ever more deeply into mystery. Thus, he found contemplation increasingly confusing and obscure, yet undeniably real. Proceeding along the pathway of his transcendent experience, Merton grew in finding God's presence not only in himself, but also in the world around him, especially in nature. *The Sign of Jonas* is replete with instances of his awe before the transcendent dimension of creation. For example: he writes of a beautiful small rectangular window with its panoramic view of a valley; of the awesome flight of a hawk swooping down upon a flock of starlings; of the forest blazing transparently with the reality of God.[3]

---

[3] See *Sign of Jonas*, 250, 274-275, 343 respectively; *Entering the Silence*, 380, 407-408, 471.

B. Awareness of Poverty of Spirit

Throughout *The Sign of Jonas* we see a twofold movement in the life of Thomas Merton. That is, as he progressed along his dark path of contemplation, his inner poverty was increasingly evident to him.

Characteristic of Merton's encounters with his shadowy side is a persistent hope in God's merciful love for him. We cite from *The Sign of Jonas* two examples of that outlook:

First, in an entry dated February 1, 1949, Merton recorded an experience of his constricted ego-centered world being shaken up. It seems that a realization of some self-serving desire on his part – perhaps in regard to his wish to be a successful writer – occasioned his reflections. In any case, to describe his situation, he used the image of his finite self, encompassed by a boundary or barrier. He had a sense of quickly coming up against that limit of himself. For years he had operated as if that limited self was co-extensive with the whole universe. He had even been somewhat complacently comfortable in that posture. However, now he viewed that perspective as illusory. Now he perceived his narrowness of vision as restricting him and accusing him of his nothingness. Now he felt the need to expand, to broaden his boundaries, to transcend himself by dying to himself. Yet, he was unable to go that way by his efforts alone. To his surprise, when he stopped trying to resolve the problem with his own resources, he would make some little breakthrough. God's love would filter into his darkness, assuring him of the freedom to come.

Second, in an entry of May 25, 1949, the eve of his ordination to the priesthood, Merton confessed to being far from the monk or the priest that he believed he ought to be. He acknowledged his life to be a great mess, a tangle of semi-aware subterfuges which he had used to evade grace and duty. Yet, he attested that, rather than plunging him into despair, his infidelity to Christ had driven him to throw himself with more abandon into the arms of divine mercy.

Merton considered each of his books to be a mirror of his own character and conscience.[4] He cracked open the covers of each newly published work with a faint hope of finding himself agreeable, but rarely did he succeed in doing so. His comments in *The Sign of*

---

[4] See *Sign of Jonas*, 165; *Entering the Silence*, 287.

Jonas on some of his published writings, although at times unduly critical, indicate honest admission of painful truth about himself.

For instance, in a July 11, 1948 entry, Merton wrote of his book, *Exile Ends in Glory*, being read in the monastery refectory at meal time. As he listened to it, parts of the book made his stomach turn somersaults. Examining himself as to where he got all the pious rhetoric, he owned up to his posturing in that book. He admitted candidly that after his simple profession of vows he thought that a monk was supposed to write that way. Merton went on to confess that he would have felt a whole lot cleaner if he had written nothing but *Thirty Poems* and *The Seven Storey Mountain*.

When the first copy of his new book, *Seeds of Contemplation,* arrived, Merton could hardly keep his hands off the beautiful jacket. However, in a journal entry of the following day, March 6, 1949, he confessed to finding nothing to be proud of between its covers. He judged its cleverness and intricacy to be due not so much to his depth of insight as to his poor punctuation skills and tortuous line of thought. He found the book to be lacking in warmth and affection. He saw in it evidence of an underlying pride in himself which he thought had long ago vanished.

After reviewing his then unpublished novel, *Journal of My Escape from the Nazis* (written in 1941), Merton wrote on March 3, 1951, of finding it to be a very inhibited book, despite its invented language which still appealed to him. In his assessment the book lacked action that moved toward a resolution. Its immobility was a confession at the time of its writing of his sense of nonentity and identity confusion.

By 1951 not even the ever popular, *The Seven Storey Mountain*, escaped Merton's reappraisal. As he corrected the proofs of the French translation of that book, the story sounded to him completely alien. He wrote on June 13, 1951, of feeling like a proofreader working for a publisher and going over the galleys of someone else's work. He concluded that his autobiography was the work of a man of whom he had never heard. That lack of identification with the main character of this autobiography indicates the radical change occurring in his sense of identity.

C. Contemplation and Self-knowledge

How do we reconcile, on the one hand, Merton's sense of deepening contemplative intimacy with God and, on the other hand, his growing awareness of himself as flawed and sinful?

Some interpreters attribute Merton's increasing realization of his imperfection principally to psychological dynamics which occur in the course of individuation; for instance, confrontation with unacknowledged or undeveloped dimensions of personhood as one grows older.[5] Other commentators conclude that Merton's growing awareness of his limitations and sinfulness is evidence that his spiritual path had been misguided and that his mysticism had been a failure.[6]

Factors such as mid-life realignment, low self-esteem and personal failure may indeed have been operative to some degree at this time in Merton's life. However, the primary dynamic at work seems rather to have consisted of these factors:

First, Merton was awakening to the dark side of himself precisely because of his growth in intimacy with God immanent yet transcendent. His increasing awareness of his poverty of spirit was itself enlightenment that emerged from his communion with Jesus.[7] Many Christian mystics attest that the more intimate the union in love between a person and God, the more that individual becomes aware of the depths of his/her limitation, sinfulness and contingency as a creature. That illumination is a fruit of contemplation, not a contradiction to it.[8] Thus, in Christ, the Light, Merton was seeing himself as he truly was – a man with exceptional gifts, but also a person of immense poverty.

Second, Merton's acute sense of his imperfection and woundedness pertained to God's work of healing him. In the dark night of contemplation God set in motion the healing of Merton's core infirmity, which was beyond his full comprehension and power to change. An integral dimension of that process was the surfacing into Merton's consciousness of the truth of himself in order for him to undergo it, to let go and to receive increased freedom of spirit.

Third, Merton was undergoing God's purgation especially in two areas: pride and perfectionism. Merton's excessive concern about the lack of excellence in his literary style is one indication of

---

[5] See, for instance, Robert G. Waldron, *Thomas Merton in Search of His Soul: A Jungian Perspective* (Notre Dame, IN: Ave Maria Press, 1994).

[6] See, for example, David D. Cooper, *Thomas Merton's Art of Denial: The Evolution of a Radical Humanist* (Athens, GA: The University of Georgia Press, 1989), 15-88; 133-191.

[7] In *Conjectures,* 23, Merton wrote that those who hope in God must be willing to let God's lamp shine suddenly upon the darkest corner of their souls.

[8] See *Contemplation,* 85-96; 116-124; *O Blessed Night,* 79-87; *The Spiritual Journey,* 99-124; 163-198.

those immaturities. He wanted desperately to be humble, and in some respects he was so. Yet, a profound pride persisted. He wanted also to strive conscientiously for "the perfection that comes through faith in Christ, and is from God and based on faith" (Phil 3:9). Yet, to some measure he was still pining after his own brand of perfection – perfection by his own efforts. Merton's awareness of the innate limitation of himself and of the work that he was producing was one means through which God mellowed that pride and self-styled perfectionism.

D. A Renewed Perspective Toward the World

No area so blatantly reveals Thomas Merton's change of heart and expansion of identity during the period 1948-1955 as does his attitude toward the world.

Before entering Gethsemani, Merton had concluded that the whole world was evil. Consequently, the world had first to be ridiculed, then spat upon and finally rejected with a curse.[9] He described himself as one spawned by the spirit of selfishness and irresponsibility which, according to him, so characterized the twentieth century.[10] Boarding the train on the first leg of his journey to enter Gethsemani was in his view a snapping and breaking of his ties with the world.[11] The Merton who wrote *The Seven Storey Mountain* and the poetry of the 1940's considered the world with contempt and disdain. As a new Roman Catholic and as a young monk, a crucial concern of Merton was detachment from creation out of what he thought was love of God. His concept of detachment was along the lines of "*either* God *or* a creature," rather than learning to love and to enjoy a specific creature in God with God's own freedom.[12] Merton's sense of detachment at that time was one of rupture with and flight from the world and its values.

During the years 1948-1955, however, Merton's perspective toward the world changed radically. One incident epitomizes that conversion. On August 12, 1948, he went to Louisville as interpreter for the French Vicar General of the Cistercian Order who had come on visitation to Gethsemani. It was Merton's first trip outside the monastery in seven years. *The Sign of Jonas* contains two very

---

[9] See *Sign of Jonas*, 322-323; *Entering the Silence*, 451.
[10] See *Seven Storey Mountain*, 133.
[11] See *Seven Storey Mountain*, 369.
[12] See *O Blessed Night*, 47-68, 155-177.

different reflections upon that trip.[13]

First, we have Merton's journal entries at the time of the trip. On the day after the outing, he portrayed it as a rather ordinary event. Then, the next day, August 14, 1948, he noted that although he felt completely alienated from the world and its activity, he was not without sympathy for the people whom he had seen walking around the city.

Second, we have Merton's introduction, written around 1952, to the section of journal entries for the year 1948.[14] There he recalled wondering as he drove into Louisville how he would react meeting again "the wicked world." He remembered having found it less wicked than he did before he entered Gethsemani. He reminisced that in the city he became aware for the first time in his life of the goodness of people and their immeasurable value to God. He saw beyond exterior details of people and looked upon them with love, respect and pity. In a word, he beheld the world with compassion.

What did Merton actually experience in Louisville? Are his two accounts of the trip reconcilable? We believe so. The two versions represent two faith perspectives upon the same event – one immature, the other maturing. In 1948 Merton was preoccupied with the importance of a static and disdaining form of detachment from the world. Therefore, his immediate reflection upon the visit was through the lens of that value, with the aspect of sympathy for people taking second place. Four years later when Merton wrote the introduction for the 1948 entries, he had undergone considerable interior change. As he reconsidered his 1948 visit to Louisville, he reinterpreted it from his new perspective, this time accentuating identification and compassion.

Thus, in his contemplative living Merton formed a renewed perspective toward the world and his place within it. For the rest of his life he continued to protest against injustice, materialism and superficiality with regard to the world. Yet, Merton came to acknowledge that much of what he had labeled as "the wicked world" was a figment of his imagination, a psychological game that began when he was about ten years of age.[15] He confessed that many things that he had resented about the world were actually a

---

[13] See *Sign of Jonas*, 114-115 and 91-92 respectively; also *Entering the Silence*, 223-224.
[14] See *Sign of Jonas*, 89-92.
[15] See *Sign of Jonas*, 162; *Entering the Silence*, 283.

projection upon it of his own defects.[16]   He realized that being a monk meant finding his place in the world and allowing the world a share in his new life.[17]

E. The Desert of Compassion

Integral to Thomas Merton's experience of himself in encounter with God was the question of vocational lifestyle. How was God calling him to live?   What style of living was compatible with his identity and conducive to his self-actualization?

Trappist life was communally oriented.   While increasingly committing himself to God according to the Cistercian constitutions, Merton experienced during the years 1948-1955 a relentless drawing to a more eremitical or solitary form of contemplative living.

Certain changes at Gethsemani after World War II further exacerbated Merton's living situation.[18]   For one thing, numerous aspirants to the Trappist life descended unexpectedly upon the monastery.   Consequently, two hundred seventy men seeking silence and solitude packed into a building designed for seventy monks. Moreover, the community itself was undergoing transition.   In Merton's words, it was a furnace of ambivalence.   Modernization of its medieval structures was in progress, especially in its agricultural and forestry operations.   One result of that modernization was an increased level of noise and activity incessantly permeating the enclosure.   Paradoxically, income from Merton's writings provided the primary source of funding for those renovations.

Throughout his journals of 1948-1955 we see Merton fluctuating on the issue of a possible call to a more solitary life.   His fluctuations made him at times a nuisance to his superiors.   Abbot James Fox was generally sensitive to Merton's need for more silence and solitude than ordinarily possible in the Trappist life.   For example, in early January 1949 Fox gave Merton permission to do his writing in a vault near the abbot's office as a means of providing him more solitude.   In 1953 the Abbot offered Merton for a certain portion of each day the use of an old tool shed in the nearby woods. Merton enthusiastically accepted this arrangement, and named that solitary place, "St. Anne's."

---

[16] See *Sign of Jonas*, 91-92.
[17] See *Sign of Jonas,* 322-323; *Entering the Silence*, 451-452; *Conjectures*, 47, 256-257, 284, 324-325.
[18] See *Sign of Jonas*, 5.

Nonetheless, Merton's longing for ever greater solitude persisted. Events came to a head in 1955. In May of that year Merton applied to the Congregation of Religious in Rome for official transfer to the Camaldolese, an order of hermits. In case that request did not receive approval, Merton devised a back-up plan: that of leaving Gethsemani and secretly going to Monte Corona where he would live as an unknown solitary and give up writing. In an unexpected turn of events Abbot Fox offered Merton in June 1955 the opportunity to live as a hermit while remaining at Gethsemani. According to Fox's plan, Merton could live as watchman at a fire-lookout tower set up by the State Forestry Department on Gethsemani property. Merton liked the idea. In the fall of 1955 Fox received approval for the undertaking from the Abbot General of the Cistercian Order. The one condition laid down by Merton's superiors was that he cease writing and publication on taking up residence at the tower.

With official approval for the fire-tower hermitage, Merton had his back against the wall. He was forced to make a decision. For years he had been expressing the desire to live as a hermit and to stop writing. Yet, just at the moment when that dream was about to become reality, Merton did a complete about-face. He opted to go in a reverse direction. Three days after the Abbot informed him of permission to proceed with their plan for the fire-tower hermitage, Merton showed up at the Abbot's office and offered to serve in the recently vacated position of Master of Novices. The Abbot accepted his offer and appointed him to the position.

Thus, Merton opted in effect to immerse himself even more in the common life. As Novice Master he assumed responsibility for maintaining Trappist traditions and for guiding the formation of future monks of Gethsemani. By means of Merton's increased involvement with his brothers at Gethsemani, God would lead Merton into greater interior solitude. By means of compassion for the world he would enter further into the desert of the heart.

Merton's choice of continuing to journey by means of the "desert of compassion"[19] may seem to be entirely opposite to his desire to live as a hermit. However, time would reveal that option to be another step in the process of his being born by God into the eremitical life. A calling to the hermit life presupposes that one has first lived fully some form of the contemplative life. Merton's

---

[19] See *Sign of Jonas*, 333-334; *Entering the Silence*, 463-464.

decision seems to have been based on an intuitive realization that further growth in communal contemplative living was necessary for him. The position of Master of Novices did enable him more exterior aloneness within community than was possible for him previously. He resided with the novices in a building apart from the other monks. There he had his own bedroom, an office and the availability of the novices to type manuscripts for him.

F. The Instinct for Self-expression

A writer's words must spring up from his/her interior depths in order to produce a work of value.[20] That principle, which Thomas Merton readily accepted, had the potential to point him toward reconciliation of his contemplation and his writing. That principle could have taken Merton in the direction of seeing his writings as a fruit of his transcendent experience and of respecting his words as a springboard to deepening encounter with the mystery of God. Yet, between 1948-1955 Merton continued to undergo conflict between those two gifts. Only in sporadic moments of insight did he accept that his path to holiness required both contemplation and writing. On those occasions Merton realized not only that he had to remain a monk, but also that he had to write down what he had become.[21]

During winter and spring of 1949 Merton's anxiety about writing took another twist. Whereas previously writing had been the source of an imaginary difficulty, then it became a real problem. Merton suddenly discovered that he could barely write at all. His instinct for self-expression had dried up or become paralyzed. Merton identified four reasons for his writer's block:

- His focus was elsewhere on preparation for major orders and the priesthood.
- He was tired and stale. He had been writing too much, and the very thought of writing repelled him to the depths of his soul.
- He was ashamed of the fame that had come his way with the publication of *The Seven Storey Mountain*. He thought public success was counter to being a good Trappist monk.
- He was overloaded with fan mail, which for a while he had to

---

[20] See *Sign of Jonas*, 125.
[21] See, for example, *Sign of Jonas*, 154, 207, 233-234, 269; *Entering the Silence*, 276, 338, 365, 400; *Road to Joy*, 22-23.

sort out and to answer on his own.[22]

After his ordination as a deacon in March 1949, Merton decided to stop composing poetry altogether. He had concluded that his verse lacked quality. Moreover, for the sake of integrity he wanted to get rid of what he considered a useless interference with his prayer life. Thereafter, he wrote poetry only on rare occasion when he thought charity demanded or permitted it. Another volume of his poetry did not appear in print until 1957.

When writer's block overcame Merton, he had in the works a manuscript that he had began under the title, *The Cloud and the Fire*. Part of that text was eventually published as *The Ascent to Truth* (1951). Merton had started the project with the intent of presenting the dogmatic essentials of mystical theology, with reference to scripture, tradition and the liturgy. The final published manuscript was a study primarily of the mysticism of St. John of the Cross, as seen through the lens of scholastic theology.

Many entries in *The Sign of Jonas* describe Merton's struggle with that project. In one passage dated February 9, 1949, for example, he described himself at sea in a mass of half-digested notes, hoping to work out his ideas on paper as he went along. To his dismay, the more he rewrote the text, the more he lost the freshness of the original expression. For him writing was hopeless without the impetus of new ideas. In an entry for April 29, 1949, he portrayed himself sitting at his typewriter, his fingers wound up in a cat's cradle of strings, overwhelmed by a sense of inadequacy and encompassed by a mass of literary dilemmas. It took two years before that manuscript was ready for press. The text took shape easily and rapidly near the end of that period. However, in later life Merton judged *The Ascent to Truth* to be among his worst books.

Merton came to several insights in laboring over that text. He deduced that the technical language of metaphysics and dogmatic theology which he had employed in the manuscript did not reach ordinary people. That mode of expression failed to communicate what for him was most personal and vibrant in religious experience. Furthermore, it did not fit his natural mode of self-expression. He began to trust his inclination toward a style more suitable to his gifts and personality, one that emerged from his traveling down the byways of poetry and intuition. That style consisted in sharing his

---

[22] See *Sign of Jonas*, 126-127.

reflection upon the spiritual life in the language of personal experience.[23]

We see a preliminary effort in that direction in the book, *Seeds of Contemplation* (1949), which Merton described as a collection of notes and personal reflections on the spiritual life.[24] He experimented further with that inductive approach in his journal, *The Sign of Jonas* (1953). With the publication of *No Man is an Island* (1955), the methodology of using experience as the basis of faith reflection had become for Merton full-blown and irreversible. He proclaimed in the introduction to that book his intention to leave systems to others and to refrain from attempting to articulate universal principles. His sole aim was to share with his readers his reflections on certain aspects of the spiritual life.

With Merton's option for personal experience as the basis of his writing, the content of his work henceforth sprang from whatever issue of spiritual significance held his attention at a given time. His creative expression flowed from his experience of transcendence in the context of his day-to-day living. For instance, Merton wrestled with his dilemma of participating in a communally oriented contemplative life, while he desired greater aloneness. From that experience came two of his most insightful works on the meaning of solitude: *Thoughts in Solitude* (written around 1953), together with an essay first published in French as "*Dans le desert de Dieu*" (1955) and later included under the title, "Notes on a Philosophy of Solitude," in the book, *Disputed Questions*. In those writings Merton broke away from the view of solitude as a means for an elite few to do penance and to withdraw from the world. He developed the perspective of solitude as available to all God's people for the purposes of healing, intimacy and unity.

---

[23] See *Sign of Jonas*, 8-9.
[24] See *Seeds of Contemplation* (Norfolk, CT: New Directions, 1949), xiv-xv.

CHAPTER 17

The New Person

According to Thomas Merton, the central character in *The Seven Storey Mountain* was now dead. The writer of *The Sign of Jonas* had passed away. But who was the new Merton rising up from the ashes?

During the years 1956-1960 the interior revolution that Merton had undergone took solid hold in his attitudes and actions.[1] We examine in this chapter the work of self-actualization and creative expression that took shape in conjunction with his experience of the transcendent throughout that period. Specifically, we focus upon the following themes:

- Merton's expanded understanding of contemplation;
- new directions emerging from his experience of the transcendent, such as:
    - solidarity with the peoples of the world,
    - involvement in ecumenical endeavors,
    - awareness of the feminine principle in God,
    - a newfound sense of mission;
- Merton's strange and solitary path.

A. Contemplation: The Fullness of an Integrated Life

In Thomas Merton's correspondence between 1956-1960, we catch glimpses of his inner journey. Awareness of God's love for him and consciousness of God's invitation to ever deeper intimacy were constants in his life. He grew in appreciation of God's gifts to

---

[1] On this period in the life of Thomas Merton, see his journal, *A Search for Solitude*, 43-394.

him and in recognition of his inner poverty.[2] Merton continued to
seek God by way of the somewhat strange and solitary path that was
his.[3]   Merton described himself to several correspondents as still
having both the desire and the opportunity for prayer, silence and
solitude.[4] He saw himself as maturing in depth, simplicity and
honesty with himself.[5] Merton found certain longstanding conflicts
continuing to ferment: to write or not to write; to remain at
Gethsemani or to take part in a monastic foundation elsewhere; to
live the cenobitic life or to become a hermit. However, in living out
those questions he had within himself deepening peace, joy and trust.

Merton's evolving experience of transcendence becomes
especially evident in his expanded understanding of Christian
contemplation. Prior to 1958, Merton thought of the practice of
contemplation to some degree as an objectified reality that other
aspects of human life could obstruct. By 1958, however, he realized
that contemplation was not a thing, an object or a possession.
Rather, contemplation belongs to the more mysterious realm of who
a person is. Prior to 1958, Merton tended to compartmentalize the
various dimensions of human life. He was inclined to think of
contemplation in terms of rest and the other aspects of life as activity
of one form or another. By 1958, however, Merton experienced
contemplation as inseparable from life and essential to the dynamism
of life, which for him included work, creation, production,
fruitfulness and most of all love. He understood contemplation then
as the fullness of an integrated life, as the crown of life and of all
life's activities.[6]

That broader understanding of contemplation did not negate
the importance of extended periods of time for silent loving
communion with God. Merton experienced solitary prayer as a
value and a necessity up to his death. Yet, by 1958 he had a keen
intuition of God's immanent transcendence animating all daily
existence and routine activity. His prayer had become grounded in
life, and life had become for him prayer.

Merton's expanded experience and understanding of
contemplation became a principle of synthesis in his life, pulling
together what had been for him seemingly irreconcilable opposites.

---

[2] See, for example, *School of Charity*, 98.
[3] See *School of Charity*, 101.
[4] See *School of Charity*, 103, 131, 134.
[5] See *School of Charity*, 98-99.
[6] See "Poetry and Contemplation: A Reappraisal," in *Literary Essays*, 339.

One example of his newfound balance is evident in his reassessment of the relationship between contemplation and art, specifically the composition of verse. His approach as expressed in the July 1947 edition of the periodical *Commonweal* had been a clear-cut "either/or" choice between mystical prayer and poetry. He had exhorted artists, when brought to the brink of direct immediate communion with God, to sacrifice art for the sake of contemplation.[7] By 1958, however, he believed that there was no universally applicable answer to the question of balancing contemplation and art. How to integrate the two gifts was dependent upon God's will for a person in a specific circumstance.[8]

Nonetheless, some residue of Merton's former "either/or" stance remained. He contended that in an individual human life it is inevitable that at some point the impulse toward creative expression and the call to contemplation come into conflict. Merton did not offer any solution for that dilemma other than to state God can and does resolve the conflict, without needing any advice from us.[9] He cited St. John of the Cross as an example of a Christian who attained the heights of both poetic creation and mystic prayer, without any apparent contradiction between the two. In his personal life Merton would continue for his remaining years to grow in the integration of contemplation and creative expression.

B. New Seeds from Contemplation

By the mid-1950's Thomas Merton's experience of the transcendent gave rise to an explosion of interests. Some subjects were entirely new to him; for instance: developmental psychology, modern art, nuclear physics, social justice and world peace. Other attractions had roots in his past, but they had been put aside on his entrance to Gethsemani; for example:

- works by contemporary writers and poets;
- writings on Eastern mysticism, which Merton had discovered while at Columbia University;
- Gandhi and non-violence, an interest that began at Oakham Public School;

---

[7] See Thomas Merton, "Poetry and the Contemplative Life," in *Figures for an Apocalypse* (New York, NY: New Directions, 1947), 95-111.

[8] See "Poetry and Contemplation: A Reappraisal," in *Literary Essays*, 352-353.

[9] See "Poetry and Contemplation: A Reappraisal," in *Literary Essays*, 353.

- the countries of Latin America, an affinity nurtured by his visit to Cuba during Easter 1940.

Certain values or interests that asserted themselves in Merton during the latter half of the 1950's were exceptionally significant. They were like seeds sprouting forth from his contemplative life that would mature and bear fruit only in the next decade. Merton's exploration of or involvement with those directions gave rise to creative expression in the form of prose, poetry, essays and letters. Specifically, these areas included: solidarity with the peoples of the world; ecumenism; a sense of mission; and intuition of the feminine principle in God.

(1) Solidarity with the Peoples of the World

The silence and solitude of Thomas Merton's contemplative life was a catalyst for communion with both God and the world. The more deeply Merton encountered God in contemplation, the more profoundly he experienced himself in communion with other people. In God Merton discovered himself to be one with all. In Christ Jesus he discovered all persons as brothers and sisters both to him and to each other.

We cite now two striking testaments of Merton to that truth: a description of an experience in Louisville and a preface to an Argentine edition of his writings.

a.   Louisville, the Corner of Fourth and Walnut

On March 18, 1958, Thomas Merton had occasion to go into Louisville.[10] At the corner of Fourth and Walnut, in the heart of the city's shopping district, he was suddenly overwhelmed with the awareness of his love for all the people whom he saw around him and with the realization of his union with them. It was as if he could see each person as s/he is in God's eyes.

Merton noted in describing this event that neither his vocation nor the monastic life itself was at issue. However, the idea that being in a monastery constituted a separation from the world came under his intense scrutiny. Monastic thinking at that time assumed that profession of vows and ordination to the priesthood put

---

[10] See *Conjectures*, 156-158; *A Search for Solitude*, 181-182.

a monk into a class of the spiritual elite. The experience in Louisville was for Merton like an awakening from a dream of separateness. It emancipated him from an illusory sense of difference that he had carried with him for sixteen or seventeen years. It jolted him out of fictitious self-isolation in a special world of renunciation and presumed holiness. It called forth in him gratitude to God for being like other ordinary human beings. It released in him joy in the discovery of being simply a member of the human family wherein God had become incarnate.

Merton insisted also that the reality of his oneness with those people in Louisville did not run counter to his solitude. On the contrary, precisely because of his solidarity with them, he owed it to them to remain alone. He proclaimed that in his solitude they were not strangers but rather his own self.

b.   The Preface to the Argentine Edition of
The Complete Works of Thomas Merton

In this preface Merton identified the life of God as the central reality of his existence. In the mystery of God's life he found the meaning and the significance of all things.

Merton noted that as his life hidden with Christ in God unfolded, his horizons expanded both historically and geographically. He attested that in the silence of the natural world around him and in the solitude of his monastery he had come to an experiential awareness of the whole western hemisphere. Without traveling from place to place or flying over rivers and mountains, he had by God's grace explored the new world.

Merton described this reality with specific reference to Latin America. As he lived out his silent and solitary life, Merton found within himself communion with the lands and the peoples of that region. He heard from within the depths of his personhood a voice speaking with a numinous clarity. It was as if he had in his heart the Bolivian plateau's glittering hoarfrost, the Incas' mountainous dwelling places, Quito's grandeur, Bogotá's frigid plains and the Amazon's mysterious jungles. It seemed to Merton that residing within him were whole cities adjacent to each other, filled with the paradoxes of extravagant wealth and extreme destitution. Merton felt as if within the inexpressible silence of his heart resided Mexico's ancient Aztec and Mayan civilizations. In the profound silence of Peru he heard the echo of ancient wisdom that contained in its secrets a symbolic and prophetic image of truth, similar to Jesus Christ.

Merton experienced Latin America with its beauty and potential as stirring within him like a giant sleeper. That presence within him seemed to speak often with God's own voice. That presence awakened him from indifference. It caused him to struggle for some comprehension of the destiny of the new world. However, when insight eluded him, he could only profess its destiny to be still hidden in the mystery of God's providence.[11]

(2) Ecumenism

By the mid-1950's Thomas Merton was acutely conscious of a need to move beyond the narrow, rather elitist Catholicism of his early monastic years toward a more universalistic Catholicism. He believed that Catholicism is not the prerogative of any one culture, nation or economic class. He felt that to identify exclusively with any one group – whether the Irish Catholicism of the Eastern United States, the then vibrant Catholicism of his native France or that of Latin America – would make him a partial Catholic. Thus, his Catholicism reached out to all the world and to all times.[12]

Conjectures of a Guilty Bystander includes a passage, the gist of which Merton wrote initially in a private journal entry dated April 28, 1957:

> If I can unite *in myself* the thought and the devotion of Eastern and Western Christendom, the Greek and the Latin Fathers, the Russians with the Spanish mystics, I can prepare in myself the reunion of divided Christians. From that secret and unspoken unity in myself can eventually come a visible and manifest unity of all Christians. If we want to bring together what is divided, we can not do so by imposing one division upon the other or absorbing one division into the other.... We must contain all divided worlds in ourselves and transcend them in Christ.[13]

---

[11] See *Honorable Reader*, 40. See also *A Search for Solitude*, 168-169.
[12] See *Honorable Reader*, 41.
[13] *Conjectures*, 21; *A Search for Solitude*, 87.

Merton's statement reveals an openness to the diverse currents within Christianity. It bespeaks his reaching out in compassion to the divided world of Christendom not only to witness to his truth, but also to let Christian traditions other than his own nurture his faith. His receptivity extended also to nonchristian religions, especially Zen Buddhism.

Throughout the years 1956-1960 Merton began encounter with other religious traditions through a variety of means; for instance:

- personal study of the different religious traditions;
- feedback from people who read his books and who wrote to him sharing their personal experience;
- dialogue at Gethsemani with Protestant groups;
- correspondence with the Russian writer, Boris Pasternak;
- interchange with Daisetz Suzuki on Zen Buddhism;
- contact with Abdul Aziz from Pakistan on Sufi mysticism in the Islamic religious tradition.

In a letter dated December 5, 1960, we see an example of how Merton's expanding horizons in the area of ecumenism were interrelating with his creative process.[14] He shared with a correspondent his plan to do a thorough revision of his book, *Seeds of Contemplation* (1949). The impetus for this project came from Merton's contact with Abdul Aziz. He could not send the book to Aziz, because it contained an insensitive remark about Sufis. The fruit of that revision would be Merton's outstanding work, *New Seeds of Contemplation* (1962).

(3) The Feminine Principle in God

Did Thomas Merton's insight into the feminine principle in God come through his efforts to integrate into his sense of self-identity what the psychologist Carl Jung termed the *anima* (the contrasexual side of man, or the feminine principle)? Was Merton's insight a direct fruit of his contemplation? Or did that awareness arise from a combination of psychological development and experience of the transcendent? Most probably the source of Merton's perception of the feminine principle in God was an

---

[14] See *Road to Joy*, 237.

interpenetration of the psychological and the spiritual. In any case, Merton's image of God during the years 1956-1960 went beyond the traditional male representation of the divine.

Merton recorded in his journal a dream of February 28, 1958. He described being embraced by a young Jewish girl who tells him that her name is Proverb. On March 4, 1958, Merton followed up on the dream by writing Proverb a letter in which he expressed gratitude to her for loving in him a lost part of himself. He revealed his admiration for the mystery, simplicity and secrecy of her name. He wrote one final time to Proverb in a journal entry dated March 19, 1958.[15]

Merton brought up the dream also in a letter of October 23, 1958, to Boris Pasternak, associating the young girl "Proverb" with Lara in Pasternak's novel, *Doctor Zhivago*. In that letter Merton connected his dream of Proverb with his experience in Louisville at the corner of Fourth and Walnut. He recalled suddenly realizing as he was walking around in the city that every person was Proverb, that her singular beauty, purity and shyness were transparent in each one, that people were unaware of their identity as the Child precious to God who before the beginning of the world played in the divine presence.[16] The latter image is an allusion to *Proverbs* 8:30-31, which describes Wisdom at play in the divine presence, delighting God before the creation of the world.

The following year a related event occurred. On April 21, 1959, Merton visited in Lexington, Kentucky, Victor Hammer, a friend who was an artist. Merton saw on the panel of a triptych which Hammer had begun a woman in dark robes setting a crown on a young man's head. That woman fascinated him. Who was she? Merton identified her as *Hagía Sophia* (Holy Wisdom). In a letter to Hammer on May 14, 1959, on the subject of Holy Wisdom, Merton referred to the feminine principle in the cosmos as the origin of the creative actualizations of the Father's presence in this world and the revelation of his glory.[17]   Merton's insights into Holy Wisdom coalesced into the poem, *Hagía Sophia*.[18]

---

[15] See *A Search for Solitude*, 176, 182.
[16] See *Courage for Truth*, 90.
[17] See *Witness to Truth*, 2-6.
[18] See *Collected Poems*, 363-371.

(4) An Apostolate of Friendship

By the year 1958 Thomas Merton as a contemplative was attempting to reformulate his responsibility to the world. Contemplation itself is the prime ministry of a contemplative. What happens in one member affects the whole body of Christ. The love of God operative within a contemplative exerts through that person a transforming and purifying effect within creation.[19] However, Merton was experiencing stirrings also in another ministerial direction. His solidarity with all peoples and his compassion for the world in its brokenness impelled him toward another kind of service. In a word, his contemplation gave birth to a new mission.

Merton did not experience that missioning as a need to leave monastic life. Rather, he felt drawn to bring his contemplative vision to bear upon the world of his time, while continuing to live his Trappist life with prayer at its center. A letter of November 10, 1958, to Pope John XXIII specified how Merton integrated that direction into his contemplative life. With the permission of his superiors he exercised a small and limited ministry to a circle of intellectuals – artists, writers, publishers, poets, etc. – from all over the world without ever having to leave his cloister. He named this endeavor an "apostolate of friendship."[20]

C. Merton's Strange and Somewhat Solitary Path

When he had the opportunity in 1955 to live as a hermit, Thomas Merton reversed himself and offered his services as Master of Novices. Yet, that option by no means quelled Merton's irrepressible longing for solitude.

As Merton conscientiously fulfilled the responsibilities of Novice Master, he secured as much silence and solitude as possible within the scope of that duty. Toward the end of 1960 an opportunity for additional aloneness came his way. A cottage for small group retreats was erected at a secluded location on the Cistercian property. When the cottage was not in use, Merton had permission to spend time there on a daily basis.

During the years 1956-1960 Merton had periodic outbreaks of plans to start up elsewhere a renewed form of monastic living.

---

[19] See *Contemplation*, 141-146.
[20] See *Hidden Ground of Love*, 481-483.

For instance, in the fall of 1958 he wrote to a friend about an idea of founding in Ecuador something akin to an ashram.[21] In 1959 he brainstormed with another correspondent about the possibility of going to live as a hermit-missionary among a Native American group.[22] His scheming reached such a pitch in 1959 that he petitioned the Congregation for Religious in Rome for a dispensation to leave Gethsemani and transfer to a monastery in Cuernavaca, Mexico. When in December 1960 the authorities in Rome denied that request, Merton peacefully reconciled himself yet again to remaining at Gethsemani.[23]

Merton's spiritual journey was evolving between 1956-1960 in two seemingly opposite, yet thoroughly interconnected directions: that of compassionate turning toward the world and that of being born gradually into deeper solitude. One work that mirrors both directions is *Disputed Questions* (1960), a collection of essays. Some essays in that book are on topics directly related to contemplative living, while others pertain to Merton's emerging interest in the world of his time. Merton identified the thread connecting the selection of essays in *Disputed Questions* as the relation of the person to the social organization.[24]

By 1960 Merton was confident about the form that his creative expression would henceforth take. His methodology in *Disputed Questions* was simply that of thinking out loud about certain ideas and events which he deemed spiritually and intellectually significant.[25] He judged himself at his best as a writer when using the form of journals or notebooks. He was again writing poetry on topics covering the wide range of his interests. Moreover, his apostolate of friendship opened up a new way to exercise his creative process: letter writing.

D. The New Merton

Who then was the new Thomas Merton who came to the fore during the years 1956-1960? Who was this person now embarking upon the decade of the 1960's? Among the salient characteristics of

---

[21] See *Hidden Ground of Love*, 17.

[22] See *Hidden Ground of Love*, 136; also *A Search for Solitude*, 287-288.

[23] See, for instance, *Courage for Truth*, 111-122; *A Search for Solitude*, 302, 306-328, 358; *Witness to Truth*, 200-226.

[24] See *Disputed Questions*, viii.

[25] See *Disputed Questions*, vii.

the new Merton are these:

Thomas Merton remained faithful to contemplation, yet tried to be contemplative to others who were contemplatively inclined. He lived the contemplative life, yet perceived the need to bring the wisdom of contemplation to bear upon the great political, social and spiritual issues of his day. In his encounter with God as mystery he intuited the feminine principle in the divine. He leapt far beyond the narrow Catholicism of his early monastic years to a broader universalistic Catholicism. Merton remained Roman Catholic, while entering into dialogue with other Christian affiliations and with nonchristian religions. He continued to reside at Gethsemani, yet extended his spiritual boundaries to include the whole world. He sought out silence and solitude, while deepening his solidarity with all people. He continued to live the communal life, yet found in himself greater solitude of heart. He envisioned new forms and expressions of contemplative living, yet labored to actualize change from within the structures of the Cistercian Order.

Thomas Merton was still a man of contradictions, finding in himself: humility and pride; acceptance and intolerance; faith and doubt; hope and near despair; love for others and impatience with them. He still bore remnants of his old conflicts: to be a monk or to be a writer; to live in community or to be a hermit; to remain at Gethsemani or to go elsewhere. Yet, he was being thrust forward on his pilgrimage in ways that he could never have foreseen.

Thomas Merton was a man struggling to balance truth as he understood it with obedience to his superiors. He was one willing to let his perception of truth be expanded, modified or corrected by dialogue with superiors, friends, confreres, anyone who touched his life.

Thomas Merton's interests had expanded to include a widening range of human pursuits: physics, psychology, languages, literary criticism, modern art, sociology.

Thomas Merton was a man seeking to become more holy by becoming more human. As an artist of words, he had found the form of creative expression that best suited his personality and best expressed his experience of transcendence.

CHAPTER 18

Becoming The Universal Person

As he embarked upon the decade of the 1960's, the new Thomas Merton moved in the direction of becoming the universal person. He experienced life proceeding inexorably toward crisis and mystery.[1] He recognized the need for the slow finishing of the work of God in him.[2] From his fresh start Merton journeyed toward final integration.[3]

The notion of final integration fascinated Merton in the last year of his life. Between January 1968 and March 1968, he read the book, *Final Integration in the Adult Personality: A Measure for Peace* (1965), by A. Reza Arasteh, a Persian psychoanalyst. Merton was so impressed by the book that he wrote an essay in which he applied the concept to the monastic life.[4]

In that essay Merton took up Arasteh's description of final integration as a state of maturity defined by rebirth of the self into a new transcultural identity. In the Christian sphere Merton understood transcultural integration to be eschatological. It entails our dying and rising, our disintegration and reintegration. It designates our rebirth into the transformed time of the Spirit and our re-creation in Christ. Receptivity, detachment, solitude and poverty of spirit dispose us for that regeneration. The dark night of the soul forms the matrix wherein we undergo death to the social and cultural self and emergence of our true self. Merton considered final

---

[1] See *Dancing in the Water*, 151.
[2] See *Dancing in the Water*, 203.
[3] These journals of Thomas Merton pertain to the years 1960-1968: *A Search for Solitude*, 367-394; *Turning Toward the World*; *Dancing in the Water*; *Learning to Love; The Other Side.*
[4] See "Final Integration: Toward a Monastic Therapy," in *CWA*, 205-217; also Merton's letter to Arasteh in *Hidden Ground of Love*, 42; *The Other Side*, 45, 71; *Merton in Alaska*, 143-155.

integration to be an aspiration not of an elite few, but of all people.

Among the qualities of the fully integrated person, Merton identified these:

- S/he is completely unique, personal and creative.
- S/he apprehends his/her life fully and wholly from an inner ground that is both individual and collective.
- S/he is in a sense the cosmic or the universal person; that is, one who identifies with all persons but without being dominated by anyone; one who embraces the full richness of ordinary life, while yet going beyond all limiting forms; one who accepts all humankind, not just his/her own society or culture.
- S/he is fully catholic; that is, one who intuits the one truth in its myriad manifestations and sees the various expressions of truth as complementary.
- S/he is capable of bringing wisdom, freedom and spontaneity into the lives of other people.
- S/he is a peacemaker.

Many significant events occurred in Merton's life during the period 1961-1968; for example: the formation of new friendships and the deepening of long-standing relationships; service as Master of Novices at Gethsemani; physical illness; involvement with the peace movement; becoming a hermit; falling in love with a young student nurse; his journey to Asia.

As the events of his life unfolded throughout the 1960's, much of Merton's energy revolved around certain primary values. In this chapter we focus on the interplay of transcendence, self-actualization and creative expression in relation to these values of his:

- contemplation,
- solitude,
- the feminine,
- justice and peace,
- dialogue with world religions.

A. Contemplation: Beholding the Dark Face of God

The catalyst for Thomas Merton's entrance into the Roman Catholic Church had been threefold: (1) He had an awareness of God's presence within himself, this life and this world. (2) He believed that his responsibility as a Christian was to live in full and vital consciousness of that transcendent ground of his being and of the world's existence. (3) He found in the Christian tradition – specifically, in the writings of the Greek and the Latin authors of Christian Antiquity, St. Thomas Aquinas and St. John of the Cross – the strongest encouragement for access to immediate and direct communion with God in daily life.[5]

That immediate and direct encounter with the indwelling Father, Son and Spirit, Merton understood to be transcendent experience or Christian contemplation. Throughout his life Merton's contemplative encounter with God deepened and found new forms of expression.

Merton continued during the 1960's to be drawn to what he termed, "the dark face of God."[6] One of his images of God was that of the abyss of being who transcends all division and nothingness.[7] He spoke of contemplation as God's burning presence in mystery.[8] He experienced his solitary prayer as a time of a silent deepening in which the interior truth of his nothingness in God impressed itself upon his consciousness.[9] He remained convinced of the need within the Church for a solitary, bare, dark, imageless and wordless type of prayer. In fact, he believed that way of communing with God to be his vocation.[10] Among the fruits of contemplation Merton identified the full awakening of self-identity and cosmic unity. He believed that contemplation enabled the Christian to find his/her place in the whole of creation, in the entire divine plan of salvation, in the full mystery of Christ.[11]

On January 2, 1966, Thomas Merton wrote to his Islamic friend, Abdul Aziz, a letter that was particularly revealing of Merton's transcendent experience at the time. In the letter Merton described through several images his ordinary way of praying. It was attentiveness to the presence of God, to God's will and to God's love. It was wordless adoration of God who is invisible and infinitely beyond human comprehension. It was an orientation toward realizing God as all. It was praise rising up out of the center of nothingness and silence. Merton shared that in praying he did not

---

[5] See *Conjectures*, 320.
[6] See *Vow of Conversation*, 177; *Dancing in the Water*, 233.
[7] See *Vow of Conversation*, 174; *Dancing in the Water*, 229.
[8] See *Conjectures*, 70.
[9] See *Vow of Conversation*, 170; *Dancing in the Water*, 224.
[10] See *Hidden Ground of Love*, 73.
[11] See *Vow of Conversation*, 184; *Dancing in the Water*, 250.

"think about" anything. Rather, his prayer was "a direct seeking of the Face of the Invisible." He remarked to his friend that a person cannot find that Face without being lost in God, the Invisible One.[12]

B. A Desert Existence

A lifelong characteristic of Thomas Merton's transcendent experience was his preference for the desert. In a Pentecost 1967 circular letter to his friends Merton wrote of having always tended toward a deepening of his faith in solitude. A desert or wilderness way of life wherein he did not seek after extraordinary experiences had been integral to his personal vocation.[13] Up to his death Merton continued to journey along that contemplative path.

In both 1955 and 1959 Merton came within a hair's breath of embarking upon a more eremitically oriented life. However, at both decisive moments he had opted to remain in community at Gethsemani, while securing more opportunities for personal solitude. After the construction in 1960 of a cottage for small group retreats on the Abbey grounds, Merton spent time alone in silence and solitude at that facility when retreatants were not using it. By 1961 he began spending a portion of each day there, sometimes the entire afternoon. In the autumn of 1964 he started remaining overnight in that cottage whenever he felt so inclined.[14] Finally, on August 20, 1965, relieved of all official leadership responsibilities at the monastery, Merton moved into the cottage on a permanent basis. Thus, he reached another crossroads in his desert existence. Merton had begun to live as a hermit. Those gradual intensifications of solitude came about as a consequence of Merton's discernment of his vocation with those persons who held positions of authority in his Order, especially James Fox, then Abbot of Gethsemani.

Merton's eremitical life was an extension and a transformation of his contemplative lifestyle. As such, it marked a critical threshold in the process of his death to self and rebirth in Christ Jesus. Merton's allusions to daily life in his hermitage reveal both the sorrow and the joy, the struggle and the peace of his solitary transcendent experience.[15] On the one hand, he contended with his

---

[12] See *Hidden Ground of Love*, 63-64.
[13] See *Road to Joy*, 102; also *Contemplative Prayer*, 89.
[14] See *Hidden Ground of Love*, 47, 369; *Road to Joy*, 97.
[15] See, for example: *Vow of Conversation*, 17, 45, 140, 161; *Hidden Ground of Love*, 62-64; 497-516; *Dancing in the Water*, 280-349; *Learning to Love*, 1-348; *The Other Side*, 3-88.

shadowy side: loneliness, pride, self-doubt, dread, rebelliousness, illusion, sensitivity to rejection, feelings of abandonment, dissatisfaction, suspicion and fear. On the other hand, Merton's experience of the hermit life was one of liberation. In eremitical solitude he let go the masks, the roles, the functions that defined his self-identity in society in order to abide in the freedom of his true identity in God. Every living creature around his hermitage – the birds, the trees, the deer, etc. – by being true to itself encouraged Merton to be faithful to who God was calling him to be.

Merton did not find the solitary life in any way esoteric, extraordinary or artificial. It was for him supremely simple, ordinary and real. It reduced him to the basic condition of humankind. It reminded him of his personal incompletion and insufficiency. From that ground of being his daily living evolved. From that position of being merely human Merton entered into renewed relationships with God, with society, with every aspect of creation. The condition of mere humanity, Merton believed, is capable of being realized by any person anywhere in any walk of life. It is not reserved to the hermit. Yet, Merton maintained that by virtue of his vocation the eremitical life was for him the way to attain full humanity in Christ Jesus.

Merton's life as a hermit was an ever deepening actualization of a spirituality of the ordinary. Living close to nature, he was liberated from the regulations and the preoccupations of organized society. His daily routine was reduced to simple tasks: eating, sleeping, studying, writing, praying, preparing food, cleaning up. In an ensemble of realities – his dwelling place, his day-to-day rhythm of life, the landscape and nature around his hermitage; relationships with his brothers in the Abbey, professional contacts and personal friends – Merton let God further develop his self-identity as an ordinary human being living an ordinary life. From that inner and outer ground of being Merton came to experience with increasing depth the radiance of God transparent in all creation. Merton perceived ever more keenly the glory of God within all creation, as it engages in one great cosmic dance in praise of its Creator.

C. Toward a Resolution of Merton's Incompleteness in Relation to the Feminine

Certain experiences in Thomas Merton's childhood, adolescence and early adulthood left him with some deficiency in his rapport with the feminine. Those experiences included: a mother whom he remembered as strict and distant, the death of his mother when he was a young boy, the absence of any sisters, and attendance at all boys' schools. Throughout his adolescence and early adulthood Merton had a tendency toward conquest with regard to the women whom he dated. Nonetheless, in the course of his development there were women with whom he had healthy relationships.

While he had felt rejection from his mother, Merton had favorable impressions of "mother figures" like Mrs. Privat and his Aunt Maud. As an adolescent and a young adult, Merton viewed many women primarily as objects of pleasure. Yet, there were exceptions. When Merton was a student at Oakham Public School in England, he met Anne Winser, a sister of one of his classmates. Although she was only twelve or thirteen years old at the time, she made a lasting impression on him. When he was a student at Columbia University, he experienced friendships with Dona Eaton, Jinny Burton and Peggy Wells. While at St. Bonaventure's he became good friends with Catherine de Hueck. After he entered monastic life, Merton formed friendships – primarily through correspondence – with women from a variety of interests, backgrounds and walks of life; for example: Etta Gullick, Sister Mary Luke Tobin, Sister Emmanuel de Souza e Silva, Naomi Burton Smith, Sister Therese Lentfoehr, Carolyn Hammer, Tommie O'Callaghan, Dorothy Day, Rosemary Radford Ruether.

By August 1965 when Merton became a hermit, he had moved well beyond seeing women primarily as objects of pleasure, and he could relate to them on the basis of respect and equality. Moreover, in his relationship with God he had come to a realization of the feminine principle in the deity, which he designated as *Hagía Sophía* (Holy Wisdom).

Yet, a sense of unfinished business in the area of the feminine and of female relationships asserted itself upon Merton's consciousness. Three areas of reference indicate the content of that unfinished business: (1) By January 1965 Merton had come to a realization not only of his need to love but also of his need to be loved. Looking back at the relationships that he had at the age of eighteen, he confessed that he used a lack of love, a selfishness and a glibness to conceal his deep shyness and his need to be loved. When a girl did love him, he could not believe it. He kept seeking absolute

assurance and perfect fulfillment.[16]   (2) In June 1965 Merton referred
to Ann Winser as symbolic of the true woman with whom he had
never come to terms prior to entering monastic life.   He
acknowledged that because he never worked through a relationship
with that type of quiet woman, there remained in him an
incompleteness that could not be remedied.[17]   (3) Moreover, Merton
had come to recognize the importance of responsibly integrating into
affective relationships the physical, sensory dimensions of love.[18]

In addition to Merton's awareness of unfinished business
with respect to relationships with women, a sense of alienation
affected his overall well-being during his first year as a hermit
(1965-1966).   At times, he felt abandoned by the monks at
Gethsemani.   His views on the Viet Nam War left him feeling
increasingly at odds with large segments of American society.
Differences of opinion and misunderstandings arose between Merton
and some of his friends in the peace movement over the issue of a
staff member at *The Catholic Worker* who had immolated himself in
front of the United Nations building in New York City.

The convergence of those circumstances in Merton's life left
him ripe for a relationship which unexpectedly occurred when he
was fifty-one years of age: that is, his falling passionately in love
with a young woman.   She was a student nurse who attended him
after he had back surgery in March 1966 at St. Joseph's Hospital in
Louisville, Kentucky.   The young woman in turn reciprocated his
love.[19]

The most intense phase of that relationship lasted a period of
approximately four months.   Merton had contact with the woman on
a number of later occasions, the final time being by phone during the
summer of 1968 shortly before he commenced his Asian journey.
Throughout the four peak months of the relationship, Merton
schemed to telephone the student nurse and to meet with her.   At
times he used his friends as means of making contact with her.
Some friends were understanding, even approving; others warned
him that he was playing with fire.   Although Merton continued to
have an affection for the woman, he eventually opted to remain at

---

[16] See, for instance, *Vow of Conversation*, 140; *Love and Living*, 25-37; *Dancing in the Water*, 197-199.

[17] See *Vow of Conversation*, 194, and *Dancing in the Water*, 259, 281.

[18] See *Conjectures*, 20, and *Love and Living*, 112-119.

[19] With regard to Merton's experience of this relationship, see *Learning to Love*. See also the synthesis in Michael Mott, *The Seven Mountains of Thomas Merton*, 435-454; 461-462.

Gethsemani and to recommit himself to his eremitical life.

With respect to transcendence, self-actualization and creative expression, how was the relationship with the student nurse significant to Merton? In terms of transcendence, he experienced at a radically new depth God present in another human being and God in one person loving God in another. As for self-actualization, Merton experienced in himself untold capacity to love and to be loved, to give and to receive. The relationship was transformative of him and of his way of seeing the world around him. In terms of creative expression, Merton's experience of that love generated many letters to the woman, two journals written especially with her in mind and a selection of poems.[20]

Thusfar, this woman whom Merton loved so passionately has maintained her privacy. Yet, the question of Merton's fairness to her persists. It seemed inevitable from the outset of the relationship – not only to his close friends, but also to Merton himself – that he would remain a monk. Nonetheless, he plunged into the relationship with reckless abandon, at one point even discussing with the student nurse the possibility of marriage.

D. Face to Face with the God of History

In the late 1950's Thomas Merton understood his contribution as a contemplative to be, in addition to his life of prayer, that of an apostolate of friendship to people who were attempting to address the social and moral issues of the times. During the 1960's Merton's sense of mission took on yet another dimension. He began to engage directly in the discussion of the critical issues of his day by means of correspondence, small group discussions at Gethsemani, the writing of essays, articles and poetry.

Among the burning controversies in American society of the 1960's were: (1) the Cold War between East and West, specifically the Soviet Union and the United States; (2) American involvement in Viet Nam; (3) racial equality; (4) appropriate means by which to work for justice and peace.

Merton's involvement in those political and social concerns came at a time when both leadership and laity in the Roman Catholic Church were reluctant to take a stand. He lamented the awful silence

---

[20] See *Learning to Love*, especially 301-348, and Thomas Merton, *Eighteen Poems* (New York, NY: New Directions, 1985).

and apathy of Catholics toward the Cold War and the possibility of nuclear destruction.[21]   In a moment of supreme exasperation he described both clergy and laity behaving as if they were lotus eaters, as if they were under a spell, as if they could see vaguely through a comatose fog their oncoming destruction while being incapable of lifting a finger to prevent it.[22]   He decried American violence in Viet Nam.   He was an advocate of racial equality for both Native Americans and Black Americans.   He maintained that Christians must seek justice and peace by nonviolent means.

Merton engaged in the discussion of those issues from a marginal position in relation to society.   His gift was the contemplative wisdom which he brought to bear upon specific moral questions of his time.   Merton affirmed the good, true, compassionate and just aspects of the world as he saw it.   At the same time he protested against the aggressiveness, violence and greed which kept numerous people in poverty and servitude.[23]

Yet, Merton found himself laboring under a tremendous handicap.   His position as a monk put restrictions on his access to information and dialogue.   Frequently, by the time he had made up his mind about a critical event the whole situation had changed, and he had to begin all over again discerning a truthful approach.[24]

The effort to promote discussion on issues of justice and peace cost Merton dearly.   Expressing his convictions became for him a source of intense anxiety.   Although his views during the 1960's were to draw a new following, many long-time readers dropped him.   He was the subject of criticism in the Catholic press. The highest authorities within his religious order believed that it was not the role of a monk to be speaking out on social issues.[25]

In January 1962 Gabriel Sortais, then Abbot General of the Cistercian Order, put Merton under a ban of silence.   Sortais ordered that Merton cease his anti-war writing and that he not submit to the censors any material on war and peace with a view to publication. James Fox, Abbot of Gethsemani, put off giving Merton this obedience until April 26, 1962.[26]   That delay made it possible for Merton to get into circulation through letters and essays most of

[21]   See *Hidden Ground of Love*, 139.

[22]   See *Courage for Truth*, 129-130.

[23]   See *Honorable Reader*, 65-66.

[24]   See *Hidden Ground of Love*, 161.

[25]   See, for instance, *Hidden Ground of Love*, 78-79; 266-268.

[26]   See *Turning Toward the World*, 186-216; *Hidden Ground of Love*, 188-189.   For Merton's letter of response to Sortais, see *School of Charity*, 141-143.

what he wanted to say on the subjects of war and peace.[27]

Merton had the last word in another, rather humorous way as well. Pope John XXIII issued in April 1963 an encyclical, *Pácem in Térris (Peace on Earth)*. That document made it clear that in light of nuclear proliferation war is not an appropriate instrument for the pursuit of peace in the modern world. Merton reminded Sortais in a 1963 Easter Sunday letter that during the preceding year when Merton himself had proposed that idea, the American Cistercian censors had judged his position on the issue to be wrong and scandalous. He wryly observed to Sortais how fortunate it was for the pope that the promulgation of *Pácem in Térris* did not require prior approval from the American Cistercian censors.[28]

Merton's involvement in justice and peace issues was intimately related to his process of self-actualization. The positions that he took on pivotal issues indicate that he possessed sufficient freedom of spirit and inner authority to speak from his own truth, even at the risk of rejection by other people. His writings in the area of justice and peace were not merely a personal interest or an intellectual concern, but rather a question of conscience and prophetic stance. He believed that in times such as his own it was not enough to go on writing only about prayer or monasticism. He had to confront the life and death issues of his era.[29]

Furthermore, Merton's engagement in social criticism was intimately related to his experience of the immanent transcendence of God in our world. His contemplative experience bore fruit in compassionate care. He saw no contradiction between living a contemplative life and promoting in ways compatible with that vocation justice and peace in this world. Merton maintained that being a contemplative carried with it responsibility for the rights of all people and for the truth of God within the Church and the world.[30] He believed that at least some contemplatives had to attempt to understand the providential events of the time. In fact, he contended that because God works in history, the contemplative who has no sense of history or of historical responsibility is not a fully Christian contemplative. Christ, the Lord of history and the Light of the world, comes from the Father into our midst and returns to him. Therefore, Christian contemplatives must seek to discover the

---

[27] See, for instance, Merton's "Cold War Letters," in *Witness to Freedom*, 17-69.

[28] See *School of Charity*, 166.

[29] See *Hidden Ground of Love*, 140.

[30] See *Hidden Ground of Love*, 79.

transforming presence of the risen Jesus in the awful paradoxes of their day.[31]

E. Dialogue with World Religions

The Second Vatican Council placed importance upon dialogue with peoples of other faith experiences, both within Christianity itself and in relation to the other world religions. Thomas Merton's study of other traditions and his dialogue with both Christian and nonchristian seekers of God were thus in keeping with the spirit of his times. He had contact not only with persons of other Christian denominations such as Baptist and Methodist, but also with people who practiced Judaism, Hinduism, Islam, Buddhism, Taoism, Confucianism. His journey to Asia in 1968 was the outgrowth of his study of religious traditions and his ecumenical dialogue.

The following principles form the starting point in Merton's approach to ecumenical dialogue:

- We must be rooted both experientially and intellectually in our own spiritual tradition.
- It is from the basis of contemplative experience rather than doctrine that ecumenical dialogue can proceed most effectively.
- With regard to doctrinal issues, all traditions share a common ground, but significant differences remain.
- Two points of convergence in all religious experience are these: the ultimate unity of all creation in the Creator and the ultimate inability of words or images to convey the fullness of the mystery of God or even of a specific experience of that mystery.[32]

Key catalysts for Merton's pursuit of ecumenical study and dialogue during the 1960's were his experience of the transcendent and his expanded sense of self-identity. We see both those influences merge in this celebrated text:

> The more I am able to affirm others, to say "yes" to
> them in myself, by discovering them in myself and
> myself in them, the more real I am. I am fully real if

---

[31] See *Hidden Ground of Love*, 186-187; 410-411.
[32] See, for example, *Asian Journal*, 309-317.

my own heart says *yes* to *everyone*.... I will be a better Catholic, not if I can *refute* every shade of Protestantism, but if I can affirm the truth in it and still go further.... So, too, with the Muslims, the Hindus, the Buddhists, etc.[33]

F. Ideas Moving Around One Center

By the early 1960's Thomas Merton had come to a basic reconciliation between his contemplative vocation and his gift for writing. He no longer saw a contradiction between contemplation and creative expression in his Trappist life. That sense of integration deepened during his final years. Writing became increasingly for him a way to meditate on paper. Of course, there was still in daily life the challenge to maintain an appropriate balance of activities.[34]

Merton's deepening encounter with God as mystery, together with his ongoing self-actualization, was the wellspring of his creative expression throughout the 1960's. It was Merton's unfolding inner journey and his expanding geographical horizons that impelled him to express himself on a variety of subjects: prayer, monasticism, racial equality, justice and peace, contemporary literature. His forms of expression included letter writing, essays, articles, poetry, photography, calligraphic paintings.

In relation to the historical reality of the 1960's, the first stage of Merton's creative process consisted of identifying the correct question.[35] Then, through discussion of ideas, writing and feedback from his readers, Merton worked out his position on the issue at hand. The outcome was always subject to revision, pending further insight or change of circumstances. Merton acknowledged his awareness of his need for constant self-evaluation and personal growth. In relation to that developmental process, he used the image of changing ideas always revolving around one center. Merton described himself as forever seeing that center from differing vantage points.[36]

Merton's overextension of himself with various activities detracted from the quality of some of his creative expression. He tended to accept too many requests for articles, to have too many

---

[33] *Conjectures*, 144.
[34] See *Road to Joy*, 88-89; 96-97; 100-101.
[35] See *Hidden Ground of Love*, 156.
[36] See *Dancing in the Water*, 67; *Vow of Conversation*, 19; *Road to Joy*, 104, 111.

projects in the works at one time, to be spread too far and wide in his interests. He believed that he said too much too soon and that his work suffered as a consequence.[37]   As the sixties wore on, he increasingly saw the need to simplify his life and activities. By August 1967 he had resolved to focus his creative energy on poetry, meditations, literary criticism, together with something on cargo cults[38] and Albert Camus.

Reviewing his work during the last year of his life, Merton expressed to a correspondent the view that all his writing contained for better or worse something of his thinking. Yet, he felt that much of his writing had been beside the point, and had not been done in the creative mode most suitable to him. He felt most happy with work that was simultaneously more personal, literary and contemplative.   As examples he cited the following books: *Conjectures of a Guilty Bystander, New Seeds of Contemplation, The Sign of Jonas* and *Raids on the Unspeakable.* He favored also his literary essays and his poetry, together with his introductions to the writings of persons such as Chuang Tzu, Gandhi and the desert fathers. Essay collections such as *Disputed Questions* and *Mystics and Zen Masters* he judged to have considerable unevenness. Some content was close to the heart of the matter, and other material in such books was far removed from what he had been trying to articulate.[39]

G. Going Home

On October 15, 1968, Thomas Merton set out for Asia. As his plane took off from San Francisco, he was ecstatic. He had a great sense of destiny, as if at last after years of tarrying he was on his way to the home that he had never found.[40]

Merton's Asian journey held many meaningful moments for him. For example, in Calcutta, India, he spoke on October 23, 1968, at the Temple of Understanding Conference. He went on to New Delhi and then to the Himalayas where during November 4-6, 1968,

---

[37] See, for example, *Vow of Conversation*, 46; *Hidden Ground of Love*, 132, 277, 307.

[38] Cargo movements originated in Melanesia and New Guinea near the close of the nineteenth century. Certain primitive peoples believed that they could acquire manufactured goods by an appeal to the spirit world. They saw attainment of "cargo" from the gods as a reward for their rejection of their own culture. See *Collected Poems*, 603-605.

[39] See *Hidden Ground of Love*, 641-642; *Learning to Love*, 193-194; *Honorable Reader*, 149-151.

[40] See *The Other Side*, 205, and *Asian Journal*, 4-5.

he had three lengthy meetings with the Dalai Lama. Another treasured moment came his way in Sri Lanka. On December 2, 1968, he set out in that country for the ancient ruins of Polonnaruwa, a city revered by both Buddhists and Hindus. Merton was profoundly moved in that sacred place by three huge Buddha figures carved out of stone. Beholding those figures, he was jerked out of his blurry vision of things. An inner clarity, which seemed to explode from the stone figures themselves, became evident to him. Everything was simultaneously emptiness and compassion. As Merton reflected afterwards upon the event, he could not remember a time in his life when he had felt such an intense fusion of beauty and spiritual energy in one aesthetic enlightenment. According to Merton, at Polonnaruwa he came to know and to see what he had been obscurely seeking when he set out on his Asian journey.[41]

Merton went to Asia with a sense of calling to remain a Trappist monk, priest, hermit and writer. The question was where and how to live out that direction in the future. He was a seeker of God to the end, never fully content, always testing the limits, forever advancing further into the unknown and the untried. His image of the Asian journey as a "going home" represented his hope for fresh penetration of the mystery of God, himself, his world, together with his desire for deeper communion with all creation in God. He did not realize it at the outset of his journey, but the home to which he was going was the fullness of God.

Tom, Thomas, Louis Merton died suddenly in Bangkok, Thailand, on December 10, 1968. Earlier that day he gave a presentation entitled, "Marxism and Monastic Perspectives," at an international conference on monastic renewal. After that session he retired to his room. He was found later, lying on his back with an electric fan across his chest. The fan switch was still on. The exact cause of death is unclear. He may have showered, then had a heart attack near the fan, and in falling knocked the fan over against himself. Another possibility is that in his bare feet on a stone floor he received a fatal electric shock from the fan.[42] Thomas Merton was one month and five days short of his fifty-fourth birthday.

---

[41] See *Asian Journal*, 233-236.
[42] See *Asian Journal*, 344-347; *The Other Side*, xviii-xix.

Part III:

Georgia O'Keeffe

(1887-1986)

CHAPTER 19

O'Keeffe's Uncatholic Soul

The transcendent, hidden yet revealed, shines through the artistic expression of Georgia O'Keeffe. Her paintings bespeak in color and line something of her encounter with mystery, with the numinous. The living spring that most nourished her quest for the Ultimate, for the Infinite, for the Unknown – in a word, for God – O'Keeffe discovered within herself and within the world around her. Transcendence, self-actualization and creative expression were profoundly interrelated in the becoming of Georgia O'Keeffe.

O'Keeffe pursued her own unique spiritual path. She was not a practicing member of any institutional religion. Yet, she found that certain religious currents resonated to some degree with her personal experience of transcendence, and at times she drew inspiration from those sources.

In this chapter we synthesize the principal religious traditions and faith expressions with which Georgia O'Keeffe had significant contact over the course of her life:

- her familial religious affiliations,
- Christianity,
- Native American spirituality,
- certain Eastern religions,
- theosophy,
- primitivism,
- American transcendentalism.

A. Familial Religious Affiliations

Georgia O'Keeffe's father, Francis, was of Irish descent. His family was Roman Catholic. Georgia's mother, Ida Totto O'Keeffe, was of Hungarian and Dutch ancestry. While Ida's maternal side of the family was Episcopalian, her paternal side was Lutheran. Ida and her siblings were brought up according to their mother's religious affiliation.

Francis O'Keeffe and Ida Totto married in an Episcopalian ceremony at Ida's home in Madison, Wisconsin. They took up residence on a six hundred acre farm near Sun Prairie, Wisconsin. Throughout their married life they derided each other's religious affiliations. Yet, Francis rarely bothered going to the Catholic Church in the town of Sun Prairie. The nearest Episcopal Church was in Madison, too far away for Ida to attend on a weekly basis. Georgia was baptized at Grace Episcopal Church in Madison. When she was a child, her uncle, Bernard O'Keeffe, would occasionally take her in his horse and buggy to Mass at Sacred Hearts of Jesus and Mary Catholic Church in Sun Prairie. Most Sundays, however, Georgia and her siblings went with their aunt, Jane Varney, to the simple Congregational services at the church near their farm.

As a teenager O'Keeffe attended two educational institutions that were under the auspices of groups associated with organized religion. From autumn 1901 to spring 1902, she studied at Sacred Heart Academy, a convent boarding school in Madison, run by the Dominican Sisters. She spent her high school years of 1903-1905 at Chatham Episcopal Institute in Chatham, Virginia.[1]

B. Christianity

In a Christmas 1917 incident in Canyon, Texas, we see an example of Georgia O'Keeffe in confrontation with what was generally accepted there as a Christian value. O'Keeffe's pacifist tendencies clashed with the town's war-fever. At the local drug store she saw on sale two Christmas card designs that she found offensive. One referred to a desire to annihilate Germany and the other had a verse expressing hatred of the Kaiser. O'Keeffe asked the owner of the store to remove them. As a consequence, she became the talk of the town and was judged to be unpatriotic. Describing the incident

[1] Throughout the nine chapters in this third part of our study, the basic sources for biographical data on Georgia O'Keeffe are these: *Lovingly, Georgia*; *A Woman on Paper*; Laurie Lisle, *Portrait of an Artist: A Biography of Georgia O'Keeffe* (Albuquerque, NM: University of New Mexico Press, 1986); Roxana Robinson, *Georgia O'Keeffe: A Life* (New York, NY: Harper-Perennial, 1990).

in a letter of January 1918, O'Keeffe remarked that "the good Christians" were up in arms. She asserted that the two cards in question were against basic principles of Christianity, and definitely not in keeping with the Christmas spirit.[2]

In her adult years Georgia O'Keeffe felt an affinity with some dimensions of the faith experience of Roman Catholicism, while retaining reservations about the institutional elements of that religious tradition.

O'Keeffe was intrigued on an August 1932 visit to the Gaspé Peninsula in Quebec, Canada, by the French Canadian faith experience as expressed in the crosses which she saw dotting the landscape. In New Mexico crosses expressive of the Spanish faith experience had captivated her interest. While she interpreted the French view of Catholicism as cheerful and witty, she perceived the Spanish view of Catholicism as somber and dark. She expressed her encounter with both traditions in paintings of crosses.[3]

After O'Keeffe had become a renowned artist, she discovered in the village of Abiquiu, New Mexico, a dilapidated house in a garden surrounded by an adobe wall with broken sections. As she walked through the ruins, she came upon a patio that had a long wall with a door on one side. From the moment O'Keeffe first saw that door in the patio wall, she was determined to acquire the property.[4] A local family was its immediate owner. O'Keeffe made an inquiry about purchase of the property, but she found the price too steep. The property became eventually the possession of the Catholic Church in Abiquiu. In due time O'Keeffe sought to purchase the property from the Church, but it refused to sell. She persisted in her attempt to acquire the estate, until finally in December 1945 her will prevailed. With the property came certain water rights. The townspeople had water for their needs on weekdays. She had watering for her garden on Sundays. She wrote of this being a suitable arrangement since she was "an outsider and a heathen."[5]

O'Keeffe had some business interaction also with members of the United Presbyterian Church. Arthur and Phoebe Pack were the owners of Ghost Ranch, which was adjacent to O'Keeffe's

---

[2] See *Art and Letters*, 166-167.
[3] See *CR*, 812-813, 667-671; *Georgia O'Keeffe*, 64, 67, 68; *O'Keeffe: In the West*, 8-10; Katherine Kuh, *The Artist's Voice* (New York, NY: Harper and Row, 1962), 202.
[4] See *Georgia O'Keeffe*, statement opposite plate 82.
[5] See *Art and Letters*, 248.

202 O'Keeffe's Uncatholic Soul

property in New Mexico. In 1955 the Packs were making final arrangements to donate their property to the United Presbyterian Church. They neglected to inform O'Keeffe of their plan. The Packs were at a meeting with church representatives to finalize the agreement when O'Keeffe came bursting in, demanding to know why the Packs would not give their ranch to her. When she realized that she could not change their minds, she stormed out, declaring that she never had any use for Presbyterians anyway. O'Keeffe got from the Catholic Church in Abiquiu what she needed in order to create her desired living milieu. O'Keeffe perceived the United Presbyterian Church at Ghost Ranch to be detracting from her solitude and privacy. By the 1960's, however, O'Keeffe and the Presbyterians were friendly neighbors. When a fire destroyed the headquarters at Ghost Ranch, O'Keeffe immediately donated fifty thousand dollars toward a rebuilding fund.

In the village of Abiquiu O'Keeffe was respectful of the seasonal liturgical rituals. She wrote to a friend of the beauty of Christmas Eve, with fires of pitch wood flaring brightly in front of the houses and the townspeople gathered in her home, sitting by the indoor fires for a while, drinking and talking after the Midnight Mass.[6] During Lent and Holy Week, O'Keeffe never failed to be fascinated by the rituals of the Penitentes, a Catholic sect in New Mexico whose first members had arrived four centuries earlier with the Spanish colonialists. From the rooftop of her home O'Keeffe observed the sect praying, processing and dolefully singing. It seemed to her that the Church overpowered the village.[7]

Writing to another friend in 1943, O'Keeffe described her visit to a Penitente morada (a place of worship for the sect) which had walls painted a pale sweet pink, an altar full of gory christs and saints, a startling death figure dressed in black carrying a bow and arrow, seven crosses each large enough for a human crucifixion, an iron chain and a wall splattered with blood. She remarked on the intermingling of the suffering in the Penitente practices and the love evident in the care of the place. She compared it to their chili: painfully hot, yet very sweet.[8]

In a letter dated July 28, 1950, Georgia O'Keeffe wrote of feeling that her world was a rock. She went on to tell her

[6] See Roxana Robinson, Georgia O'Keeffe: A Life, 486-487.
[7] See Art and Letters, 251-252.
[8] See Art and Letters, 234-235.

correspondent how a prominent Catholic priest who was head of the chemistry department at Fordham University in New York City had tried to convert her to the Catholic Church. She expressed her amazement at the fact that the priest could do no more than make the Church look like a "mound of jelly compared to [her] rock."[9]

Two years later (July 25, 1952) and to the same correspondent, O'Keeffe described another encounter with a priest:

> Ive had a priest – Catholic – visiting me for a week – it was very pleasant but when he is gone I realize how uncatholic – in his sense – my soul is – as I read a little book he left me – "The Cloud of Unknowing" by an unknown monk of the 14th century – I am startled to realize my lack for the need of the comfort of the Church –
>
> When I stand alone with the earth and sky a feeling of something in me going off in every direction into the unknown of infinity means more to me than any thing any organized religion gives me.
>
> The church, to me, seems to assume a fear of death – and after – and I think I have no fear.[10]

Several points are noteworthy in O'Keeffe's account: (1) The visit of this priest was "very pleasant" in contrast to the encounter with the priest from Fordham a few years earlier. Apparently, this visiting priest did not try to convert her to the Catholic Church. Nor did he make the Church seem to her like a mound of jelly. Moreover, the fact that he stayed with her "for a week" suggests that they engaged in some in-depth sharing. (2) Yet, after his departure O'Keeffe realized clearly just how "uncatholic – in his sense" was her "soul." She realized that she did not fit into the organizational or doctrinal structure of the Church and that her concept of catholicity, ecumenism and religious freedom was radically different from that of pre-Vatican II Catholicism. (3) On at least one specific matter she perceived an immense gulf between her experience and the outlook of the church that the visiting priest represented. At issue was what

---

[9] *Art and Letters*, 253.
[10] *Art and Letters*, 263.

she considered a disturbingly pessimistic assessment of death and final judgment. O'Keeffe had "no fear" of death or of what might happen "after." Whatever her understanding of God in her mid-sixties, she did not perceive God as one who judges us after death and consigns some people to hell for all eternity. (4) Before the priest left, he gave her a copy of a fourteenth century spiritual classic entitled, *The Cloud of Unknowing*. As she read it, she became aware of her own lack of need for the Church's "comfort" and support. With that remark, she implies that her communion with the Transcendent did not depend upon or require institutional affiliation with "any organized religion."

Despite intellectual and emotional reservations about Roman Catholicism, that religious tradition continued to have appeal for O'Keeffe. In the late 1960's, for instance, she was so moved by the architectural simplicity and the solitary setting of the chapel at the Monastery of Christ in the Desert – a short distance from her home in Abiquiu – that she attended services there occasionally.[11]

In contrast to the meaningful simplicity found at the Monastery of Christ in the Desert was O'Keeffe's experience of the extravagant religious trappings of Rome. Returning to the United States from the Middle East in 1959, O'Keeffe stopped over in the Eternal City. She found nothing there to be on a human scale. For example, she described the angels on the Vatican walls as dreadfully huge naked things. In fact, everything in Rome struck her as supremely vulgar – as if hugeness in itself were intrinsically aesthetic.[12]

C. Native American Spirituality

Georgia O'Keeffe had a strong attraction toward the values and the religious rituals of Native Americans. Shortly after her 1929 arrival in Santa Fe, New Mexico, she attended the Corn Dance at San Felipe Pueblo and three days later the Indian relay races at Taos. Her hostess, Mabel Dodge Luhan, was married to Tony Luhan, a member of a local tribe. Tony gave Georgia immediate access to Native American country and life. After an outing to Las Vegas, O'Keeffe wrote of being deeply moved by tribal ceremonial dances.

---

[11] Thomas Merton was also immensely impressed by this chapel. He considered it the "best monastic building in the country." See *The Other Side*, 104; Thomas Merton, *Woods, Shore, Desert: A Notebook, May 1968*, 26-28.
[12] See Charlotte Willard, "Georgia O'Keeffe," in *Art in America* (October 1963).

The metamorphosis in the dancers from almost stoical indifference to tremendous vitality captivated her.[13] At one event O'Keeffe was enthralled by a native dancer's circular ornament spinning and flashing in the sunlight. She expressed her experience of that ornament in her vibrant mandala-like painting entitled, *At the Rodeo, New Mexico, 1929.*[14]

O'Keeffe's affinity with the Native American spiritual approach to life was longstanding. Writing to a correspondent in 1950, for example, she told of how she had attended two all-night dances – one in a Zuni village, two hundred fifty miles away, to celebrate the blessing of a home; the other, about the same distance in another direction to attend a Navajo ceremony for the curing of the sick. She was filled with wonder in the presence of the singing, dancing, greenness of nature, smoke, fire and stars.[15]

D. Eastern Religions

Some oriental spiritual traditions appealed to Georgia O'Keeffe. She was familiar with Hinduism through Elizabeth Stieglitz Davidson, a niece by marriage, and through other acquaintances. O'Keeffe found meaning in the Hindu philosophy of acceptance. Yet, she gravitated most toward Zen Buddhism, as it found expression in Chinese and Japanese art.

Between 1914-1915 O'Keeffe attended art classes given by Arthur Wesley Dow at Columbia University, New York City. Dow recommended to his students Ernest Fenollosa's book, *Epochs of Chinese and Japanese Art*, as well as Gonse's work, *L'Art japonais.*[16] O'Keeffe was most likely familiar with both works. The serene Japanese prints in Dow's art collection appealed to her. Dow's approach to painting introduced her also to the Japanese form of composition known as *notan* (abstract arrangement of light and dark patterns).

Later in her life O'Keeffe saw firsthand the Japanese wood blocks of her friend, Louis Ledoux. She secured rare illustrated material on Japanese art, including painted scrolls, for her personal library. She read translations of Chinese and Japanese literature.

---

[13] See Roxana Robinson, *Georgia O'Keeffe: A Life*, 334.

[14] See *CR*, 650; *O'Keeffe: In the West*, 7.

[15] See *Art and Letters*, 257.

[16] See Barbara Rose, "Georgia O'Keeffe's Universal Spiritual Vision," in *Catalogue of Georgia O'Keeffe Exhibition in Japan* (Santa Fe, NM: Gerald Peters Gallery, 1988), 98.

Among her favorites were *The Book of Tea* and the poet Basho's, *Narrow Road to the Deep North.* She read Osvald Seren's, *History of Early Chinese Painting.* On a visit to France during the spring of 1953, she marveled at the Buddhist sculptures that she saw at the Louvre in Paris.

O'Keeffe's attraction to the oriental spiritual outlook led her to undertake many journeys in her elder years. Within the United States she made short trips to cities across the country for the purpose of seeing Asian art in various museums. In 1959 she made a three and a half month trip, which included stops in Japan, Southeast Asia and a period of seven weeks in India. In 1960 she made a six-week trip, which included time in Japan and Southeast Asia. Moreover, her love of the Orient influenced the way in which she saw her immediate environment. For instance, she noticed how when the light hit the mountains around Abiquiu simultaneously from in front and behind, they had the look of Japanese prints; that is, of distances in layers.[17]

E. Theosophy

The word "theosophy" comes from two Greek words: *theós* (God) and *sophós* (wise). Theosophy designates religio-philosophical systems that offer their members secret knowledge of God and of the cosmos in relation to its Creator.[18] People access that wisdom by means of mystical intuition, philosophical inquiry or a combination of the two. Attainment of occult knowledge comes only after a person passes through an intense initiation. Those who seek the wisdom of God in that manner are referred to as theosophists or spiritualists.

Georgia O'Keeffe's teacher, Arthur Wesley Dow, was a committed practicing spiritualist. Although no significant evidence exists that Dow sought to awaken O'Keeffe's interest in his occult beliefs or practices, she would have known of his orientation. Furthermore, at the suggestion of an associate of Dow, O'Keeffe studied Wassily Kandinsky's book, *Concerning the Spiritual in Art.* Kandinsky referred in that book to the theosophist Frau Blavatsky.

---

[17] See Beth Coffelt, "A Visit with Georgia O'Keeffe," in *San Francisco Sunday Examiner & Chronicle* (11 April, 1971).

[18] On theosophy, see Antoine Faivre and Jacob Needleman, eds., *Modern Esoteric Spirituality*, vol. 21 of *World Spirituality: An Encyclopedic History of the Religious Quest* (New York, NY: The Crossroad Publishing Company, 1992), 311-329.

He described therein his visual concept of vibration, which he derived from theosophical teachings. According to Kandinsky's theory, nature causes in the soul vibrations that form the basis of all human emotion. The artist's task is to stimulate those vibrations in the beholder. O'Keeffe's direct exposure to Kandinsky's ideas possibly awakened in her some insight into her own spiritual experience. However, she did not become a member of any theosophical society.

From 1915 onward, O'Keeffe read back issues of *Camera Work,* published by Alfred Stieglitz at his 291 Gallery in New York City.[19] Therefore, she was most likely familiar with an essay by Max Weber in a 1910 edition on the topic of the "fourth dimension" in theosophy. Weber described this concept as the immensity of all creation and as the consciousness of space and magnitude in all directions simultaneously.[20] The idea must have caught O'Keeffe's attention, since space and immensity remained primary characteristics of her transcendental experience.

During the mid-1920's Claude Bragdon was a resident at the Shelton Hotel in New York where O'Keeffe and Stieglitz lived. He joined them frequently for breakfast in the hotel cafeteria. Bragdon was an architect with myriad interests, chief among them spiritualism. He believed geometry and number to be the foundation of all effective decoration. He described the task of the artist as that of putting geometric forms into sensuous images that make music to the eye. He maintained that to accomplish this effect the artist would need to conceive of a space or a fourth dimension of reality which constituted a beyond that is within all things.[21]

O'Keeffe had used geometric forms in her paintings for approximately ten years before she met Bragdon. Her shapes crystallized in her mind, consciously, unconsciously or in some interaction of the two. When she began painting abstractions, her intent was to create forms evocative of universal feeling. Her contact with Bragdon's metaphysical ideas possibly awakened insight into what she was already doing.

Jean Toomer, a black writer, played a significant role at a

---

[19] With regard to the contact of Alfred Stieglitz and his circle of artists with theosophy, see Sarah Whitaker Peters, *Becoming O'Keeffe: The Early Years* (New York, NY: Abbeville Press Publishers, 1991), 63-79.

[20] See Max Weber, "The Fourth Dimension from a Plastic Point of View," in *Camera Work* 31 (July 1910): 25.

[21] See Claude Bragdon, *Architecture and Democracy* (New York, NY: Alfred A. Knopf, 1918), 104-120.

pivotal moment in O'Keeffe life. Toomer was a disciple of a spiritualist named Gurdjieff.[22] O'Keeffe declined to study Gurdjieff's ideas when another friend gave her a translation of his book. Yet, some of his approach may have filtered down to her through Toomer. She was deeply touched by Toomer's personal integrity, by his healing presence and by the feeling of balance that he gave her – qualities integral to Gurdjieff's approach.

F. Other Spiritual Currents

Georgia O'Keeffe connected with certain currents of religious experience through the study and practice of art itself. For example, aspects of the spirituality implicit to primitivism and American transcendentalism were similar to her encounter with the transcendent within life.

(1) Primitivism

Primitivism refers to the religious experience of indigenous people, as well as to artistic expressions of that form of encounter with the divine. The basic spiritual intuition of many native peoples is that of time, space and nature charged with a numinosity both fascinating and terrifying. In that experience no clear boundaries separate the spiritual and the natural world or the sacred and the profane. Everything and everyone exist in one great cosmic unity. Within that milieu the religious person seeks to abide at the center of the world and at the source of ultimate reality. There that person remains as close as possible to the opening which allows communion with the divine. In taking on responsibility for creating his/her world, the person seeks to live in a cosmos as pure and holy as when it first came forth fresh from the hands of its Creator.[23]

While in Canyon, Texas, O'Keeffe read *Egyptian Decorative Art* by the archaeologist, Sir Flinders Petrie. O'Keeffe had exposure to primitive art in Stieglitz's publication, *Camera Work.* She admired the primitivist paintings of Henri Rousseau.

At the 291 Gallery in New York City O'Keeffe attended exhibits that included primitive art. During her years in New

---

[22] On Gurdjieff and his school, see Antoine Faivre and Jacob Needleman, eds., *Modern Esoteric Spirituality*, 359-380.

[23] See Mircea Eliade, *The Sacred and The Profane* (New York, NY: Harcourt Brace Jovanovich, 1959), 65.

Mexico many Native American artifacts caught her attention. On her first trip to Europe in 1953, as she drove from France to Spain, O'Keeffe made a point of visiting the prehistoric caves in the Dordogne-Lascaux region where she saw wall paintings approximately thirty thousand years old.[24]

Related to primitive art is the art of children. For a few years O'Keeffe taught art to children. Children's drawings also evoked her sense of wonder.

(2) American Transcendentalism

Nineteenth century American transcendentalism promoted the hope that the increased personal autonomy possible in a democratic society would foster the development of a creative, integrated and morally responsible individual. The transcendentalists believed in the presence of God within the self and within the universe. They held that people have little need for the mediation of organized religion since the divine reveals itself through human intuition. Thus, they emphasized individual experience as the point of encounter with God. They encouraged the expression of spiritual experience in art forms such as painting, prose and poetry.[25]

Artists of the Stieglitz circle aimed to create art that was specifically American. In that vein they looked to the transcendentalists, Henry David Thoreau (1817-1862), Ralph Waldo Emerson (1803-1892) and Walt Whitman (1819-1892). O'Keeffe's library in Abiquiu contains copies, which had belonged to Alfred Stieglitz, of Van Wyck Brooks' *The Life of Emerson* (1932) and Thoreau's *A Week on the Concord and Merrimack Rivers*, *The Transmigration of the Seven Brahmans,* and *Walden*. Whether or not Georgia O'Keeffe read firsthand those books or any other writings of the American transcendentalists, she would certainly as a member of the Stieglitz circle have been exposed to the ideas of the transcendentalists. O'Keeffe's value system, approach to life and philosophy of art had much in common with the basic tenets of American transcendentalism. However, rather than having used the transcendentalists as guides or teachers, it may have been a case of

[24] See *A Woman on Paper*, 260.
[25] See Jon Alexander, "Spiritual Insights of the American Transcendentalists," in *Western Spirituality: Historical Roots, Ecumenical Routes*, ed. Matthew Fox (Santa Fe, NM: Bear & Company, Inc., 1981), 386-400.

her recognition of correspondences between her experience and their outlook.

G. Summary

Having surveyed Georgia O'Keeffe's contact with various forms of religious experience, we identify these qualities within her:

- *Broadness of view*: O'Keeffe's father was Catholic, her mother Episcopalian, her aunt Congregationalist. Thus, from her earliest years she was exposed to a variety of religious expressions. As an adult she had contact with religions of the Orient, together with spiritual currents related to the field of art.
- *Openness*: She was willing to look beyond the familiar and to explore the unknown that came her way.
- *Ecumenical:* Her openness of heart led her to be ecumenical in her spiritual orientation. She was receptive to truth wherever she encountered it.
- *Inner-directed*: She trusted her personal experience of transcendence. That experience became her guiding principle in her exploration of various religious approaches.

O'Keeffe had such trust in her own experience of transcendence that she felt no inclination to be a practicing member of any religious group. In relation to organized religious traditions, some combination of Roman Catholicism and Zen Buddhism seems to have had special appeal to O'Keeffe. Moreover, O'Keeffe expressed in paint some of her perceptions of the faith experience of Spanish Catholicism, French Canadian Catholicism, Native American spirituality and Zen Buddhism.

CHAPTER 20

The Faraway Nearby

One evening during a stroll outside her home in Abiquiu, New Mexico, Georgia O'Keeffe and her caregiver, Christine Taylor Patten, broached the topic of religion. Christine asked Georgia what she thought of God. O'Keeffe responded: "I don't think much of God." Christine, rather puzzled, pressed for an explanation. Georgia reiterated in her typical straightforward manner: "I mean exactly what I said: I don't think much of God!"[1] O'Keeffe was ninety-six years old at the time.

O'Keeffe's words are open to various interpretations. They could imply a low opinion of God or indifference toward the divine. Yet, another explanation is most likely. O'Keeffe was simply stating that she was not in the habit of trying by means of verbal reasoning to understand God or to grasp the divine purpose in creation.

Two factors converge on why O'Keeffe did not "think much of God" in that sense. First, she tended to commune silently, wordlessly with the numinous transparent in the world around her, especially in nature. Second, she processed her experience of the numinous primarily by means of spatial intelligence rather than by words, thoughts or concepts. Her manner of reflecting upon encounter with the transcendent consisted ordinarily of exploring and synthesizing the living relationship of color, shape, space and line with respect to a specific subject. Thus, her paintings and drawings expressed in visual language something of her transcendent experience.

O'Keeffe found shapes and colors more meaningful modes

---

[1]   Christine Taylor Patten and Alvaro Cardona-Hine, *Miss O'Keeffe* (Albuquerque, NM: University of New Mexico Press, 1992), 115-116.

of expression for herself than words. She was frequently astounded at what she considered to be the "odd things" said and written about her.[2] Consequently, in an attempt to reveal to others something of the true meaning of her art, she did on occasion employ words. Selective interviews, letters to family members, close friends and business associates, a short book about some of her drawings and another book about her paintings contain eloquent forms of her verbal expression.

To flesh out O'Keeffe's experience of transcendence, we draw upon her words. We reflect in this chapter upon certain key phrases in her thought; specifically:

- the distance always calling,
- adventure of spirit into the unknown,
- the unknown of infinity,
- the faraway nearby.

A. The Distance Always Calling

When Georgia O'Keeffe was eighty-nine years old, a book that she had written about her paintings, entitled *Georgia O'Keeffe*, appeared in print. She recalled therein a scene dear to her heart during her high school years at Chatham Episcopal Institute in Virginia:

> always on the horizon far away ... the line of the Blue Ridge mountains – calling – as the distance has always been calling me.[3]

In that text O'Keeffe's memory of a specific scene opens out to the identification of a fundamental thrust in her life. A geographical landscape of her youth becomes a symbol of the enduring landscape of her spirit. Just as the faraway horizon of the Blue Ridge Mountains always beckoned her in her youth, so "the distance" continuously called her throughout her life. Even as she wrote those words she felt "the distance" up ahead still luring her.

Several words in O'Keeffe's statement merit reflection. They are: distance, calling, always, and the faraway horizon line.

---

[2] See *Georgia O'Keeffe*, first page of text (unnumbered).
[3] *Georgia O'Keeffe*, ninth page of text.

Distance: In O'Keeffe's experience distance was immense. Moreover, it was full of emptiness. She grew up in the open prairie land of Wisconsin. She lived in an area of New Mexico where the space is so vast that visually there is only a nearby and a faraway, without any appreciable middle ground. The distance of which O'Keeffe spoke was on the "faraway horizon line." Horizontally, the point most remote from us is the line where sky (that is, the heavens) and the earth meet. Distance then is a metaphor for transcendence. It bespeaks the meeting of the divine and the human, the uncreated and the created. It denotes the beyond which is within our view but which still transcends us.

Calling: O'Keeffe described the distance as calling her. She experienced it as drawing her to itself, luring her to come toward it, moving her in its direction. Moreover, that calling was irresistible. It would not let her rest content. She could not but freely seek after the distance. That calling motivated her to explore the untried and the uncharted. It awakened in her a searching for something more, something beyond. It made her a pilgrim and her life a spiritual journey.

Always: The distance calling was for O'Keeffe a voice persistently beckoning her. Its sound was ceaselessly reverberating within her being. Its presence echoed through all the events of her daily life. It invariably set the direction for her life, both inwardly and outwardly.

The faraway horizon line: O'Keeffe designated the place from which the distance called her as the faraway horizon line. Thus, the distance calling was within sight, but beyond immediate reach. Yet, in seeing the distance and listening to its calling, O'Keeffe sensed connectedness between here and there, now and forever.

While we can move toward the distance, it remains elusive. Just when we think that we have arrived at our destination, we find distance again stretched out before us. We reach the faraway place that we had been seeking only to see a new horizon line beyond us. We find that a specific response to the distance calling us at any given time is but one stretch on the way to the goal.

O'Keeffe's image then of the distance on the faraway horizon always calling her denotes her awareness of a consistent spiritual direction to her life. The expression refers to her sense of the numinous within creation, but always more than it. The phrase bespeaks what we have termed God's immanent transcendence.

B. Adventure of Spirit into the Unknown

The distance always calling Georgia O'Keeffe became the catalyst for an adventure of her spirit into the unknown. Distance always calling – that is, her experience of transcendence – became the impetus for her spiritual journey. That quest was the milieu out of which burst forth her creative expression.

In a letter to Sherwood Anderson that was written probably in September 1923, O'Keeffe addressed the relationship of spiritual adventure to the creation of art:

> I feel that a real living form is the natural result of
> the individuals effort to create the living thing out of
> the adventure of his spirit into the unknown.[4]

Thus, O'Keeffe identified the unknown as that which generates the desire to create a work of art. The unknown is itself the life-giving source from which emerges "a real living form." The artist taps into that unknown by undertaking "an adventure" – O'Keeffe's word for a quest, pilgrimage, search. While this journey into the unknown involves the whole person, O'Keeffe designated it as above all an "adventure of ... spirit." This search involves the transcendent depths of the human person and of creation. This quest pertains to the divine abiding within all creation.

(1) The Real Living Form

In the letter of September 1923 to Anderson, Georgia O'Keeffe proceeded to comment further on the manner in which the desire to creatively express oneself emerges from this adventure of spirit into the unknown:

> [One's spirit] has experienced something – felt
> something – it has not understood – and from that
> experience comes the desire to make the unknown –
> known.

---

[4] *Art and Letters*, 174-175. All quotations in this section are from this letter. Although there is some uncertainty about the exact date of this letter, for the sake of simplicity we refer to it henceforth as the letter of September 1923.

In effect, O'Keeffe noted the following: From the inmost depths of our personhood we encounter a reality beyond comprehension. That experience gives rise to a desire to express something of the unknown. Creating a "living form" –whether poetry, painting, prose, etc. – thus embodies the process of wrestling with mystery. It is our attempt to make sense, for ourselves and for others, of an encounter with transcendence.

O'Keeffe went on to explain to Anderson her understanding of the word "unknown" and to describe the effect of the unknown upon the artist's will to create:

> By unknown – I mean the thing that means so much to the person that he wants to put it down – clarify something he feels but does not clearly understand – sometimes he partially knows why – sometimes he doesn't – sometimes it is all working in the dark – but a working that must be done.

For O'Keeffe, the unknown referred to personal value and meaning in life. It is in essence the "I-don't-know-what"[5] treasured above all else. It is the ineffable thing so cherished that it has to be embodied in a form. It is the mystery held so dear that it must be clarified by means of a creative expression. This value/treasure/mystery-requiring-expression became for O'Keeffe a burning inner necessity and an all-consuming passion. Her artistic form was simply the inevitable outcome of her ongoing adventure of spirit into the unknown.

Georgia O'Keeffe valued movement toward the "distance calling" over arrival at the destination. Journeying was more significant to her than reaching the end. Therefore, while emphasizing in her September 1923 letter to Anderson the supreme importance of making the unknown known, she warned him that the artistic responsibility did not end with creating a real living form. She pointed out to him the equal importance of the following factor:

> [that of] keeping the unknown always beyond.

O'Keeffe was thereby reminding her correspondent that by its very nature a real living form does not bring the artist to a point of

---

[5] St. John of the Cross, *The Spiritual Canticle*, stanza 7.

ultimate rest or clarity. Rather it serves to open the artist to a deepening participation in mystery and an intensifying awareness of transcendence.

(2) Two Consequences

In Georgia O'Keeffe's view a real living form is the natural result of the adventure of one's spirit into the unknown. She identified in her letter of September 1923 to Sherwood Anderson two consequences of that truth.

First, there is no such thing as success or failure with respect to the expression of the spiritual adventure. Those standards of judgment are irrelevant for true artists. In their own time artists cannot know the quality of their vision. Neither can they know whether or not a work has an enduring meaning to communicate to society.

Second, artists must risk letting their work stand on its own. They must let a creative expression speak or not speak to contemporaries, without attempting to know for certain its message or to control the response of its beholders. Thus, the work formed in the course of a spiritual quest demands of the artist a relinquishing, a surrendering, a letting go once it is completed. In that situation O'Keeffe advocated that the artist maintain personal integrity according to his/her sense of balance with the world.

(3) Personhood as an Expression of the Unknown

Georgia O'Keeffe believed that the quest for the unknown or "what you vaguely feel ahead" is innate to being human:

I some way feel that everyone is born with it clear
but that with most of humanity it becomes blasted –
one way or another.

In concluding her letter of September 1923 to Anderson, O'Keeffe spoke to him of "the thing that is yourself." That is, she injected the issue of identity and self-actualization. She reminded him that ultimately his personhood was the only thing he had. She advised: "Keep it as clear as you can – moving." Then she posed this enigmatic question:

There are several million of us – have we all a *form*?"

With that query O'Keeffe broadened the scope of her thoughts on form. She intimated that whatever else we create, authentic personhood itself is an expression of the unknown. Who we are becoming is inextricably linked to mystery. Our tangible self is the "form" or embodiment of our spirit or hidden self. The more we encounter the transcendent depths of our personhood, the more we experience an inner necessity to let the unknown within us express itself in our identity.

C. The Unknown of Infinity

The primary catalyst for the adventure of Georgia O'Keeffe's spirit into the unknown was the world of nature. In the context of commenting on her stance vis-à-vis organized religion, O'Keeffe referred to her spiritual experience with nature in a letter written from New Mexico on July 25,1952:

> Ive had a priest – Catholic – visiting me for a week
> – it was very pleasant but when he is gone I realize
> how uncatholic – in his sense – my soul is – as I
> read a little book he left me – "The Cloud of
> Unknowing" by an unknown monk of the 14th
> century – I am startled to realize my lack for the
> need of the comfort of the Church–

> When I stand alone with the earth and sky a feeling
> of something in me going off in every direction into
> the unknown of infinity means more to me than any
> thing any organized religion gives me.

> The church, to me, seems to assume a fear of death –
> and after – and I think I have no fear.[6]

The word "unknown" refers in common parlance to that which we do not yet comprehend but are capable of understanding. However, by adding the qualifier "of infinity" to the word

---

[6] *Art and Letters*, 263. The correspondent is William Howard Schubart, a nephew of Alfred Stieglitz. See pp. 202-204 above for observations on other aspects of this letter.

"unknown" in the above letter, O'Keeffe clearly went beyond ordinary usage of the term.   Her phrase, "unknown of infinity," implies ultimate mystery, immanent transcendence, divine ineffability – in a word, God.   O'Keeffe shared with her correspondent an issue of immense personal meaningfulness: that standing "alone with the earth and sky" she experienced a participation in the "unknown of infinity."   Moreover, that experience was more important to her than anything which organized religion had to offer. Elsewhere O'Keeffe identified that unknown of infinity as "the intangible thing in myself" and as "the unexplainable thing in nature."[7]

(1) O'Keeffe and "God"

Although the reality of God as immanent transcendence was an intensifying constant in both her life and her creative expression, the word "God" was not part of Georgia O'Keeffe's ordinary vocabulary, thought processes or daily experience. Undoubtedly, her reticence to use the term arose in part from the conceptualizations of God and the dogmatization about God which predominated in organized religious contexts.   Many of those images of and ideas about the deity detracted from the purity and the simplicity of her experience of the divine transcendence and immanence within her and all around her. More appealing and personally meaningful than the way that she perceived the word "God" used around her were expressions such as "the distance always calling," "adventure of the spirit into the unknown," "the unknown of infinity," "the intangible thing in myself," and "the unexplainable thing in nature."

Another significant reason for O'Keeffe's infrequent use of the word "God" pertained to her preference for spatial intelligence over linguistic intelligence. Her most connatural way of expressing something of her quest for "the unknown of infinity" was by means of visual images rather than by spoken or written language. In fact, her use of the verbal expressions that she found personally meaningful was more by way of exception than the rule.

It was by standing "alone" – that is, in solitude – "with the earth and sky" –in other words, with the transcendent immanent in nature – that O'Keeffe came face-to-face with "the unknown of infinity" – that is, the mystery of God. Silence and solitude opened

---

[7] *Georgia O'Keeffe*, statements opposite plates 88 and 100 respectively.

her to much more than a cosmic sense of oneness. They brought her into direct encounter with divine numinosity transparent in nature. Silent and solitary communion with nature provided the ambiance par excellence for her experience of transcendence. In the above quoted letter, O'Keeffe specified in terms of geographical landscape her inner quest for the beyond. She named it: "a feeling of something in me going off in every direction into the unknown of infinity." That description sounds remarkably similar to what some Christian mystics term contemplation.

(2) O'Keeffe and "Contemplation"

In the above quotation from Georgia O'Keeffe's July 25, 1952 letter, several significant elements of her contemplative experience stand out:

First, O'Keeffe's contemplative experience involved a reality existing within her, but originating beyond her and not of her. It related to that which was most mysterious, deepest and elusive in her personhood. It spoke of that depth which she could describe only as "something in me."

Second, those depths of O'Keeffe "went off in every direction." The image that comes to mind is activation of a centrifugal force, like an explosion. Yet, the bursting forth was not in the direction of fragmentation or disintegration. Quite the contrary, this movement was in the spiritually positive direction of going out of self, of losing self, of dying to self. The movement was in relation to "the unknown of infinity" – that is, in the direction of ultimate mystery who is God.

Third, the dynamic at work in O'Keeffe's contemplation of God in, through and beyond nature was none other than that of the finite pointing to the infinite, the created opening the human heart to the uncreated. O'Keeffe found "the infinite" to be the beyond within all things, including her own self. All creation was radiant with the immanent transcendence of God.

Fourth, O'Keeffe's "going off in every direction" was not only outward, but also inward. Her opening out to mystery was not only in terms of the vast expanses of space – to the infinite out there, as it were – but also in terms of the infinite within, deeper than consciousness can penetrate, deeper even than the unconscious – to God more intimate to her than she was to herself.

Fifth, in that way O'Keeffe's adventure of spirit into the unknown was ecstatic, wonder-filled and awe-inspiring. It was, in a word, contemplative.

(3) O'Keeffe and The Cloud of Unknowing

If then Georgia O'Keeffe was so contemplatively inclined, is it not ironic that by her own admission (in the above quotation from her letter of July 25, 1952) an enduring classic on contemplation – *The Cloud of Unknowing* – struck no resonant cord within her? The irony is compounded all the more by the fact that the anonymous fourteenth century author of that work described contemplation in a way profoundly compatible with O'Keeffe's experience. Moreover, the contemplative approach of *The Cloud* has great affinity with meditation in Zen Buddhism, a tradition that had immense appeal for O'Keeffe.

Several explanations for that lack of resonance present themselves:

First, O'Keeffe herself noted that on reading the book she was "startled" by her "lack for the need of the comfort of the Church," and that she did not share the Church's "fear of death – and after." Although those themes are not stressed in *The Cloud*, they recur throughout the work. O'Keeffe may have found the presence of those motifs annoying.

Second, the theology of sin and of last judgment that underlies the book probably struck in O'Keeffe a negative cord and possibly distracted her from appreciating its positive teaching on contemplation.

Third, the literary construct of *The Cloud* is that of a master (presumably a priest or a monk) giving spiritual guidance and practical advice to a neophyte on the contemplative way. O'Keeffe's keen sense of not needing that kind of reassurance may have been such that the author's profound insight into the contemplative experience escaped her attention.

Fourth, perhaps the idea of a master-disciple relationship within a hierarchical, male-dominated ecclesial structure was itself so distasteful to O'Keeffe that she could not get beyond it to the book's description of the contemplative experience.

Fifth, in general *The Cloud* puts such strong accent on the utter transcendence of God that it may have confused O'Keeffe or simply turned her off. Her connatural way of approaching divine transcendence was always through the divine immanence in the geographical landscape or in a specific aspect of it, evident to her by means of her visual perception.

Sixth, The Cloud is clearly in the long line of apophatic mystical writings; that is, those which stress the kenotic or emptying aspect of the spiritual life. Probably O'Keeffe confounded this approach – which in reality is paradoxically quite positive – with the pessimistic attitude of the Church at the time toward death and final judgment.

(4) O'Keeffe 's Contemplative Experience and Her Art

With regard to the expression, "going off in every direction," Georgia O'Keeffe used elsewhere a related turn of phrase. In a letter dated December 24, 1945, she wrote of her experience of "going off in space" when doing paintings such as her canvases of bones and sky in colors of blue and red:

> It is a kind of thing that I do that makes me feel I am going off into space – in a way that I like.... I always feel that sometime I may fall off the edge – It is something I like so much to do that I dont care if I do fall off the edge – No sense in it but it is my way– [8]

Those words reveal the interconnection of O'Keeffe's contemplative experience and her art. Standing "alone with earth and sky" was an integral aspect of O'Keeffe's spiritual adventure into "the unknown of infinity." Her attempt to make the unknown known in her painting flowed from and redounded to her experience of mystery. In another context O'Keeffe expressed that evolving circular pattern this way:

> The unexplainable thing in nature that makes me feel the world is big far beyond my understanding – to understand maybe by trying to put it into form. To find the feeling of infinity on the horizon line or just over the next hill. [9]

---

[8] *Art and Letters*, 242-243.
[9] *Georgia O'Keeffe*, statement opposite plate 100.

In other words, O'Keeffe's art was an expression of her being drawn by God through nature in the direction of divine transcendence. And her art in turn reflected back to her and to its beholders something of that experience of being drawn by God to God's own self.

D. From the Faraway Nearby

Throughout her life Georgia O'Keeffe was fascinated by the immensity and the wonder of nature in the environment in which she lived. In that world she was especially drawn to "the distance always calling" her, to "the unknown of infinity," to "the inexplicable thing in nature," and to "the intangible thing" in herself.

O'Keeffe employed two other metaphors for transcendence: "the faraway" and "the faraway nearby." As always, her perception of a geographical landscape became a metaphor for her inner landscape. She used the phrase "the faraway" (or "the Far Away") in two geographical contexts:

(1) She spoke of her life in New Mexico as being in the "far away" in relation to New York City and the eastern states. For instance, on August 15, 1940, she wrote to her close friend Ettie Stettheimer of her delight to be back in Abiquiu which was "so far away that no one ever comes." She went on to allude to her love for "the far away," even if that love seemed odd to others. She then noted how in her "far away country" there was no radio or newspaper, except for *Time* magazine.[10] In this spatial sense O'Keeffe wrote again to Ettie on June 10, 1944, expressing her feelings of being "very small – and far away – and unimportant."[11]

(2) A second geographical context in which O'Keeffe used the phrase "the faraway" (or "the Far Away") was in reference to an aspect of her immediate environment within New Mexico itself. Even when she traveled around the world, she was always happy to return to her "Far Away" in Abiquiu. That Far Away within her world of Abiquiu inspired in her wonder, fascination and love. For instance, writing to her husband on August 26, 1937, of the moon coming up over the landscape, O'Keeffe mentioned a strange white light creeping across "the faraway" to the dark sky.[12] To another

---

[10] See *Art and Letters*, 231.

[11] *Art and Letters*, 239.

[12] See *Georgia O'Keeffe: Catalogue of the Fourteenth Annual Exhibition of Paintings with Some Recent O'Keeffe Letters* (New York, NY: An American Place, 1938).

correspondent on January 19, 1951, she wrote of being the most fortunate of people in that she loved "the sky – and the Faraway."[13] O'Keeffe sometimes camped overnight at an area near Abiquiu which she designated "the Black Place." Commenting on that locale, she wrote:

> Such a beautiful, untouched lonely-feeling place – part of what I call the Far Away.[14]

In addition to her own words, the visual language of O'Keeffe's paintings sheds light on her notion of the Far Away. O'Keeffe titled one painting from 1937, *From the Faraway Nearby.*[15] The basic design of this painting is that of a narrow band of earth surface in which undulating hills soon give way to distant horizon. Approximately seven-eighths of the canvas surface is sky. A deer skull with a rack of antlers rises from near the bottom to the top edge of the canvas, as well as from edge to near edge horizontally. The painting is done in hues of gray, brown, red and blue. The antlers sweep upward in a V-shape, reversing the upside down V-shape of the hills. The beholder sees the nearby and the faraway, but no middle ground. O'Keeffe's visual integration of the nearby and the faraway is striking. She presents the skull with antlers in three-quarter view, the lowest left antler looming up close to the front and almost hooked around a small hill, while the skull and right rack veer back into the faraway. The visual effect of that composition is marriage of the here and the there, the now and the forever, the close and the distant, the nearby and the faraway.

Thus, the painting depicts "the faraway nearby." In spiritual terms, the unknown of infinity is already radiant in what is close at hand. Transcendence is immanent in creation. However, what is perceived is *from* the Faraway Nearby. Creation does not and cannot contain the fullness of transcendence. The painting expresses something of the mystery of the faraway, but that expression keeps beckoning the beholder further into the beyond. The distance always keeps on calling.

---

[13] See *Art and Letters*, 258.
[14] *Georgia O'Keeffe*, statement opposite plate 60; see also statement opposite plate 70.
[15] See *CR*, 914; *Georgia O'Keeffe*, plate 72; *O'Keeffe: In the West*, 40.

CHAPTER 21

Making the Unknown Known

"Making your unknown known is the important thing."[1] That statement of Georgia O'Keeffe was more than a word of advice to a friend. It articulated the spiritual direction of her own life. From her adventure of spirit into the unknown arose an irresistible urgency to express herself in paint. She felt a compelling imperative to communicate what she saw, as she saw it.[2]

O'Keeffe's experience of transcendence and her compelling desire to express something of it on canvas affected every detail of her daily life and guided all her choices. Her painting was the factor that integrated all the events and encounters of each day into a unified whole. On one occasion she compared painting to a thread that ran through all the reasons for all the other things that she did day in and day out: baking, gardening, taking care of business, receiving visitors, spending time with friends, etc.[3] Her art was the focus of her life – indeed, the very love of her life – and all other activities took on significance in relation to it. Her passion to make her unknown known was all-consuming, and it provided her consistently with meaning, purpose and direction.

In this chapter we ponder the creative process of Georgia O'Keeffe. By "creative process," we mean that mysterious longing to express herself in painting; that energy which enabled her to communicate her experience in line and color; that dynamic by which she brought forth from her inmost depths something uniquely her own. Specifically, we examine:

---

[1] *Art and Letters*, 174.
[2] See B. Vladimir Berman, "She Painted the Lily and Got $25,000 and Fame for Doing it!..," *New York Evening Graphic* (12 May 1928), in *O'Keeffe...and the Critics*, 287.
[3] See Lee Nordness, ed., *Art: U.S.A.: Now* (New York, NY: Viking Press, 1963), 35-36.

- nature as catalyst for her transcendent experience and self-expression;
- her language of form and color;
- her urge to speak visually;
- painting as an equivalent for her world;
- the "memory or dream thing" dimension of her work;
- her approach to painting by "filling space in a beautiful way."

A. The Wideness and Wonder of the World

The grounding for Georgia O'Keeffe's experience of immanent transcendence, self-actualization and creative process was what she termed "the wideness and wonder of the world" in which she lived.[4] The phrase, "wideness of the world," alludes to extensive space, uninhabited landscape, horizons that fade off into infinity. It suggests the silence, the solitude and the freedom of prairie, desert, ocean and sky. The phrase, "wonder of the world," embraces movement, shape, light, color and diversity of creatures.

The wideness and wonder of the world sustained O'Keeffe's lifelong adventure of spirit into the unknown. Experience was her wise teacher on that spiritual quest.[5] Yet, her experience of the world's wideness and wonder always exceeded what O'Keeffe could express of it. She felt that she lost much of an experience before she could render it in drawing or painting. The content of a finished painting seemed to her infinitesimal when compared to the richness of the inspiring event.[6]

O'Keeffe saw and could not help but see the wideness and wonder of the world.[7] She felt that autumn was always her best time for painting.[8] She painted what were to her the most ordinary things that she had beheld. Yet, she was aware that other people did not see or know those things as she did.[9] Her work as a whole reveals her solitary perspective on her world. Her interpretation of a subject on canvas emerged from her contemplation of it in solitude for a lengthy period of time. With rare exceptions she chose her subjects

---

[4] *Georgia O'Keeffe*, statements opposite plates 71 and 107.
[5] See *Art and Letters,* 210 and 267.
[6] See O'Keeffe's statement in *Georgia O'Keeffe: Exhibition of Oils and Pastels* (New York, NY: An American Place, 1940); also *Art and Letters,* 179.
[7] See *Art and Letters,* 241.
[8] See *Art and Letters,* 192.
[9] See *Art and Letters,* 254.

from nature. People, living creatures and human-made objects did not ordinarily find their way into her paintings.

O'Keeffe's artistic expressions reveal three basic vantage points from which she encountered transcendence immanent in the wideness and wonder of the world around her. Those perspectives are:

- standing on level ground, beholding the earth at eye level and/or seeing the sky above;
- standing on a hill, beholding earth below, mountains or cliffs at a higher altitude and/or sky above;
- sitting in an airplane, viewing the earth below, the horizontal plane outside the window and/or the sky above the flying altitude.

B. Statements in Colors and Shapes

Georgia O'Keeffe described herself as having the kind of mind that sees shapes.[10] She visualized things more readily than she conceptualized them. O'Keeffe spoke and wrote with stark eloquence. Yet, she found it easier to express herself in painting than in words. She believed that she could make a more definite statement with colors and shapes than with words. The significance of a color was more exact for her than the meaning of a word.[11]

Essential to O'Keeffe's creative development was her coming to accept as true her way of seeing and thinking.[12] For years she painted in the conventional way taught in the art schools of that time. It did not occur to her to use her personal experience or visual imagery as the basis and the content of her artistic expression. While she interacted vibrantly with the world around her, she did not adequately perceive or sufficiently value the uniqueness of her own experience. Moreover, while her art teachers instilled in her in a superb manner the techniques of painting and drawing, they did not encourage her to express herself according to her way of seeing. When she came in touch with Arthur Wesley Dow's approach to

---

[10] See Mary Daniels, "The 'Real Painting Country' of O'Keeffe," *Chicago Tribune* (28 September 1975).

[11] See *Art and Letters*, 227; *Georgia O'Keeffe*, first page of text and statement opposite plate 13.

[12] See *Some Memories*, first page of text (unnumbered); *Georgia O'Keeffe*, statement opposite plate 1.

painting, she began to recognize her unique visual images, to value them and to express them. Thereafter, she proceeded unwaveringly in that direction.

Some of O'Keeffe's visual images had realistic or natural bases, while others were just beautiful images formed by her imagination. She would put together at times a string of visual forms, seemingly out of nowhere. She believed that her visual language spoke for itself. She would not paint anything that she judged capable of expression in another form.[13] She believed that the meaning of a painting was evident on the canvas.[14] On one occasion an interviewer asked her why she painted skulls. She replied that to answer his question she would probably have to do another painting with a skull in it.[15] In other words, the visual language of the skull contained the power to convey its own reason for being.

C. An Urge to Speak

For Georgia O'Keeffe, making her unknown known in painting and drawing was an inner necessity.[16] She carried within herself a persistent desire to put down in visual form the things that meant so much to her. She had a relentless longing to say in shape and color the meaning of her experience. She felt impelled to give visual expression to her communion with the unknown transparent within the wideness and wonder of the world in which she lived. In her words, she felt an urge to speak in drawing and painting.[17]

That interior imperative directed O'Keeffe's creative process. She did not decide primarily by means of logic and analysis on a specific form for an artistic expression. Rather her inner need was the determining factor in her work. That innate prompting to make

---

[13] See *Art and Letters*, 202.

[14] See Edith Evans Asbury, "Silent Desert Still Charms Georgia O'Keeffe, near 81," in *New York Times* (2 November 1968).

[15] See Allen Keller, "Animal Skulls Fascinate Miss O'Keeffe, but Why?" in *New York World Telegram* (13 February 1937).

[16] See *Art and Letters*, 174-175. O'Keeffe studied thoroughly Wassily Kandinsky's *Concerning the Spiritual in Art*. Kandinsky designated an artist's inevitable impulse for outward self-expression as "inner need" or "inner necessity." According to Kandinsky, the convergence of three mystical elements constituted that need: something within the artist which calls for expression (the element of personality); the artist's inclination to express the spirit of his/her time and culture (the element of style); and the artist's urge to further the cause of art (the element of pure artistry).

[17] See *Art and Letters*, 227.

the unknown known in a specific context gave birth to a form that was real and living.

When O'Keeffe was most in tune with her inner need, her experience of herself at work painting was that of her whole being moving from the inside outward. She had then a sense of harmony between herself and her work. When she was somewhat off-center within herself, she had to exert effort of mind and will toward the task at hand.[18] On some occasions she was unable to paint at all because of a lack of sharp interest at her center.[19]

O'Keeffe's everlasting urge to speak in drawing and painting sprang from her inmost being, her deepest self, her sense of identity. Ultimately, she made drawings and did paintings not to convey a distinct message but to express herself.[20]

D. Painting: An Equivalent for the World and for Life

Georgia O'Keeffe was enthralled by the wideness and wonder of the world not only on a grand scale, but also as seen in microcosm in individual people, things and places. She once advised a fellow artist to try to paint the world – the wind, the cold, the heat, the dust, the starlight night – as if he were the first person looking at it.[21] No doubt, that suggestion came from her own experience of beholding nature.

O'Keeffe's aim in painting was to make known the unknown as she saw it manifest in a specific subject:

> I have picked flowers where I found them – have picked up sea shells and rocks and pieces of wood where there were sea shells and rocks and pieces of wood that I liked.... When I found the beautiful white bones on the desert I picked them up and took them home too.... I have used these things to say what is to me the wideness and wonder of the world as I live in it.[22]

---

[18] See *Art and Letters*, 175.
[19] See, for example, *Art and Letters*, 213.
[20] See *A Woman on Paper*, 123-124.
[21] See *Art and Letters*, 214.
[22] *Georgia O'Keeffe*, statement opposite plate 71.

O'Keeffe relied on intuition in her choice of subject. Out of her experience would come images of shapes and colors. She would then focus on a prominent image that drew forth feeling and held meaning. She would make quick positive decisions, and discover only later the reasons for her choices.[23]

It was O'Keeffe's love for a specific subject that motivated her to paint it. "Why paint something if you don't love it?" she once asked.[24] Her work of creative expression, although difficult and demanding, was her pleasure. She worked for the sheer joy and the love of creating.[25] Making known the unknown within her wide and wonder-filled world was its own reward.

Over the course of her life O'Keeffe used flowers, rocks, pieces of wood, sea shells, bones from the desert, hills, buildings, clouds, etc. in order to convey her experience. She intended those treasured subjects to be "equivalents" for the world in which she took delight and for life as she saw it.

> I know I can not paint a flower. I can not paint the sun or the desert on a bright summer morning but maybe in terms of paint color I can convey to you my experience of the flower or the experience that makes the flower of significance to me at that particular time.... [Painting] ... is my effort to create an equivalent with paint color for the world – life as I see it.[26]

Although they usually symbolized the natural world, O'Keeffe used equivalents – for instance: leaves, trees or an abstract form – sometimes to portray her experience of a person or a situation.[27] Explaining why she did not paint people or living creatures, she expressed her belief that she could by means of suggestion get into a painting the life lived in a specific place.[28]

---

[23] See *Art and Letters*, 184.

[24] See Harold Butcher, "Georgia O'Keeffe," *Santa-Fean* (September-October 1941).

[25] See B. Vladimir Berman, "She Painted the Lily and Got $25,000 for Doing it!..." *New York Evening Graphic* (12 May 1928), in *O'Keeffe...and the Critics*, 287; Carol Taylor, "Lady Dynamo," in *New York World Telegram* (31 March 1945).

[26] *Art and Letters*, 202.

[27] See *Georgia O'Keeffe*, statement opposite plate 55; *Art and Letters*, 218.

[28] See Daniel Catton Rich, *Georgia O'Keeffe* (Chicago, IL: Art Institute of Chicago, 1943).

E. That Memory or Dream Thing

After she had selected a subject for painting, Georgia O'Keeffe usually required a lengthy incubation period. Ordinarily, she proceeded slowly to the actual painting. She spent considerable effort and energy familiarizing herself with her subject. Working with a visualization was for her like getting acquainted with a person. Neither came easily to her. She needed time to formulate clearly into shape and color the new experience.[29]

Integral to O'Keeffe's preparation for painting was communion with the subject of interest to the point of identification. To paint a flower she became the flower, in a sense; to paint desert and sky she became that landscape. In that act of communion she entered into the spirit of the subject. She discovered a presence radiating through it, from beyond it: that "unexplainable thing in nature" and that "intangible thing" in herself.[30]

In pondering subjects for painting, O'Keeffe worked toward simplifying the forms to their essential shapes. She believed that it was only by selection, elimination and emphasis that she could get to the true meaning of things.[31] To make the unknown known meant expressing her subject in its most basic shape and most revealing color. Rarely did she start a painting before the visual image was clear to her. She knew what she was going to do before she put the brush to the canvas. If she did not know, she simply did not try to paint.

Before starting to paint, it was O'Keeffe's custom also to draw in pencil a small line composition. She worked out in that way the form for the painting. It was not unusual for her to do several possible versions of the composition. Moreover, she selected in advance her color scheme. When she was ready to begin, she organized her colors on a glass palette, each at a distance from the other. She set out a different brush for each color.[32]

It often happened that one painting would lead to another. Thus, O'Keeffe would end up doing a series on a specific subject. That approach entailed working through a question, exploring a set

---

[29] See O'Keeffe's statement in *Georgia O'Keeffe: Exhibition of Oils and Pastels* (New York, NY: An American Place, 1940).

[30] *Georgia O'Keeffe*, statements opposite plates 100 and 88 respectively.

[31] See "I Can't Sing, So I Paint!..," *New York Sun* (5 December 1922), in *O'Keeffe...and the Critics*, 180.

[32] See *A Woman on Paper*, 265; Frances O'Brien, "Americans We Like: Georgia O'Keeffe," *Nation* 125 (12 October 1927): 361-362, in *O'Keeffe...and the Critics*, 269.

of relationships and reducing a subject to its essential form through a process of visual thinking. Ordinarily, she began a series by painting her subject in a realistic manner. Then, as she went on from one painting to another of the same subject, she would simplify her design until the final painting was either entirely abstract or almost so. O'Keeffe referred to that creative approach with the phrase, "that memory or dream thing I do."[33] Her final numbering of a series did not always follow the order of her painting.

One example of O'Keeffe's series approach is a group of six jack-in-the-pulpit paintings done in 1930.[34] The first painting consists of a small 12" x 9" realistic image of the plant. In the second painting (40" x 30") of this series O'Keeffe magnified the plant and placed emphasis upon lines radiating outward from the pulpit. The third painting (40" x 30") has a simpler design, which consists of the flower set against a background space. In the fourth painting (40" x 30") O'Keeffe did a magnified view of the flower-pulpit area. The fifth painting (48" x 30") is almost abstract, with the colors and curving lines of the earlier paintings still present. In the sixth painting (36" x 18") she reduced the original image to the black shape of the pistil against a white halo-like shape, which has behind it an expanding and darkening halo-like form.

O'Keeffe's intent was not to reproduce a thing exactly as it was in itself. Her purpose in painting was to express how she saw it. Getting to what most people judged to be abstract was O'Keeffe's reason for painting. She considered that essential form to be the clearest visual statement of the unknown that she was seeking to make known. She wrote to a friend:

> That memory or dream thing I do ... for me comes
> nearer reality than my objective kind of work.[35]

It surprised O'Keeffe that many people separated the objective from the abstract in painting. She believed that nothing was less real on canvas than so-called "realism." She maintained that details were confusing and obscured meaning. Lines and color put together in order to express meaning instead of being merely representational was of ultimate importance to her. O'Keeffe

---

[33] *Art and Letters*, 206.
[34] For illustrations, see *CR*, 715-720; *Art and Letters*, plates 78-81; *Georgia O'Keeffe*, plates 38-42; *One Hundred Flowers*, plates 60-66.
[35] *Art and Letters*, 206.

described abstraction in that sense as the most definite form for the intangible unknown in herself which she could only clarify in paint.[36]

O'Keeffe's creative process sprang out of who she was as a person. Yet, she recognized that it took more than a gift or a talent to be an artist. It required what she called "nerve" and hard work, together with commitment to a certain definite line of action, perseverance in that direction, training in the school of experience.[37]

F. Filling Space in a Beautiful Way

In the western perspective of reality people tend to view space in terms of void or absence. However, in the eastern outlook people conceive space not as a lack of something, but as the fullness of nothing. That is, the void of space has value in its own right.

Georgia O'Keeffe experienced empty space more in an oriental than occidental fashion. She liked empty space; for instance, the seashore in Maine and the desert landscape of New Mexico. Since her various homes had only the essentials, there was plenty of nothing in her living environment. She preferred a blank wall because she could imagine whatever she liked on it. The holes in bones that she found on the desert floor inspired her. The openness beyond the patio door of her home in Abiquiu captivated her. The empty space of a canvas called her to visually explore and express the unknown that she felt in one experience or another. By her own admission there was "some thing" in space that she loved almost as passionately as she could love a person.[38]

O'Keeffe's key to self-expression was the idea of art as "filling a space in a beautiful way."[39] She committed herself decisively to that artistic approach as a result of her encounter with Alon Bement, who was teaching art according to the principles of Arthur Wesley Dow. Dow's method accentuated three elements – line, *notan* (abstract arrangements of light and dark patterns), and

---

[36] See *Georgia O'Keeffe*, statement opposite plate 88; "I Can't Sing, So I Paint!...", in *O'Keeffe...and the Critics*, 180-182.

[37] See Mary Lynn Kotz, "A Day with Georgia O'Keeffe," in *ARTnews* (December 1977): 36-45; Lillian Sabine, "Record Price for Living Artist...," *Brooklyn Sunday Eagle Magazine* (27 May 1928), in *O'Keeffe...and the Critics*, 288.

[38] See *Art and Letters*, 207.

[39] See *Georgia O'Keeffe*, statement opposite plate 11; Arthur Wesley Dow, *Theory and Practice of Teaching Art* (New York, NY: Teachers College, Columbia University Press, 1912) and *Composition*, 20th ed. (New York, NY: Doubleday, Page, 1938).

color. While Dow emphasized line among those elements, O'Keeffe accentuated color. Dow's approach to painting caught O'Keeffe's attention because it seemed so basic to daily life for every person. It had application to how one dresses, how one arranges one's home, how one performs simple ordinary tasks.

O'Keeffe began work on a canvas from the viewpoint of its unity. She considered the empty space of the canvas as a single whole. She did not work in the empty space by depicting separate forms and balancing them in relation to the framing edge. Rather, she filled the canvas by dividing its one unified space. In this respect, her work anticipated by decades the color-field painters of the 1960's like Mark Rothko, Ad Reinhardt and Clifford Still.[40]

And how did Georgia O'Keeffe fill space? She divided the whole space in a beautiful way. Most of her paintings and drawings are beautiful in a way that far transcends decorative effect. Their beauty captures a sense of wholeness, integrity and completion with respect to a subject. Their beauty flows from a color-harmony and a form-harmony that embodies meaning – especially transcendent meaning. It is the beauty of a subject radiating a mysterious energy or presence and evoking wonder in the beholder.

---

[40] See Barbara Rose, "Georgia O'Keeffe's Universal Spiritual Vision," in *Georgia O'Keeffe Exhibition in Japan* (Santa Fe, NM: Gerald Peters Gallery, 1988), 98-99.

CHAPTER 22

Keeping the Unknown Always Beyond

In September 1923 Georgia O'Keeffe wrote to Sherwood Anderson that "making your unknown known is the important thing." However, she immediately reminded him of another equally meaningful value: that of "keeping the unknown always beyond you."[1]

O'Keeffe's creative expression emanated from her encounter with immanent transcendence, especially within the natural world. In the course of her spiritual adventure into the unknown, she would feel or intuit something that she did not clearly understand. A specific encounter with mystery hidden yet revealed in a subject then generated in O'Keeffe an urge to express herself in line and color. Yet, instead of affording O'Keeffe restful satisfaction and a sense of closure, her finished canvas would impel her to explore further the unknown. Her self-expression itself confronted her once more with mystery.

In this chapter we consider the unknown that was always beyond O'Keeffe's experience and creative expression. We approach that theme from two perspectives:

- O'Keeffe's lack of satisfaction with her finished paintings;
- the transcendent which reveals itself to beholders of O'Keeffe's work.

A. Inability to Be Fully Satisfied

As an artist Georgia O'Keeffe aimed to make the unknown

---

[1] *Art and Letters*, 174.

known and to keep the unknown always beyond her. She explained that intent further with these words:

> [It is] catching crystalizing your simpler clearer
> vision of life – only to see it turn stale compared to
> what you vaguely feel ahead – that you must always
> keep working to grasp.[2]

O'Keeffe's phrase, "catching crystalizing your simpler clearer vision of life," is equivalent to her phrase, "making your unknown known." The words, "seeing it turn stale compared to what you vaguely feel ahead," paraphrase her words, "keeping the unknown always beyond you." Primarily by means of her painting, O'Keeffe engaged in the process of "catching crystalizing" a "simpler clearer vision of life." However, when she completed a work on canvas, it seemed "stale" to her.

In O'Keeffe's thought "stale" did not mean "poor quality." Like any artist she did paintings from time to time that were not up to her usual standards. O'Keeffe had many such canvases destroyed. Rather than indicating a judgment of "poor quality" with regard to a painting, the adjective "stale" designated O'Keeffe's lack of satisfaction upon completing a highly qualitative painting.

O'Keeffe's lack of satisfaction could indicate a compulsion for perfection. If indeed some perfectionism was asserting itself in O'Keeffe's judgment, that compulsion does not appear to be the dominant impetus. Of vital importance to O'Keeffe was the process itself of making known the unknown. Any painting embodied what she could perceive at a specific moment in that development. As she beheld a finished canvas, she intuited through her line and color more of the unknown. Her creative expression itself directed her toward the unknown up ahead, which she could already vaguely feel. Thus, a finished painting lacked luster in comparison to the "more" toward which it pointed. It was "stale" in light of a fresh intuition of the beyond that urged her to speak again on canvas.

O'Keeffe referred explicitly to her lack of satisfaction as an artist in a letter written in 1950:

> I am never satisfied – never really – I almost always
> fail – always I think – now next time I can do it –

---

[2] *Art and Letters*, 174-175.

Maybe that is part of what keeps one working – [3]

O'Keeffe was "never satisfied" in the sense that she was unable to rest contentedly in the experience which a painting expressed. By the time she completed a painting she herself had already gone beyond the experience that it embodied. The painting itself had thrust her toward further revelation of the unknown and richer experience of immanent transcendence. In and through her work the beyond asserted its hold ever more strongly upon her.

Thus, O'Keeffe's lack of satisfaction with her work, or her sense of "staleness" with respect to a painting, did not arise from dissatisfaction or disgruntlement. Rather, completion of a painting intensified O'Keeffe's awareness of her inability to be totally satisfied by anything but the fullness of the unknown. Her creation itself thrust her further into the realm of transcendence. A painting pointed her beyond itself to the mystery ready to reveal itself further. It impelled her always to keep working toward the beyond. O'Keeffe's series of paintings on a specific subject – like an evening star, a jack-in-the-pulpit flower or a patio door – exemplify clearly the cycle of one finished painting giving rise to a fresh intuition of the beyond, which she then expressed in yet another painting.

O'Keeffe's lack of satisfaction bespeaks her interaction with her own creative expression. She was captivated by the unknown that she perceived in her world, especially in the realm of nature. In ecstatic wonder and joy she tried to crystallize in paint what she so loved. Yet, the fullness of mystery always eluded her. Her expression of immanent transcendence had the effect of increasing her longing for more of the beyond. Her vague intuition or feeling of what lay up ahead instilled in her a yearning for more of the unknown. It thrust her forward on her spiritual adventure.

B. The Experience of the Beholder

Having considered an effect of Georgia O'Keeffe's self-expression upon herself, we turn our attention now to this question: How do her paintings touch other people?

Self-expression, whether in verbal or visual form, attempts to communicate a meaning or a message. Above all, it seeks to share with another person an experience of who one is and of how one

---

[3] *Art and Letters*, 254.

sees.   O'Keeffe's self-expression in color and line invites us to participate in her world of experience. The unknown that she reveals draws us into the transcendent which remains hidden.

In this section we identify certain prominent features of the experience of many people who behold O'Keeffe's art. We focus on these specific qualities:

- solitude,
- presence,
- light,
- two-dimensional surface,
- symbolism,
- the is-ness of each subject.

(1) Solitude

Silence and aloneness were integral to the process of Georgia O'Keeffe's self-expression in line and color. She spent much time quietly ruminating upon a subject. She usually went off by herself to a secluded place in order to paint. Ordinarily, she did not show a painting to anyone until she had finished it.

Solitude is essential for us also if we are to enter into an O'Keeffe painting. Seeing her visual language requires that we remain alone and silent for some time in the presence of the painting. That stance of beholding is the doorway to the wideness and wonder of O'Keeffe's world.

(2) Presence

Many of Georgia O'Keeffe's paintings contain one dominating subject; for instance: a flower. Other canvases depict a few shapes in relation to each other; for example: desert, bone and sky. Our encounter with the presence of a subject in an O'Keeffe painting opens us out to an all-encompassing Presence, hidden yet revealed.

Generally, O'Keeffe did not include on her canvas any indication of specific locale for a subject. In her paintings a subject's lack of association with an identifiable place leaves us with a sense of a universal and timeless presence.

In some paintings vast, empty space surrounds O'Keeffe's subject. Many paintings that present a looming close-up view of a subject, such as a cliff, a hill or a building, contain an intimation of space trailing off into the infinite beyond. Yet, the wideness of her world is neither unfriendly nor hostile. It is a nurturing and inviting spaciousness, offering us boundless freedom. We enter into an infinite emptiness fraught with presence. We see what O'Keeffe has seen, but we do not see her. She points us beyond herself and her vision to the unknown. The presence that filled her world is mysterious. It is the presence of immanent transcendence. Ultimately, it is God's presence.

(3) Light

As we abide in Georgia O'Keeffe's spacious world, light is also a significant aspect of the experience. With the exception of a small number of paintings, light shines through her canvases. In some paintings a muted light radiates almost evenly from within all aspects of the composition. In other canvases light has a concentrated focus, yet to varying degrees illumines everything. Light casts no shadows in O'Keeffe's world of line and color. Yet, while light pervades everything, its source is nowhere visible. Thus, through her representation of light O'Keeffe intimated immanent transcendence. God dwells in inaccessible light, yet the light of God's presence shines forth from within all creation.

(4) Two-dimensional Surface

Georgia O'Keeffe expressed herself on flat surface in a two-dimensional way (length and width), with some subjects appearing ready to burst over the edges of her canvas. Although a dimension of depth creeps into some paintings, O'Keeffe was not intent upon portraying depth. Using a two-dimensional surface, for instance, she portrayed in many landscape paintings of New Mexico the near and the far, without any significant middle ground. Thus, she created the effect of capturing the eternal in space and time or, conversely, of seeing space and time taken up into the eternal.

As we behold O'Keeffe's world, we have the impression of being in the unbound vibrant space of an eternal present. In and through the ordinary world around us, infinity touches us. We experience the forever in the now and the now in the forever.

(5) Symbolism

Georgia O'Keeffe painted many subjects from the world of nature: flowers, fruits, leaves, feathers, rocks, bones, hills, trees, sky, sea shells, clouds, etc. Those subjects have a dimension of archetypal symbolism. From the beginning of human history people have experienced those subjects as charged with the numinous and as having polyvalent meanings. As we behold O'Keeffe's work, her subjects exert on us that evocative power of universal symbolism.

O'Keeffe used the subjects of her paintings as symbols also of her personal experience. She painted a particular flower in a certain manner to express the way that flower had touched her. She used the image of a fractured autumn leaf to portray herself in intense pain. She painted natural subjects to represent her impressions of people. O'Keeffe herself adverted to personal symbolism with respect to her subjects. For instance, she noted how certain black rocks fashioned over time by sun, wind and blowing sand had become for her a symbol of the wideness and wonder of the sky and the earth. Moreover, she confessed to using natural subjects as "equivalents" for her world. Bones, for example, conveyed her experience of something keenly alive in the desert.[4]

In addition to both the archetypal and the personal symbolism of a specific subject, O'Keeffe employed color in a symbolic manner. She claimed that it was color that made her life worth living. She came to think of painting as her attempt to create an equivalent with color for her world and for life as she saw it.[5] White, for example, designated purity and innocence. Blue, as in the sky, represented infinity.[6] O'Keeffe's brilliant colors exert their psychological and spiritual effects upon us as we behold her world.

(6) Is-ness

Symbolism indeed entered into Georgia O'Keeffe's visual imagery. However, her foremost concern appears to have been expression in line and color of her experience of the being – the is-ness – of each subject. Her prime intent in painting was not to

---

[4] See *Georgia O'Keeffe*, statements opposite plates 71 and 107.
[5] See *Art and Letters*, 202. Kandinsky maintained in his book, *Concerning the Spiritual in Art*, that each color produces a corresponding spiritual vibration in the soul and that an artist's inner necessity should dictate the choice of colors for a painting.
[6] See, for example, *Georgia O'Keeffe*, statement opposite plate 74.

pass from the individual to the universal, from the singular to the collective, from the concrete to the abstract. Rather, O'Keeffe sought to render simply and clearly each subject as she perceived it: a rock as this rock, a flower as this flower, a bone as this bone, etc. As O'Keeffe interacted with the is-ness of her subjects, the transcendent hidden yet revealed within them was perceptible to her.

Essential to O'Keeffe's experience of transcendence was her vision of "the unexplainable thing in nature"[7] transparent in the ordinary being of the subject at hand. Her encounter with the unknown occurred for the most part in the suchness of what was extraordinarily familiar. Beholding on canvas the wideness and wonder of O'Keeffe's world, we too see transcendence immanent within the is-ness of each ordinary subject.

---

[7] See *Georgia O'Keeffe*, statement opposite plate 100.

CHAPTER 23

A Very Small Moment in Time

Time knits countless, unrepeatable, distinct moments into a whole. It situates a single human life within the broad span of history. Reflecting upon her life and her work in a letter dated July 28, 1950, Georgia O'Keeffe remarked to a correspondent:

I am a very small moment in time.[1]

O'Keeffe did not say that her work or her accomplishments constituted that very small moment, although those aspects of her life implicitly come into play. It was her unique personhood – her "I" – which she described as "a very small moment" in relation to history. Yet, in her time she believed that her work represented something unique and specifically American.[2]

In this chapter we focus principally on Georgia O'Keeffe's self-identity. We examine:

- her understanding of her deepest self;
- her description of self as the only thing a person really has;
- her accent upon personal integrity.

A. Georgia O'Keeffe's Center

Francis and Ida O'Keeffe lived on a farm near Sun Prairie, Wisconsin. On November 15, 1887, Ida gave birth to the second of their seven children. They named the dark-haired baby girl Georgia

---

[1] *Art and Letters*, 253.
[2] See *Art and Letters*, 241.

Totto O'Keeffe.

Decades later Georgia O'Keeffe recalled her earliest memories.[3]

O'Keeffe's very first recollection was that of the brightness of light all around her. Remarkably, she was only about eight or nine months old at the time. She was sitting outdoors among large pillows on a quilt spread out on the ground. Her mother and a friend were nearby. Together with light, she noticed color and shape: the cotton patchwork quilt made of white material with tiny red stars dotting it and black material with a red and white flower on it; the woman's blond hair with curly bangs, her dress made of thin white material patterned with a tiny blue flower and a sprig of green.

O'Keeffe's next memory of her early life reached back to an event which occurred probably a year later. It was her first recollection of actually taking pleasure in seeing with her eye and touching with her hand. Little Georgia had wandered across the lawn of the family home to the long entrance drive. She was fascinated by the color of the road's dust, bright in the sunlight. The dust looked so soft that she quickly got down into it and may have even tasted it. She felt its warmth and touched the smooth tiny ridges carved out in the driveway by buggy wheels. As the toddler was delighting in the moment, her frightened mother suddenly snatched her up under her arm – a turn of events which Georgia did not at all enjoy.

From her earliest years O'Keeffe was drawn to light and color, to sensory delight in the earth, to the patterns and shapes of the world around her. While the United States as a whole was moving increasingly in the direction of urbanization, technology and industrialization, O'Keeffe's childhood years were immersed in family life on a large mid-western farm. She treasured the land, the daily rhythms of nature, the changing of the seasons – so much so that the earth became for her a pivotal image for the core of her personhood. She wrote in 1934 to a close friend:

> My center does not come from my mind – it feels in
> me like a plot of warm moist well tilled earth with
> the sun shining hot on it – [4]

---

[3] See *Georgia O'Keeffe*, second and third pages of text (unnumbered).

[4] *Art and Letters*, 217. In a similar analogy (*Art and Letters*, 183), O'Keeffe described herself as a little plant which Stieglitz had watered, weeded and dug around.

In that statement O'Keeffe clearly associated her center with feeling rather than thinking. Thus, she accentuated the emotional and relational dimensions of her experience. Moreover, she located her center *within* herself, not outside herself in some work, institution, authority figure or loved one: "My center ... feels in me..." Her center refers then to that which characterized her as a unique human being, woman and artist. It denotes the solid foundation of her identity and the consistent basis of her self-actualization.

In the above quotation from the letter of 1934, O'Keeffe compared her center to a plot of earth, warm and moist, with sunlight penetrating it. A "plot of earth" represents solid ground. Metaphorically, that image designated the ground of her being and becoming. In her description of that plot of earth, O'Keeffe alluded to soil, water, light and heat. Those components favor the gestation, emergence and nurturance of new life. The proper balance of those elements prepares the earth so there can occur sprouting of the seed, formation of a root system and full development of a plant. The plot of earth thus becomes "mother earth." It is like a womb holding a new form, engendering new creation. O'Keeffe employed the image of the fertile plot of earth to designate her center as the source of her life and the matrix of her creativity. From those inner depths her identity took shape, her self-actualization unfolded, her creative expression formed.

A plot of "warm moist well tilled earth" is ideal for the gestation of new living forms. Yet, the actual engendering of that life remains mysterious. The wonder of life rising out of a dying seed occurs in the darkness and the hiddeness of the soil. The sower of the seed can only trust the process and wait in hope. By analogy, the life-engendering process operative from within our center or ground of becoming remains hidden. We cannot fully see or wholly grasp what is happening within those depths. We can foster to some extent the conditions that favor development of who we are to become, but we wait in dark faith and trust upon the process of self-actualization.

O'Keeffe's notion of center refers to that transcendent dimension of her personhood, which opened out into the transcendence of God. Her center was the nucleus of the "intangible thing" in herself that she sought to clarify in paint.[5] It was the home

---

[5] See *Georgia O'Keeffe*, statement opposite plate 88.

of the faraway nearby.[6] From within her center the distance kept always calling her.[7] From within her center the Unknown revealed itself, making itself known, while yet keeping itself always beyond.[8]

B. Self: The Only Thing a Person Has

In a letter written September 1923 Georgia O'Keeffe implied that the observable self is the form inevitably arising from a person's inmost center. After expressing her belief that everyone is born with a form, she passionately demanded that her correspondent honor his own "form."

> I ... feel incensed that you dont treat the thing that is yourself as the simple fact of yourself – there it is – just you ... the only thing you have.[9]

O'Keeffe practiced what she preached. Her attitude toward her own personhood was rather pragmatic: Here I am, as I am – no masks, no make-up, no pretense, neither super-human nor sub-human. Self-acceptance was for her a basic value. That quality was fundamental to her encounter with the transcendent dimension of life and to her creative expression.

Our form – that is, our conscious, observable self – is as yet unfinished. Until our death/resurrection we remain God's works of art in process. Our tangible self is mediator between our inner and outer world. To the extent that this self embodies something of our most elusive essence, it relates our center to the world around us. Moreover, our tangible self brings our interactions with people and things to bear upon our inner center. That dynamic was operative in O'Keeffe's personhood also. The interworking of her center, her conscious self and the world around her was integral to the development of her self-identity and the progression of her self-actualization.

C. Willingness to Bet on Herself

At the age of sixty-three Georgia O'Keeffe made the

---

[6] See *Georgia O'Keeffe*, ninth page of text and statement opposite plate 72.
[7] See *Georgia O'Keeffe*, ninth page of text.
[8] See *Art and Letters*, 174.
[9] *Art and Letters*, 175.

following observation to a correspondent:

> I have always been willing to bet on myself you
> know – and been willing to stand on what I am and
> can do even when the world isnt much with me.[10]

Of special interest is the phrase, "willing to stand on what I am and can do." With the words, "what I am," O'Keeffe designated her inmost center or core identity. The verb, "can do," denotes her capacity for action and her innate gift for painting. Her choice of the verb, "to stand on," is also significant. The object of "to stand on" is ground or grounding of some sort – land, floor, a ladder, etc. The image thus has similarity to O'Keeffe's comparison of her center to "a plot of warm moist well tilled earth with the sun shining hot upon it."[11]

O'Keeffe claimed that she was "always willing" to bet on herself. That is, she had a consistent inclination to believe in herself and in her work. She had a basic trust with regard to her sense of direction. So clear was she with respect to that direction that she stood firm even when the world was not much in tune with her. Irrespective of changing trends in the art world and the response to her work by art critics of her time, she stayed her course. She steadfastly kept moving forward, standing upon the solid ground of her center. Her work of self-actualization and self-expression was a developing, unfolding and blossoming of her experience of the unknown making itself known.

D. Integrity

Throughout her life Georgia O'Keeffe aimed to keep both her sense of identity and her work of self-expression in harmony with her center. In a word, she sought integrity. O'Keeffe considered integrity to be essential to self-actualization and creative expression. She stressed the importance of maintaining integrity, irrespective of success or failure in the judgment of other people.[12]

We highlight below four examples of O'Keeffe's practice of integrity. They pertain to:

---

[10] *Art and Letters*, 253.
[11] *Art and Letters*, 217.
[12] See *Art and Letters*, 175.

- decision-making;
- artistic desire;
- self-discipline;
- the Alfred Stieglitz photographic portrait of O'Keeffe.

(1) Decision-making

At the age of ninety Georgia O'Keeffe explained to an interviewer the method which she had followed over the course of her life for making daily choices.[13] It went back to 1907-1908, her year at the Art Students League of New York. There O'Keeffe found herself confronted with the choice of being her own person or being everyone's pet. She came across a book that taught decision-making in a practical way. The method consisted of writing "Yes" at the top of the left-hand side of a blank page and "No" at the top of the right hand side. In the Yes-column one wrote down the reasons for doing a particular thing. In the No-column one spelled out the reasons for not doing it. That approach made sense to O'Keeffe. It enabled her to see on paper what she truly desired to do.

For O'Keeffe the essential question was always: If you want to do *this,* can you do *that*? To illustrate the point, O'Keeffe cited the effect of dancing upon her artistic expression. As a young art student she had loved dancing. Yet, if she danced all night, she was unable to paint for three days afterwards. Because she wanted to paint at her best, she gave up dancing.

(2) Artistic Desire

Georgia O'Keeffe's sense of identity profoundly affected her creative expression.

In 1928 O'Keeffe named for an interviewer her one desire as an artist. She wanted to paint what she saw, as she saw it, in her own way. Thus, she sought fidelity to her unique vision, irrespective of the preferences of professional dealers and collectors of art.[14]

O'Keeffe worked in a field dominated in her time by men. That situation caused her to be especially vigilant with respect to

---

[13] See Mary Lynn Kotz, "A Day with Georgia O'Keeffe," in *ARTnews* (December 1977): 36-45.
[14] See B. Vladimir Berman, "She Painted the Lily and Got $25,000..," *New York Evening Graphic* (12 May 1928), in *O'Keeffe...and the Critics*, 287.

speaking with her own voice and to painting as she herself saw things. During the spring of 1930 O'Keeffe publicly debated Michael Gold, editor of *New Masses*. She pointed out to him that she had gone to men as artistic sources because of the dearth of women's work flowing from their unique feminine perspective. She accentuated her effort to paint in a way that was truly her own both as a person and as a woman. To ensure the integrity of her work, O'Keeffe questioned herself thus before ever putting her brush to canvas: Was the idea really hers? Did it come from her center? Or had she been unconsciously influenced by some man's photograph or idea?[15]

(3) Self-discipline

Georgia O'Keeffe was a high-spirited and passionate person. As a young woman she was emotionally intense toward every aspect of life. Her affective energy led her at times to excess in activities and relationships. She came to recognize a need for balance and moderation in order to sustain qualitative life. To that end O'Keeffe practiced what she called "conservation of energy"; that is, the focusing of her feelings upon what was really important to her, instead of dissipating those energies upon insignificant things.[16]

(4) The Stieglitz Photographic Portrait of O'Keeffe

Alfred Stieglitz did a series of photographs of Georgia O'Keeffe, spanning approximately two decades.[17] Long before Stieglitz knew O'Keeffe, he had the idea of doing a portrait of woman as woman. From the beginning of Stieglitz's photographing of her, O'Keeffe believed in the aesthetic significance of his project and was willing to be the subject. The Stieglitz portrait of O'Keeffe ranged from nudes, to close-ups of body parts, to photos of her with her paintings. Stieglitz presented her as *femme fatal*, artist and muse.

The photographs in that series from the late 1910's and the early 1920's were highly controversial. Influenced in part by the sensuality of the portrait, art critics interpreted O'Keeffe's drawings

---

[15] See Gladys Oaks, "Radical Writer and Woman Artist Clash on Propaganda and Its Uses," in *New York World* (16 March 1930).

[16] See *Lovingly, Georgia*, 52.

[17] See *Georgia O'Keeffe: A Portrait by Alfred Stieglitz* (New York, NY: Metropolitan Museum of Art, 1978); *A Woman on Paper*, 168.

and paintings of that period primarily as an expression of her sexuality. That interpretation appalled O'Keeffe.

Many people have questioned the motivation and the wisdom of O'Keeffe's decision to pose for Stieglitz's portrait of a woman. Why would a publicly recognized artist subject herself in that way to the male gaze? Was she motivated by a sense of integrity? Or did her involvement display a lack of self-esteem, together with personal dysfunctionality and loss of integrity? O'Keeffe's comments indicate that she herself thought the portrait enhanced rather than detracted from her sense of self-worth.

Throughout her life O'Keeffe had a number of different reactions to the portrait. When she received the prints of the first photos taken in 1917, she was so excited at seeing such photographs of herself that she took them to her school at Canyon, Texas, and showed them to her students. In an interview during 1977 she acknowledged that seeing the photos changed her perception of herself. Prior to viewing the first photos, she had not known what she looked like or given the matter much thought. She was amazed to find her face was not round but lean and structured.[18] O'Keeffe described Stieglitz's portrait of her as having enhanced her sense of individuality. Her ability to see her uniqueness had in turn facilitated her creative expression. At the age of ninety-one, however, she experienced distance from the woman whom she beheld in the Stieglitz portrait. She wrote of looking over the photographs and wondering who that person was. She felt as if in her life she had lived many lives.[19]

---

[18] See Mary Lynn Kotz, "A Day with Georgia O'Keeffe," in *ARTnews* (December 1977): 36-45.

[19] See introduction to *Georgia O'Keeffe: A Portrait by Alfred Stieglitz* (New York, NY: Metropolitan Museum of Art, 1978).

CHAPTER 24

Working into Her Own

O'Keeffe's book about her paintings, entitled *Georgia O'Keeffe*, was first published when she was eighty-nine years of age. O'Keeffe noted on the opening page of her text that her focus was not on where she had been throughout her life, but in what she had done with where she had been.[1] Facts such as place of birth, cities or towns of residence, details of her everyday living were not her primary interest. Of more importance to her was her response over the years to both her inner stirrings and her outer world. To use an analogy, her concern was not with naming the cards which she had held in her hand, but rather with how she had played out the hand which she was dealt.

Transcendent experience, self-actualization and creative expression are dimensions of what O'Keeffe did with where she had been. Thusfar, we have seen O'Keeffe primarily as the independent woman and talented artist expressing with her own voice and her unique vision her adventure of spirit into the unknown. But how did she become that person? How did she work into her own: spiritually, humanly and artistically?

In this chapter we address those questions by highlighting the following themes:

- certain significant events which prepared O'Keeffe for her fundamental creative breakthrough;
- that critical threshold of her development wherein she accepted as true her own thinking, feeling, seeing, and proceeded to do art expressive of her center;
- certain movements in the early twentieth century which helped

---

[1] See *Georgia O'Keeffe*, first page (unnumbered).

to create a milieu favorable to O'Keeffe's self-actualization and unique creative expression.

A. Pencil and Brush: But What to Say with Them?

Georgia O'Keeffe's interest and training in art went back to her early years. As children, Georgia and her sisters were driven on Saturdays into the town of Sun Prairie to take painting lessons. When Georgia was in the eighth grade, she declared to a school friend that she was going to be an artist when she grew up. Looking back upon her life, O'Keeffe could not identify the exact origin of that desire. She recalled having seen a beautiful drawing entitled, "The Maid of Athens," which had set something moving in her. As a young girl Georgia did not have a clear idea of how to go about becoming an artist. Nonetheless, by the age of twelve she was certain of what she wanted to be.

During O'Keeffe's first year of high school at Sacred Heart Academy in Madison, Wisconsin, she received private art instruction from a Dominican Sister. O'Keeffe remembered the sister as having criticized one of her drawings for being too small and too dark. When Georgia was a high school student at Chatham Episcopal Institute in Virginia (autumn 1903 to spring 1905), the art teacher, Elizabeth May Willis, recognized and nurtured her talent. Mrs. Willis encouraged Georgia's mother to send the young woman to the Art Institute of Chicago after her graduation from high school.

O'Keeffe began studying in Chicago with the leading art instructors of the time. Of special interest to her were John Vanderpoel's classes in drawing. Yet, after she had completed the 1905-1906 school year at the Art Institute of Chicago, O'Keeffe's training in art was rudely interrupted. That summer, while visiting her family who had moved to Williamsburg, Virginia, she contracted typhoid fever. After a period of convalescence, Georgia resumed her studies in the fall of 1907, at which time she chose to attend the Art Students League in New York City. Her instructors that year included William Merritt Chase, F. Luis Mora and Kenyon Cox. As winner of the Chase Still Life Scholarship, Georgia attended the League's 1908 outdoor summer school at Lake George, New York.

While at the Art Students League, Georgia visited for the first time Alfred Stieglitz's Little Galleries of the Photo-Secession, known as "291" because of its Fifth Avenue address. Stieglitz was making available to the general public primitive art, children's art and modernist European art. Those currents were counter to the traditional approach to painting then taught in art schools.

O'Keeffe remained at the League for just one year. Because of her family's deteriorating financial situation, she had to begin supporting herself. She found employment in Chicago as a commercial artist from 1908-1910, drawing pictures of lace and embroidery for advertisements. That venture ended when a severe case of measles affected her eyesight.

By the beginning of 1910 O'Keeffe found herself in a crisis that would span several years. She realized that she had been taught to work like other artists, and was dutifully following their example. Yet, she felt that she could not paint any better than those master artists. O'Keeffe knew that she was not expressing herself according to her unique way of seeing and thinking. Yet, she did not have a clear sense of what she wanted to say visually. She was certain of one thing, however: She did not intend to spend the rest of her life doing what other artists had already done.

O'Keeffe knew that she excelled in the use of her artistic tools. Charcoal, pencil, pen and ink, watercolor, pastel and oil were materials that she had been using since childhood. She had become so fluent with them from her earliest years that they were simply another language that she handled easily. Yet, she was left with the question of what to say with them.[2]

B. Something She Had to Say

On sporadic occasions in her early life Georgia O'Keeffe expressed visually in craft, drawing or painting something of personal meaning. In contrast to what she was obliged to do in classes, her art sprang in those instances from her experience. Those works represented what she termed "something I had to say."[3] Chief among them were the following:

(1) The first drawing that O'Keeffe could remember was that of a man lying on his back with his feet up in the air. She used a black lead pencil on a tan paper bag. She had tried to draw him standing and bending over. However, she could not get his legs bent properly at both hips and knees. Then, she turned the paper bag around and saw that he looked right as a man flat on his back with

---

[2] *Some Memories*, first page (unnumbered); *Georgia O'Keeffe*, statement opposite plate 1.

[3] *Georgia O'Keeffe*, fourteenth page of text (unnumbered).

his feet up in the air. O'Keeffe recalled working intensely at that drawing – probably as hard as she had ever labored at anything in her life. Although the outcome was not what she had intended, her effort left her with a sense of achievement.

(2) As a child O'Keeffe had a family of small china dolls with little-girl bodies and long golden hair. She made dresses and a portable doll house for them. She would take them outdoors during summer and set up a park to go with the house. She cut grass with scissors, left tall weeds for trees, made walkways with sand and stones, used a pan of water for a lake and an old shingle floating on it as a boat. O'Keeffe remembered that family of dolls as her greatest enjoyment during childhood.

(3) O'Keeffe made two drawings of a lighthouse. First, she copied a drawing of a lighthouse from a geography book. Because the paper looked quite empty, she added a horizon line, some palm trees and the sun. Then she painted the sun yellow, the sky and the waves blue, and the lighthouse white. Not satisfied with the sun which looked dirty rather than glowing, Georgia did a second lighthouse painting. This time by rendering the sky cloudy, she made the sun look brighter.

(4) About the same time as she did the lighthouse paintings, Georgia stood one winter night at an upstairs window of her home. Outside she saw in the yard a tall pointed spruce tree, across the road a burr oak tree black against the snow, in the distance a smaller oak and a soft line of woods. By lamplight she tried then to draw what she could remember of that scene and to paint the picture in color.

(5) At the Art Students League O'Keeffe did a painting of the back of a standing man. She had prepared the canvas with something white and had done the painting in bright color. After completion, she put the canvas in her window to dry. Visiting a friend who lived across the street from her, Georgia looked over in the direction of her room and was astounded to see her painting. She noticed how fresh and clean it seemed in comparison to the drab projects that she did at art school.

(6) When O'Keeffe was at the Art Students League, she and some friends walked up Riverside Drive in New York City on a clear moonlit night. They sat down on the grass near the Soldiers and Sailors Monument. Looking up at the night, Georgia saw two poplar trees breathing/rustling in the light spring air, the nearby river, the faraway twinkling lights on the other side. She studied carefully the outlines of the trees and the openings where the sky came through.

Next morning she tried to paint the scene from memory. She was particularly pleased with her rendering of the trees. However, when she showed the canvas to another student, he painted over her trees in the style of the Impressionists. To Georgia's disappointment she was unable to re-paint the scene like the beautiful night that she had experienced.

(7) During O'Keeffe's summer school of 1908 at Lake George she and a young man rowed across the lake one night to go shopping. He was already furious with her because she had wanted to let another male student come along. Her companion became still more annoyed after their shopping. They discovered their boat missing, and they had to walk back around the end of the lake to their residence. Heading back, O'Keeffe stood for a moment to gaze across the marshes. The scene looked just like she felt: wet, swampy and gloomy. Next morning she expressed the experience on canvas. She judged that painting to be probably her best work that summer. It was definitely something she had to say.[4]

C. Chatham Episcopal Institute

Georgia O'Keeffe's sporadic experiences of painting subjects of personal meaning were instrumental in bringing her to her crisis of 1910 and the years that followed. Those experiences, together with her proficiency in the use of pencil and brush, awakened within her a longing to walk her own path. Initially, she had three points of clarity regarding that emerging direction:

- her dissatisfaction with the idea of spending her life repeating what other artists had already done in paint;
- her awareness of a need to express herself according to her own way of seeing;
- her realization that she did not as yet have a visual language uniquely her own.

O'Keeffe became caught in a vortex of somewhat conflicting desires: a tendency to conform to her teachers' expectations, a driving need for self-actualization, a yearning for success as an artist. Feeling at a dead-end, she decided in the winter of 1910-1911 to quit art altogether.

---

[4] See *Georgia O'Keeffe*, third - fourteenth pages (unnumbered).

However, an unexpected event in the spring of 1911 drew O'Keeffe back to her art. Her former teacher, Elizabeth May Willis, decided to take a six-week leave of absence from Chatham Episcopal Institute in Chatham, Virginia. She asked O'Keeffe to teach the art classes during that period. O'Keeffe accepted the invitation. During those weeks Georgia discovered that she had a gift for teaching and truly enjoyed the work. Moreover, she saw that teaching art offered her a way to pursue her painting, to secure financial independence and to reside in a country setting. She considered those factors to be essential to the living situation that she sought to create for herself.

D. An Idea of Use to Everyone

Georgia O'Keeffe's renewed interest in painting was further enkindled during the summer of 1912. Her sisters, Ida and Anita, had registered for a summer school art class at The University of Virginia in Charlottesville. Their instructor was Alon Bement, a teacher from Columbia Teachers College in New York City. Anita, intrigued by Bement's peculiarity and novel ideas, persuaded Georgia to attend a class.

Georgia's meeting with Alon Bement marked another decisive threshold in the process of working into her own. Through Bement she came across an idea that motivated her to begin anew. She described his significance in her life this way:

> He had an idea that interested me. An idea that
> seemed to me to be of use to everyone – whether
> you think about it consciously or not – the idea of
> filling a space in a beautiful way. Where you have
> the windows and door in a house. How you address
> a letter and put on the stamp. What shoes you
> choose and how you comb your hair.[5]

Bement was teaching according to the principles of Arthur Wesley Dow. Profoundly discouraged by the sterility of his artistic training and work, Dow had found renewed inspiration in his discovery of Japanese art. He found encouragement from Ernest Fenollosa who had taught in Tokyo and who had become curator of Oriental Art at the Boston Museum. Rather than copying the

---

[5] *Georgia O'Keeffe*, statement opposite plate 11.

expression of other artists, the Dow method encouraged students from the beginning of instruction to produce original work. To that end Dow offered exercises in rhythm, subordination and balance. He taught also arrangement of line, *notan* (harmonious interplay of light and dark) and color.

O'Keeffe enrolled in Bement's advanced class that summer of 1912. She was then twenty-five years old. Bement taught her the basics of the Dow method. For O'Keeffe who had been trained in traditional realist painting and in drawing casts and the human figure, Dow's approach became the key to the discovery of her unique visual language. What she learned that summer became the basis of her artistic expression for the rest of her life. As well as introducing O'Keeffe to the Dow approach, Bement suggested to her things to see and to read; for instance: Wassily Kandinsky's book, *Concerning the Spiritual in Art*, and Jerome Eddy's work, *Cubists and Post-Impressionism.*

Impressed by her work, Bement invited O'Keeffe to teach in the Art Department of the University of Virginia the following summer. The University required of its instructors teaching experience in the public schools. To satisfy that requirement, O'Keeffe eagerly accepted a position as art supervisor and teacher in the schools of Amarillo, Texas. In O'Keeffe's mind, Amarillo typified the American West, a source of endless fascination since her childhood.

O'Keeffe taught in Amarillo for two years, 1912-1914. From the fall of 1914 to spring 1915, she attended Teachers College, Columbia University, New York City. There Arthur Wesley Dow was himself one of her teachers. There she began a long-lasting friendship with another student, Anita Pollitzer. During the summers of 1913-1916 O'Keeffe taught at the University of Virginia.

E. Alone and Singularly Free

In August 1915 Georgia O'Keeffe stood indecisively at a crossroads. She had to choose between going back to college or moving to Columbia, South Carolina, in order to take up a teaching position which she had accepted at Columbia College. By mid-September O'Keeffe had decided on South Carolina.[6]

A first motivation underlying that option was financial

---

[6] The source for this section, unless otherwise indicated, is *Lovingly, Georgia*, 14-119.

independence. O'Keeffe doubted that income solely from her art would be sufficient to support herself. She concluded that the best course for her would be one that provided some money, yet left her mind free to work as she pleased. In New York City all her time and energy would have to be spent on just making a living. Teaching art in South Carolina, on the other hand, would provide an income, while leaving her free to paint.

A second motive for her option to teach at Columbia College was the aloneness and freedom which that opportunity afforded. O'Keeffe welcomed the challenge of living on her own, of being away from the excitement of New York City and of not having the proximity of her friends. She reasoned that working for a year by herself without any stimuli other than books, distant friends and her own capacity to enjoy life would test her worth.

On arrival in South Carolina, O'Keeffe got off to a bumpy start. Late September found her in an emotional slump. She wrote to her friend, Anita Pollitzer, that she was just existing, not living. Moreover, O'Keeffe felt an emptiness unlike anything she had previously experienced. Pollitzer responded by reminding her that she was not jailed in Columbia for life, but only to serve a one-year sentence. Pollitzer pointed out that this initial reaction was bound to come. She counseled O'Keeffe to grit her teeth and bear it. O'Keeffe decided to follow her friend's advice. Yet, she questioned whether she was capable of the tremendous effort necessary to keep from stagnating.

By October O'Keeffe felt at home. She was enjoying her students and taking cherished walks in the country. In her drawing and painting, however, she found herself still in a conflict between her desire for self-expression and her wish to please certain friends and respected teachers. The person whose opinion she valued above all others was Alfred Stieglitz. She confessed in a letter to Pollitzer that she would rather have Stieglitz than anyone else she knew like something of hers. However, her urgency for self-expression prevailed over her desire to please. From her center came the decision during October to put away everything she had ever done and start anew.

Later in life Georgia O'Keeffe described that pivotal turning point in these words:

> I hung on the wall the work I had been doing for
> several months. Then I sat down and looked at it. I

could see how each painting or drawing had been done according to one teacher or another, and I said to myself, "I have things in my head that are not like what anyone has taught me – shapes and ideas so near to me – so natural to my way of being and thinking that it hasn't occurred to me to put them down." I decided to start anew – to strip away what I had been taught – to accept as true my own thinking.[7]

Throughout the remainder of October 1915 O'Keeffe experimented on paper with watercolor, pastels and charcoal. She drew without any plan for composition. She was willing to let some things turn out ugly and unbalanced according to her judgment. In some instances she kept doing the same thing over and over in her spare time until she was satisfied.

Near the end of October O'Keeffe switched entirely to charcoal. She wrote Pollitzer of finding landscapes that she had done in charcoal to be most satisfying. O'Keeffe experienced colors as absolutely nauseating. In the midst of her experimentation she was peaceful about the direction that she was pursuing, yet doubtful about the value of her work. Nonetheless, she was determined to press forward, not catering to anyone else's tastes.

O'Keeffe's attempt to express herself from her center continued throughout the fall of 1915. Around mid-November 1915 she sent a roll of charcoal drawings to Pollitzer for her opinion. Pollitzer encouraged her to continue working in the same vein. While Pollitzer was tempted to ask Stieglitz's opinion of the drawings, she did not believe that it was yet the proper time. Meanwhile, O'Keeffe kept on expressing her feelings in abstractions done in charcoal.

At the end of December O'Keeffe mailed another roll of charcoal drawings to her friend. This time Pollitzer recognized that O'Keeffe had worked into her own. She had expressed in her unique way personal experience that had a universal resonance. Without O'Keeffe's permission Pollitzer sought out Stieglitz's opinion. Pollitzer visited Stieglitz at his 291 Gallery, and proceeded to show him the latest roll of charcoal drawings. After studying the work, Stieglitz enthusiastically affirmed its value and uniqueness. When

---

[7] *Georgia O'Keeffe*, statement opposite plate 1; see also *Some Memories*, first page of text.

Georgia learned of this turn of events, she wrote her friend a calm and quiet "thank you."[8]

In her later years O'Keeffe looked back fondly on those months in South Carolina:

> This was one of the best times of my life. There was no one around to look at what I was doing – no one interested – no one to say anything about it one way or another. I was alone and singularly free, working into my own, unknown – no one to satisfy but myself.[9]

F. The Spirit of the Times

Aloneness, freedom and inner-directedness were catalysts that enabled Georgia O'Keeffe to work into her own. Yet, her breakthrough was situated in a specific historical context. While her creative expression was unique, she was nonetheless in continuity with a visual language that had been developing throughout human history.[10]   Moreover, the ferment of the early decades of the twentieth century provided a milieu conducive to her creative emergence. Four developments in particular converged to form an environment wherein creative endeavors such as hers could flourish.[11]

First, there was modernism. This movement embraced the idea of unending progress. It emphasized the power of the self-directed, independent person. It accentuated reason, intelligence and universal truth. It promoted human control of nature, especially by means of science and technology. On the negative side, some people and institutions considered modernism to be a seedbed of incompetence, immorality, conspiracy, revolution and anarchy.

Second, the Armory Show of February 17 to March 15, 1913, in New York City enabled Americans to see for the first time the works of European modernist artists. Included in this show were works of late Impressionists (Vuillard and Bonnard), post-Impressionists (Cézanne, Van Gogh, Gaugin), Cubists (Picasso and

---

[8] For some of O'Keeffe's early charcoal drawings, see *CR*, 45-56; *Art and Letters*, 1-5.
[9] *Georgia O'Keeffe*, statement opposite plate 1; see also *Some Memories*, first page of text.
[10] See *Lovingly, Georgia*, 305.
[11] See Katherine Hoffman, *An Enduring Spirit: The Art of Georgia O'Keeffe* (Metuchen, NJ: The Scarecrow Press, Inc., 1984), 11-24; 59-72.

Braque) and the Fauves (Matisse, Derain, Vlaminck). This show challenged the American art world to fresh ways of thinking and seeing. Some people felt modernism hailed the destruction of the art of painting. Yet, other persons welcomed its quest for a new way of seeing, founded upon individual freedom and personal perception.

Third, fostering the birth of the modern spirit in America was Alfred Stieglitz. At his gallery Stieglitz exhibited the work of modernist European artists and promoted the endeavors of American experimentalists. He took under his wing a small group of American avant-garde artists, providing them with spiritual inspiration and financial support.

Fourth, there was the burgeoning Women's Movement. The Seneca Falls Convention of 1848 stimulated discussion of the civil, social and religious standing of women. In the early years of this movement the thrust was toward gaining rights in the areas of income, property holdings, divorce proceedings, and opportunity for education and employment. Leaders of the movement exerted considerable effort toward changing the concept of female inferiority inherent in institutional religion. As the United States moved into the twentieth century, urbanization and industrialization were major social trends. Growing numbers of women entered the workplace. Women began pressing hard for the right to vote, gaining that right in 1920 with the final ratification of the Nineteenth Amendment to the Constitution.

Fifth, the discipline of psychology gained acceptance. The ideas of Sigmund Freud were widely disseminated in the early twentieth century. In the United States Freud's teachings promoted thought and discussion of the sexuality, the unconscious and the nature of women.

The above currents contributed significantly to the formation of a milieu conducive to O'Keeffe's adventure of spirit into the unknown. Thus, "the indefinable thing" in her was able to find expression in the decisive breakthrough of late December 1915. Therein, she discovered a visual language expressive of her deepest self. Thereafter, she could not but see with her own eyes. Her inner necessity demanded creative expression reflective of the truth of her experience. O'Keeffe's breakthrough of 1915 was pivotal in that her future work was to be a further development, a gradual unfolding, a maturation of this pristine vision. She made known something of the unknown. Yet, in so doing, she was drawn irresistibly to the unknown that remained beyond her grasp.

CHAPTER 25

Crystalizing A Clearer Vision of Life

The end of World War I engendered hope for peace and prosperity. However, as the United States moved through the 1920's there was an increase of disillusionment, social unrest, economic difficulty, fundamentalist thinking and isolationism in relation to other nations. Many people plunged into the pursuit of pleasure as a means of coping with the trying times. Thus, radio, movies and the automobile became quite popular. Sex magazines and contraband liquor were readily available. The decade ended with the Stock Market crash of 1929.

The propensity for experimentation which had characterized the art world of the 1910's declined during the roaring twenties. Some American artists who found the ambiance of that decade deadening moved to Europe. Yet, many artists and intellectuals persisted in their commitment to modernist ideals. Those people attempted to articulate the American experience and to gain insight into the national identity. Among them were Alfred Stieglitz and his circle of artists, which included Georgia O'Keeffe. Acceptance by Stieglitz and his associates afforded O'Keeffe support as her development continued throughout the 1920's.

In this chapter we focus on certain transitions in O'Keeffe's life between the years 1916-1929. We consider those events to the extent that they have bearing upon the interrelationship of transcendence, self-actualization and creative expression in her life and her work. Specifically, we look at these themes:

- O'Keeffe's continuing journey;
- her option for change in her visual language because of critical response to her work;

- her relationship with Alfred Stieglitz;
- the impasse that she experienced at the end of the 1920's;
- her attempt to resolve that crisis.

A. The Continuing Journey

In early January 1916 Georgia O'Keeffe expressed to her friend, Anita Pollitzer, ambiguous feelings about being in Columbia, South Carolina. Externally, O'Keeffe felt that she was walking through an environment of mediocrity. Interiorly, she sensed that something which she did not want to hurry was growing within her. That process of self-actualization was utterly mysterious, even to her.[1]

Several significant events occurred during the spring of 1916. O'Keeffe left her position in South Carolina rather abruptly in order to resume studies for several months at Columbia Teachers College, New York City. During May her mother died of tuberculosis in Charlottesville, Virginia. Stieglitz included Georgia's work for the first time in an exhibition at his gallery from May 23 to July 5, 1916.

O'Keeffe headed southwest again in September 1916, this time to assume a position as head of the art department at West Texas State Normal College in Canyon, Texas. She held this position until February 1918. Stieglitz gave the first solo exhibition of her works from April 3 to May 14, 1917. She went to New York City in late May only to find the show already dismantled. But Stieglitz re-hung the exhibition for her to see. It was during that visit that she began to model for Stieglitz's portrait of her. In August 1917 O'Keeffe made a trip with her youngest sister Claudia to Colorado via New Mexico. Later she remarked that from thereon out she was always on her way back to New Mexico.[2]

A convergence of circumstances led to O'Keeffe's departure from Canyon, Texas. Her pacifist inclinations clashed with the burning war-fever that had beset the town. She was horrified at seeing war glorified and young men going off to battle. Moreover, she was physically ill. Therefore, in March 1918 she went to a friend's ranch in Waring, Texas, for rest and recuperation. At Stieglitz's urging she decided to return to New York City in June

---

[1] See *Lovingly, Georgia*, 118.
[2] See *A Woman on Paper*, 158.

1918. Stieglitz's niece offered O'Keeffe the use of her studio apartment in the city. One day O'Keeffe told Stieglitz that rather than return to teaching she would like a year to paint. He secured the financial assistance which she needed in order to pursue that course. After the year O'Keeffe continued as a painter and earned her living by sales of her canvases.

O'Keeffe's move to New York City was to Stieglitz's advantage as well as to her own. Stieglitz's 291 Gallery closed in 1917, partly because of financial constraints and partly due to the difficulty of getting artwork from Europe during the war. With subscriptions to *Camera Work* down to a bare minimum in 1917, Stieglitz discontinued its publication. He believed that he had fulfilled his mission of getting photography widely accepted as a form of art. Yet, he did not see a new path opening up in his professional life. The relationship between Stieglitz and his wife was marked by differences in values, as well as considerable emotional distance. He seemed at an impasse in every direction. O'Keeffe and her work reawakened in him hope for the future and encouraged him to undertake new creative endeavors.

After her move to New York City O'Keeffe and Stieglitz grew more intimate. He separated from his wife in July 1918, and took up residence in the studio apartment with O'Keeffe. They were lovers and artistic collaborators. Stieglitz and O'Keeffe married in December 1924, after his divorce was finalized.

Two events which caused Georgia immense heartache occurred in the O'Keeffe family near the end of 1918. Francis O'Keeffe, her father, died accidentally in November at the age of sixty-five. He fell from a roof on which he had been working. Alexis, her favorite brother, returned home from military service in December seriously ill. He had been gassed during fighting in France.

B. Walking into Nowhere

Georgia O'Keeffe had used charcoal in her 1915 breakthrough series of abstractions. Soon afterwards she began working again in color. Throughout 1916 she returned mainly to pastels and watercolor. By 1918 she was using oil painting as her primary medium of expression.

Among O'Keeffe's paintings of 1916 were *Painting n. 21 (Palo Duro Canyon), Train at Night in the Desert, Blue Lines* and

Abstraction IX. Her 1917 works included the *Light Coming upon the Plains* series; the *Seated Nude* series; *Starlight Night*; and the *Evening Star* series. From 1918 came works entitled *Series 1, No. 4*; *Three Women*; and *Spring.* O'Keeffe experimented also in 1918 with the theory of synaesthesia: that is, one sensation (sound) translated into another medium (sight). Two paintings related to that endeavor are *Music - Pink and Blue, No. I* and *No. II.*

Characteristic of O'Keeffe's work in general from 1916-1918 was her use of simplicity of line, range of color and essence of shape. She employed those qualities to express visually a personally meaningful experience that had appeal to a broad range of people. O'Keeffe believed that the purpose of painting was putting together lines and colors in order to say something of significance.[3]

O'Keeffe's late December 1915 series of abstractions in charcoal were based primarily on inner intuitive images. However, from 1916 onward she drew also upon her experience of external things for her visual language. Beholding something of significance to her – such as a landscape, a seashell, a leaf – she would internalize it, and then paint her interpretation of it. We cite below three examples of that creative process.

(1) Painting n. 21 (Palo Duro Canyon)[4]: 1916

When Georgia O'Keeffe lived in Canyon, Texas, she and her sister Claudia would go out to Palo Duro Canyon, several miles from the town. O'Keeffe described this canyon as a small Grand Canyon. At the bottom where it was quiet, a person could look up and see the wind and the snow blow across the slit in the plains. The only trails going down into the canyon were narrow winding cow paths. Each time that Georgia and Claudia went there, they took a different trail in order to climb down into a new place. O'Keeffe reminisced:

> Those perilous climbs were frightening but it was wonderful to me and not like anything I had known before. The fright of the day was still with me in the night.... Many drawings came from days like that, and later some oil paintings.[5]

---

[3] See *Georgia O'Keeffe*, statement opposite plate 88.
[4] See *CR*, 155; *Georgia O'Keeffe*, plate 5; *Art and Letters*, 11.
[5] *Georgia O'Keeffe*, statement opposite plate 5.

(2) The Evening Star Series[6]*: 1917*

O'Keeffe and her sister would often around sunset walk away from the town into the wide open land outside Canyon. The evening star would be high in the sky, even though it was still daylight. Reflecting back on that experience, O'Keeffe commented:

> That evening star fascinated me. It was in some way very exciting to me .... I had nothing [to do] but to walk into nowhere and the wide sunset space with the star. Ten watercolors were made from that star.[7]

(3) Series 1, No. 4[8]*: 1918*

O'Keeffe's visual language tended to include rounded forms (organic shapes), jagged angular shapes (geometric design) or juxtaposition of the two in the same painting. The abstraction, *Series 1, No. 4,* illustrates an organic shape with bands of rich color. This painting suggests the upward surging of a wave or the upward thrusting of a seedling. It exemplifies O'Keeffe's skill at harmonizing sharp contrasts of color; in this case, orange and green.

C. The End of Something

From 1918-1928 Georgia O'Keeffe and Alfred Stieglitz spent a portion of each year in New York City and the remaining months, usually from late spring through fall, at the Stieglitz family's Lake George estate. Apart from that routine O'Keeffe made many short annual visits to friends in York Beach, Maine, a trip to Bermuda in the spring of 1928 and a visit also in the spring of 1928 to Wisconsin. Throughout the 1920's she carried forward her work of creative expression in art, drawing upon her experiences in those various locales.

Between 1918 and 1920 O'Keeffe did many paintings of red cannas. Of particular significance is her *Red Canna* series of 1919. This series marked the beginning of work with flowers that would continue throughout the1920's and 1930's.

---

[6] See *CR*, 199-206; *Georgia O'Keeffe*, plates 6-9; *Art and Letters*, 14 and 15.
[7] *Georgia O'Keeffe*, statement opposite plate 6.
[8] See *CR*, 255; *Art and Letters*, 29.

Around 1924 O'Keeffe began painting bee's-eye view of flowers. She explained her intent this way:

> In a way – nobody sees a flower – really – it is so small – we haven't time – and to see takes time, like to have a friend takes time. If I could paint the flower exactly as I see it no one would see what I see because I would paint it small like the flower is small.... So I said to myself – I'll paint what I see – what the flower is to me but I'll paint it big and they will be surprised into taking time to look at it – [9]

O'Keeffe's flowers constituted a new approach to still life painting, with her near abstract form and her focus on a single flower rather than on bouquets and arrangements. In the still life tradition also, O'Keeffe painted during the 1920's grapes, alligator pears, plums, apples and leaves. [10] Her unique way of seeing those subjects was influenced in part by photographic techniques employed by certain members of the Stieglitz circle.

Between 1918 and 1928 O'Keeffe painted many scenes from Lake George – for instance, *Lake George with Crows* (1921); *Starlight Night, Lake George* (1922); *Storm Cloud, Lake George* (1923). Certain trees at the lake were of special interest to her. She did paintings such as: *Maple and Cedar, Lake George* (1922); *The Chestnut Red* (1924); *The White Birch* (1925); and *The Old Maple, Lake George* (1926).

In addition to subjects from nature, O'Keeffe painted buildings. From Lake George came works such as *My Shanty* (1922), *Little House with Flagpole* (1925) and *Barns, Lake George* (1926). From New York City there was in 1919 the painting, *Fifty-Ninth Street Studio,* followed in 1920 by a work in charcoal entitled *Backyard at Sixty-fifth Street.*

In 1925 O'Keeffe and Stieglitz moved into the Shelton Hotel, New York City. From their apartment they had an aerial view of much of the city. There O'Keeffe did paintings such as *New York*

---

[9] *Georgia O'Keeffe*, statement opposite plate 23. For illustrations, see *One Hundred Flowers.*
[10] On O'Keeffe in relation to the still life tradition, see: Jan Garden Castro, *The Art and Life of Georgia O'Keeffe* (New York, NY: Crown Publishers, Inc., 1985), 157-171; Katherine Hoffman, *An Enduring Spirit: The Art of Georgia O'Keeffe* (Metuchen, NJ: The Scarecrow Press, 1984), 83-93; Sarah Whitaker Peters, *Becoming O'Keeffe: The Early Years* (New York, NY: Abbeville Press Publishers, 1991), 256-275.

with Moon (1925); *East River with Sun* (1926); *The Shelton with Sunspots* (1926); *City Night* (1926); *East River No. I* (1927 or 1928); *The Radiator Building* (1927) and *The Ritz Tower* (1928).

Simplicity of form characterizes O'Keeffe's vision of the architecture. In some works she depicted vertical structures rising up from the ground toward an intimated endless expanse of sky. Other canvases depict buildings and city life viewed from on high and made small by immense space.

Visits to York Beach, Maine, inspired works that include the *Clam Shell Series* (1926) and *Seaweed* (1927). From a visit to Wisconsin in 1928 came the painting, *Red Barn*, which for O'Keeffe represented her childhood.[11]

From the onset of the relationship of O'Keeffe and Stieglitz, significant differences existed between them. A gap of twenty-three years separated their ages. He was an incessant talker and needed people constantly around him. She required solitude for herself and her work. He needed the family togetherness and lush green landscape of Lake George. She needed privacy, silence, spacious horizons and endless sky. He tended to control those around him. She valued her independence. Initially, those differences did not pose undue tension. However, as the 1920's went on, O'Keeffe felt increasingly constricted by Stieglitz, his family and Lake George. Balancing their respective needs became quite difficult for O'Keeffe and Stieglitz.

Two women's issues during the 1920's may have had an eroding effect upon O'Keeffe's zest for life. (1) In the early 1920's O'Keeffe, then in her mid-thirties, yearned to have a child with Stieglitz. However, for a number of reasons Stieglitz would not agree to parenthood. (2) In August 1927 O'Keeffe underwent surgery for a benign lump in her breast. In December of that year she had a second biopsy. Given the surgical method used at the time for breast biopsy, O'Keeffe had to have suffered considerable disfigurement. Loss of the opportunity to become a mother when one so desires it and invasive breast surgery are experiences that can cut to the core of a woman's sense of self.

Presently, lack of sufficient evidence prevents a complete evaluation of the emotional and spiritual impact of those events upon O'Keeffe's sense of identity and upon her relationship with Stieglitz. However, those events had to have profoundly affected her life and

---

[11] See *Art and Letters*, 187; *CR*, 618.

work. Some interpreters see O'Keeffe's still life paintings of fruits such as apples and alligator pears during the early 1920's as expressive of her effort to come to terms with being childless. O'Keeffe herself commented on the significance of her painting, *Black Abstraction* (1927). She explained that it represented the fading out of light and the overpowering of darkness, as she underwent anesthesia prior to surgery.[12]

To confound even more the O'Keeffe and Stieglitz relationship, a young married woman, Dorothy Norman, entered Stieglitz's life toward the end of 1926. Stieglitz accepted Norman's offer of late 1927 to work for him. During 1928-1929 he became intimately involved with her, soon photographing her as he had photographed O'Keeffe.

Thus, by the late 1920's O'Keeffe found herself at a dead end. She knew she would never have a child. She bore the scars of at least two breast biopsies. Her relationship with Stieglitz was in crisis. She experienced life in New York City and at Lake George as oppressive and stifling. Indeed, the wellspring of inspiration for her art had dried up.

We find intimations of crisis in letters to friends. For example, O'Keeffe wrote to a correspondent in January 1927 that her upcoming exhibition was "too beautiful." She expressed the hope that her next show would be so "magnificently vulgar" that all the people who liked her work would turn away. She believed that reversal would make her a great success to herself. As for her personal life, O'Keeffe observed tersely:

> I have come to the end of something – and until I am clear there is no reason why I should talk to anyone –[13]

D. Suspended Between Crystalizations

When Georgia O'Keeffe viewed the February 4 to March 17, 1929, exhibition of her paintings, she judged her work to be mostly dead. On seeing her finished canvases stretched out before her, she knew that she either had to get back to some of her own ways or else

---

[12] See *Georgia O'Keeffe*, statement opposite plate 54 (*Black Abstraction*); *CR*, 574.
[13] *Art and Letters*, 185.

cease painting altogether.[14]   She opted for what would meet her needs. Specifically, she decided to go to New Mexico, even though that choice would entail radical changes in her relationship with Stieglitz and in their rhythm of life together.

O'Keeffe arrived in New Mexico during April 1929, accompanied by her friend Rebecca Strand. For the most part they stayed in the Taos area at the home of Mabel Dodge Luhan. O'Keeffe experienced rebirth in New Mexico. She wrote to several friends of feeling like herself again and of enjoying her sense of well-being.[15] To one correspondent she described herself feeling so alive that she might crack at any moment – in other words, so full of life that she could hardly contain herself.[16] She relished the special moments alone when unexpectedly she experienced liberation from some interior constriction.[17]   Nonetheless, in June she was still grappling to find her path. To her hostess who was away at the time, she wrote:

> I feel so suspended between one crystalizing and another – one that has finished and one that is beginning – that it is very difficult to say anything [18]

By late August 1929 O'Keeffe had found inner peace. She felt ready to return to her life in New York.[19] The light, color and spaciousness of the New Mexican landscape had revived her spirit and provided her with new sources of inspiration for her painting. During those months O'Keeffe had done canvases such as *At the Rodeo*; *Ranchos Church*; *Black Cross*; and *D.H. Lawrence Pine Tree*. Moreover, she had sorted out her personal relationship with Stieglitz. In essence, she came to a certain emotional independence from him. She decided to remain with him, but to carve out for herself a lifestyle that would meet her spiritual, emotional and artistic needs.

After she had settled in for the fall at Lake George with Stieglitz, O'Keeffe wrote Mabel Luhan the following reflection upon

---

[14] See *Art and Letters*, 195
[15] See *Art and Letters*, 189.
[16] See *Art and Letters*, 195.
[17] See *Art and Letters*, 199.
[18] *Art and Letters*, 191.
[19] See *Art and Letters*, 192.

her time in New Mexico:

> It was really perfect for what I was needing this
> summer – as this is perfect for me now.... The
> summer had brought me to a state of mind where I
> felt as grateful for my largest hurts as I did for my
> largest happiness – in spite of all my tearing about[,]
> many things that had been accumulating inside of
> me for years were arranging themselves – and
> rearranging themselves.... Maybe you understand it
> without understanding it – as I do –.[20]

E. Things So Strange and Far Removed from Her

Alfred Stieglitz believed that no great women artists had emerged over the centuries because men dominated the field of art. According to his view, the educational systems then employed in the art academies had been developed by men for men. Consequently, it was impossible for women to be what their teachers were to them. He believed also that the social order was changing, that women were evolving and that they had the potential as artists to be equal to men. He saw Georgia O'Keeffe's work as proof of his convictions.

Nonetheless, Stieglitz maintained that fundamental differences existed between male and female artists. He asserted that for both men and women the process of creativity was initiated by feeling and then actualized through the intellect. However, he believed that the original generating feeling differed in men and women. Stieglitz claimed that woman received the world through her womb and that for woman the womb was the seat of her deepest feeling.[21] Thus, from the outset and throughout his life Stieglitz saw O'Keeffe's work as expressive of her sexual feelings. Stieglitz influenced the prominent critics of his time to interpret O'Keeffe's work in that sexual vein.

Compounding the question of interpreting O'Keeffe's work on its own merit was the fact that in 1921 Stieglitz's photographs of O'Keeffe were exhibited publicly for the first time at the Anderson Galleries in New York City. The composite portrait presented many

---

[20] *Art and Letters*, 196.
[21] See Alfred Stieglitz, "Woman in Art," (1919), a portion of which is included in Dorothy Norman, *Alfred Stieglitz: An American Seer* (New York, NY: Random House, 1973), 136-138.

faces of O'Keeffe; for example: a woman bold, daring and self-assured; a vulnerable woman; an alluring seductive woman; a woman who physically embodied erotic power. The exhibition had a twofold effect: (1) O'Keeffe became immediately what one critic called "a newspaper personality"; and (2) Stieglitz's photographic portrait of O'Keeffe as seductive and sexually powerful colored the critical interpretation of her art. Male critics – and several female critics as well – interpreted her paintings in terms of the sexual feelings of the woman in Stieglitz's photographic portrait.[22]

The sexual interpretation of her work was profoundly upsetting to O'Keeffe. To her friend Mitchell Kennerley she wrote during the fall of 1922:

> The things they write sound so strange and far removed from what I feel of myself. They make me seem like some strange unearthly sort of creature floating in the air – breathing in clouds for nourishment – when the truth is that I like beef steak – and like it rare at that.[23]

Another friend, Hutchins Hapgood, had come upon O'Keeffe in a state of fury after reading two articles on her work. Hapgood pointed out that critics were writing not so much about her as about their own autobiography.[24] While that thought consoled O'Keeffe, it did not entirely calm her. In an attempt to influence critical response to her work, she decided to change her visual imagery. Writing to Sherwood Anderson of the work she did in 1923, she explained:

> My work this year is very much on the ground – There will be only two abstract things – or three at the most – all the rest is objective – as objective as I can make it.... I suppose the reason I got down to an effort to be objective is that I didn't like the interpretations of my other things – so here I am with an array of alligator pears ... calla lilies ... leaves ... horrid yellow sunflowers – two new red

---

[22] See *O'Keeffe ... and the Critics*, 55-111; 157-164.
[23] *Art and Letters*, 170-171.
[24] See *Art and Letters*, 171. The articles were written by Paul Rosenfeld. See *O'Keeffe ... and the Critics*, 171-179.

cannas – some white birches.... Altogether about forty things –[25]

As well as using recognizable natural subjects, O'Keeffe took a second line of approach in her effort to influence critical response.   In interviews throughout the 1920's she intentionally projected an image of herself as a professional artist and as a woman with a right to self-actualization.   Those efforts to counter the general perception of her as sexually provocative contributed to the creation of an opposite image. Many people perceived her as aloof, remote, androgynous. Somehow the two polarities worked together over the course of her life to create a public persona that was intriguing yet enigmatic.   O'Keeffe played that perception to her advantage. She used it as a means to secure the privacy and solitude that she needed for her adventure of spirit into the unknown.

Critical response to O'Keeffe's attempt to sway interpretation of her painting was like a pendulum swinging one way, then another. For instance, between 1924-1927 critics associated with the Stieglitz circle refrained from any mention of erotic symbolism in her work. In the early 1930's critics began again ascribing sexual nuance to her imagery. The latest cycle of critical interpretation along the lines of eroticism was during the 1970's and 1980's when art historians and feminist artists cited her work as the first expression of a specifically female iconography.[26]

Up to the end of her life O'Keeffe denied that her visual imagery was expressive of her sexual feelings.[27] The truth seems to reside in this direction: O'Keeffe's work contains allusion to sexuality in that sexuality is a normal dimension of each person and each living thing. However, that sexual aspect of nature is but one facet of a larger whole, both in life and in O'Keeffe's paintings.

---

[25] *Art and Letters*, 176.
[26] See *O'Keeffe ... and the Critics*, 157-164.
[27] For instance, see: Dorothy Seiberling, "The Female View of Erotica," *New York Magazine* (11 February 1974): 54-58.

CHAPTER 26

Moving Toward A Kind of Aloneness

Between the years 1929-1946 American society underwent the Great Depression and World War II. People exhibited strong social, civic and national concern in response to those events. Franklin Roosevelt and his New Deal legislation gained acceptance in that historical framework. The beginning of the Federal Art Project in 1935 afforded employment to many artists. The quest for and the articulation of a specifically American identity continued to be a preoccupation in art and literature. Social realism and American scene painting were prominent themes in art. However, by the mid-1930's various forms of abstract art began to appear.

Against that historical backdrop Georgia O'Keeffe held steady on her unique path. The early 1930's saw a number of women artists receiving recognition for their work. Whereas O'Keeffe had previously stood alone in the limelight, she began to share that space with other women.

In this chapter we reflect on the life and the work of Georgia O'Keeffe during the years 1930-1946. We look at her self-actualization as that process interacted with her sense of transcendence and her creative expression. Specifically, we focus on these events:

- O'Keeffe's experience of inner division;
- her breakdown during 1932-1933;
- her road to recovery;
- her movement toward a more solitary life;
- the resolution of her relationship with Stieglitz.

A. O'Keeffe's Divided Self

Georgia O'Keeffe returned to New Mexico in 1930. She remained there from mid-June to late September. She confided to a friend that she wanted to make the trip for the sake of her work. Yet, she had been unable to decide to do so until Stieglitz gave his approval.[1] When that consent was forthcoming, she felt as though she was receiving from Stieglitz the gift to be herself.

The summer months of 1930 were artistically productive. O'Keeffe painted subjects related to life in New Mexico; for example: *Ranchos Church*; *Church Steeple,* and *White Calico Rose.* She captured in line and color something of the terrain itself; for instance: *Dark Mesa with Pink Sky*; *Sandhills with Blue River*; *Rust Red Hills*; and *Black Mesa Landscape.* Together with images from the desert of New Mexico, O'Keeffe continued in 1930 to work with familiar themes. She did canvases such as *Clam Shell*; *White Iris*; *Black Hollyhock, Blue Larkspur*; and the *Jack-in-the-Pulpit* series.

O'Keeffe's joy upon returning to Stieglitz at Lake George in September 1930 quickly gave way to the pain of renewed interpersonal conflict. Stieglitz had become further involved with Dorothy Norman and more independent of O'Keeffe.

By the spring of 1931 O'Keeffe was quite unhappy. She returned to New Mexico for ten weeks, this time renting a cottage at the H & M Ranch in Alcalde. O'Keeffe worked steadily at her painting. She began during that visit to incorporate into her visual imagery bones that she had collected in the desert. Her love for New Mexico grew. Nonetheless, she returned to Lake George during July to be with Stieglitz. To her disappointment, she found him more preoccupied than ever with Dorothy Norman. By late August 1931 O'Keeffe felt "smothered with green"[2] at the lake, and regretted her early return.

O'Keeffe had found a new source of vitality for her art. However, even with respect to her paintings of 1931, she felt frustration. After seeing an exhibit of her work for that year, she assessed it thus:

> My show looked well but the two most important
> phases of it – the landscapes and the bones were

---

[1] See *Art and Letters*, 200.
[2] *Art and Letters*, 204.

both in a very objective stage of development – I hadn't worked on the landscapes at all after I brought them in from outdoors – so that memory or dream thing I do that for me comes nearer reality than my objective kind of work – was quite lacking – I hadn't worked at either the landscapes or bones long enough objectively to be able to carry them on in the other way as I wanted to –[3]

By 1932 O'Keeffe, then forty-five years old, experienced herself living a divided life – almost a split existence. On the one hand, she spent many months with Stieglitz in New York City and at Lake George. On the other hand, she spent extensive periods in New Mexico. She valued both worlds, but had difficulty reconciling them. O'Keeffe could only accept her situation, and try to live with her divided self as best she could.[4] Practically speaking, pursuing that direction meant balancing the green of Lake George and the desert of New Mexico, marriage to Stieglitz and the demands of her work. Increasingly, however, New Mexico and painting were asserting the stronger pull within O'Keeffe. As early as 1930, she expressed certitude that it was her work that was "the thing in life."[5]

B. Nothing to Say

The ongoing tensions between Georgia O'Keeffe and Alfred Stieglitz peaked in 1932. The catalyst for that climax was twofold: Stieglitz's relationship with Dorothy Norman and O'Keeffe's acceptance of a commission to paint a mural.

Dorothy Norman had become an all-pervasive presence in Stieglitz's life. She was his intimate friend, photographic model, student and business associate. Along with photographs of O'Keeffe that he had done during the preceding ten years, Stieglitz included recent photographs of Dorothy Norman in his February 1932 retrospective exhibition at his gallery, An American Place, in New York City. O'Keeffe always liked to be central in Stieglitz's life.[6] She was clearly losing first place in her husband's affections and endeavors.

---

[3] *Art and Letters*, 206.
[4] See *Art and Letters*, 207.
[5] *Art and Letters*, 200.
[6] See *Art and Letters*, 171.

For several years O'Keeffe had wanted to paint something big for a public space.[7] An opportunity presented itself in the spring of 1932 when Donald Deskey, the designer of Radio City Music Hall interiors in New York City, invited her to do a mural for the ladies' powder room – an eighteen by twenty foot interior, with eight round mirrors, three feet six inches in diameter, set into the walls. Deskey offered O'Keeffe one thousand five hundred dollars, a fee less than half the going rate for an O'Keeffe oil painting, but the maximum paid to any artist involved in the Radio City project. Without consulting Stieglitz, O'Keeffe accepted Deskey's offer.

Stieglitz flew into a rage when he found out about the agreement. He accused O'Keeffe of public betrayal, from both a marital and a professional perspective. As her husband, he expected her to stand by him in public. As her agent, he believed that the nominal fee sabotaged his efforts to maintain a strong market for her work. Moreover, he felt that her negotiation of the contract made him look superfluous. Stieglitz objected also on the grounds that O'Keeffe's involvement in a public project financed by rich people and decorated by numerous artists ran counter to his concept of art.

Stieglitz sought to revoke the contract between Deskey and O'Keeffe. Deskey insisted that his contract was with O'Keeffe, not Stieglitz. O'Keeffe stood firm. She wanted to do a large painting in public. She saw the Radio City project as her opportunity to do so. Therefore, she chose to honor her agreement with Deskey.

Because of her strained relationship with Stieglitz and her work in preparation for the mural, O'Keeffe elected not to go to New Mexico during the summer of 1932. By the end of that summer Stieglitz realized that his protestations were in vain. Perhaps to save face, he gave public approval to her Radio City Music Hall project.

O'Keeffe spent most of the fall of 1932 at Lake George working on her mural designs. Stieglitz remained in New York City, in part to oversee publication of a collection of poems by Dorothy Norman.

In addition to O'Keeffe's continuing anxiety about the Stieglitz-Norman relationship, she found the mural project itself to be a source of stress. Although Stieglitz had signaled approval in the public sphere, O'Keeffe knew that privately he maintained his reservations.[8] O'Keeffe worried about the possibility of her mural

---

[7] See *Art and Letters*, 188.
[8] See, for instance, *Art and Letters*, 207-210.

turning out to be a failure both in Stieglitz's eyes and in the view of the public.   Complicating the matter further, it was not until November 16, 1932 – a mere six weeks before the scheduled public opening of the Radio City Music Hall – that the powder room was ready for O'Keeffe to begin her work.   Deskey took O'Keeffe and an assistant to the room.   While sitting in a corner of the room and preparing for her task, O'Keeffe noticed the canvas peel away from the wall in one corner.   Deskey assured her that it could be repaired. O'Keeffe went out to lunch and returned only to find more canvas loose.   Refusing to paint on canvas with wet plaster underneath it, she walked off the job.

Stieglitz's response to O'Keeffe's quitting was self-righteous delight.   Next day he contacted Deskey to inform him that O'Keeffe was having a nervous breakdown and could not resume the project. Deskey released O'Keeffe from her contract and replaced her with another artist.

O'Keeffe indeed had a nervous breakdown.   However, the Radio City Music Hall episode was not in itself the cause.   That incident served merely as the proverbial straw that broke the camel's back.   O'Keeffe's breakdown came at the culmination of a history of conflict between herself and Stieglitz in which she finally lost her basic sense of self and her self-confidence.   Stieglitz had displayed increasing hostility toward her.   He had withdrawn from her his affection in favor of Dorothy Norman.   He had initially railed against her plan to paint the mural at Radio City.   He continued to exhibit disapproval in private, even after he had voiced public support. O'Keeffe experienced all this behavior as a rejection of her core being.   Unable to withstand the onslaught any longer, she lost her sense of grounding.

O'Keeffe's illness began in November 1932 with physical symptoms: difficulty in speaking, shortness of breath, chest pains. After a brief improvement in her condition, she regressed dramatically in early December.   At that time splitting headaches, fatigue, crying spurts and sleeplessness were added to her previous ailments.   Four days before Christmas, O'Keeffe moved out of the apartment she shared with Stieglitz and moved in with her sister Anita.   O'Keeffe was admitted in early February 1933 to Doctors Hospital in New York City.   She was treated for psychoneurosis. O'Keeffe remained hospitalized until late March 1933.   During that time Stieglitz was permitted only a weekly ten-minute visit with her, since his presence was so upsetting to her.

O'Keeffe's breakdown had a sobering effect on Stieglitz. His guilt and grief refocused him on O'Keeffe as the emotional center of his life. The romantic aspect of his relationship with Dorothy Norman waned thereafter, but she continued to work for him up to his death.

Although O'Keeffe was released from the hospital in March 1933, it was not until the period from December 1933 to early January 1934 that she regained a sense of wholeness. O'Keeffe did no painting throughout her lengthy illness; that is, from November 1932 to January 1934. To a friend she wrote in the fall of 1933 of having done nothing all summer but wait to be herself again. She explained to her correspondent the reason for not having worked at all:

> Nothing seems worth being put down – I seem to have nothing to say   It appalls me but that is the way it is – so I dont work –[9]

C. A Beautiful Feeling of Balance

In December 1933 Geo[...]kdown gave way to a breakthrough. Finally, sh[...]lf and her self-confidence. She experienced [...] to life. She regained her sense of groundin[...]

The person most i[...]wal was Jean Toomer, a black writer and [...] O'Keeffe and Stieglitz. O'Keeffe had inv[...]orge where she was recuperating. He acce[...]remained there for most of December 1933.

By O'Keeffe's own [...]verbal exchange transpired between herself and Too[...]enjoyed the quietness and stillness in the house, as the [...] fell outside. She rested much of the time. He worked all day [...] his writing. At night they would talk some or just sit and read. Toomer gave her something that had little to do with anything that he said or did. He was a follower of the spiritualist Gurdjieff. Toomer's qualities of calmness and quietness, together with the warmth and tenderness of his presence, were exactly what O'Keeffe needed to enable her to reaffirm her worth as a person and to re-claim her direction in life.

---

[9] *Art and Letters*, 213.

After Toomer left Lake George, O'Keeffe wrote him a series of letters in which she expressed something of the healing which took place in her during their time together. In a letter dated January 3, 1934, she described his role in her healing with these words:

> You seem to have given me a strangely beautiful
> feeling of balance that makes the days seem very
> precious to me – I seem to have come to life in such
> a quiet surprising fashion – as tho I am not sick any
> more – Everything in me begins to move and I feel
> like a really positive thing again – [10]

Yet, O'Keeffe was careful to point out to Toomer in that letter the mysterious quality of her restoration. She noted that while he was instrumental in her recovery, the source of her healing had little to do with either of them.

During the period in which O'Keeffe wrote those revealing letters to Toomer, she was putting herself together piece by piece. Surveying as a whole her letters to Toomer during 1934, we identify the following awarenesses that came to her as a result of her time with him:

•   a renewed sense of her own center, the core of her personhood:

> My center... feels in me like a plot of warm moist
> well tilled earth with the sun shining hot on it – [11]

•   a recognition of her personal needs:

> I do know that the demands of my plot of earth are
> relentless if anything is to grow in it – worthy of its
> quality.[12]

•   a commitment to honoring those needs, even in her relationship with Stieglitz:

> If the past year or two or three has taught me

---

[10] *Art and Letters*, 216.
[11] *Art and Letters*, 217.
[12] *Art and Letters*, 217.

anything it is that my plot of earth must be tended with absurd care – By myself first – and if second by someone else it must be with absolute trust – their thinking carefully and knowing what they do.[13]

- a sense of moving in the direction of a more solitary life:

    It also seems that I never felt more ready and willing to be alone.[14]

    I feel ... my affections – the things that I am – moving it seems – more and more toward a kind of aloneness – not because I wish it so but because there seems no other way.[15]

- a renewed interest in her painting:

    I started to paint on Wednesday – it will undoubtedly take quite a period of fumbling before I start on a new path – but Im started – and seem to settle down to it every day as tho it is the only thing I do[16]

D. Ready and Willing to Be Alone

The landscape of New Mexico exerted an irresistible allure upon Georgia O'Keeffe. She spoke of it in the spring of 1930 as calling her in a way that she had to answer.[17] Even in the throes of her illness during late October 1933 she felt the strong pull to go west.[18] On recovery from her prolonged illness, O'Keeffe knew that for her personal well-being and for her work it was essential that she spend a portion of each year in New Mexico. By late April 1934 she was again feeling its call. Still fresh in recovery, her interest at that point was rather vague and her motivation more on the level of head

---

[13] *Art and Letters*, 217.
[14] *Art and Letters*, 217.
[15] *Art and Letters*, 219.
[16] *Art and Letters*, 216.
[17] See *Art and Letters*, 200.
[18] See *Art and Letters*, 214.

than heart.[19] Nonetheless, in June 1934 she set out again for New
Mexico.

This time, instead of participating in a lively social group as
she had done in other years, O'Keeffe sought a more solitary
ambiance. Her desire for aloneness and quietness led her to visit
Ghost Ranch, located near Abiquiu, New Mexico. Ghost Ranch was
a dude ranch owned by Arthur Pack. O'Keeffe immediately fell in
love with the place – with the remoteness, spacious desert, colorful
cliffs, infinite sky and Mount Pedernal looming over the landscape.

Thereafter on her sojourns in New Mexico O'Keeffe stayed
at Ghost Ranch. Each year her roots sank deeper. Eventually, she
invested in property for two homes. In October 1940 she purchased
from Arthur Pack Rancho de los Burros, a small adobe house and
eight acres of land situated about three miles from the main complex
at Ghost Ranch. In 1945 she purchased from the Catholic Church an
abandoned house and property in the village of Abiquiu. She had
both homes renovated in an utterly simple yet eloquent style,
expressive of her inner self.

O'Keeffe's letters give indication of her great love for her
wide and wonderful world in New Mexico. For instance, to her
friend Cady Wells she described an experience in the early 1940's of
walking at sunset in the hills near her home:

> I get a keen sort of exhilaration from being alone....
> from where I stood it seemed I could see all over
> this world.... My world here is a world almost
> untouched by man.... it is so bare – with a sort of
> ages old feeling of death on it – still it is warm and
> soft and I love it with my skin – and I never meet
> anyone out there – it is almost always alone – [20]

To her friends, Ettie and Carrie Stettheimer, O'Keeffe wrote
in 1944 of how moved she was by the light and the color of the land:

> I loved walking in the low sun – evening light
> through the red and purple earth – [21]

---

[19] See *Art and Letters*, 220-221.
[20] *Art and Letters*, 243.
[21] *Art and Letters*, 238.

The "unexplainable thing in nature"[22] captivated her. At her ranch it was her custom to climb to the roof of her house and to sit for lengthy periods drinking in the sunrise and the sunset. She took long walks, and frequently camped out overnight. She gave her favorite places special names related to color: Black Place, White Place, Grey Hills. She welcomed close friends and family members to her world for occasional visits. In New Mexico she created for herself an environment that nurtured her experience of immanent transcendence, her process of self-actualization and her work of creative expression. Even her time in New York City during the 1930's and 1940's was on her own terms. She cared for the aging Stieglitz. Yet, independently of him, she maintained her interests and she had her own circle of friends.

E. The Desert

In New Mexico the focal point of O'Keeffe's experience was the desert. She perceived vibrant life within the desert, although on a tangible level the desert had qualities of vastness, emptiness, untouchability and merciless beauty.[23]

O'Keeffe wanted to paint the desert, but did not know how. She solved the problem by focusing in her work on aspects of desert life that represented her experience of it. She called those subjects "equivalents."[24] Her principal equivalents during the 1930's and 1940's were hills, cliffs, bones and sky. At times she used one or more of those subjects in combination with familiar themes like flowers, trees or shells.

O'Keeffe's hill and cliff paintings include these: *Grey Hill Forms* (1936); *White Place in Shadow* (1941); *Black Hills with Cedar, New Mexico* (1942); and *Cliffs, Ghost Ranch* (1945).

O'Keeffe began painting bones from the desert as early as 1931. *Horse's Skull on Blue* and *Cow's Skull – Red, White and Blue* are among her earliest skeletal paintings. O'Keeffe experienced the bones which she found in the desert to be as beautiful as anything she knew and as mysteriously more living than the animals walking around. In her perception the bones cut to the center of something

---

[22] *Georgia O'Keeffe*, statement opposite plate 100.
[23] See Georgia O'Keeffe, "About Myself," *Exhibition Catalogue* (New York, NY: An American Place, 1939), 2-3; "About Painting Bones," *Georgia O'Keeffe: Painting – 1943* (New York, NY: An American Place, 1944).
[24] See *Georgia O'Keeffe*, statement opposite plate 63.

vitally alive in the desert.[25]   Similarly, she experienced the blue of
the sky as representative of something eternal and enduring.[26]

In 1943 O'Keeffe began paintings of the sky as seen through
holes in animal pelvic bones.   The impetus for this project came
when she found an especially beautiful pelvis bone on a mountain.
She described her fascination regarding bones this way:

> I was most interested in the holes in the bones –
> what I saw through them – particularly the blue from
> holding them up in the sun against the sky as one is
> apt to do when one seems to have more sky than
> earth in one's world .... They were most wonderful
> against the Blue – that Blue that will always be there
> as it is now after all man's destruction is finished.[27]

At first O'Keeffe painted the pelvic bone and sky series in
colors of blue and white.   As her work progressed, she switched to
red and yellow.   Her work on the theme of pelvic bone and sky
includes these canvases: *Pelvis with the Moon – New Mexico* (1943);
Pelvis with Distance (1943); *Pelvis with Pedernal* (1943); *Pelvis
Series, I-IV (in Blue)* (1944); and *Pelvis Series, Red with Yellow*
(1945).

Several paintings from the 1930's have a dream-like quality
similar to many of the pelvis paintings.   O'Keeffe infused realism
with her "memory or dream thing"[28] in part by the unexpected
juxtaposition of subjects.   She once commented that some of her
paintings came together from seemingly unrelated things around
her.[29]   Examples of that creative approach include: *Ram's Head,
White Hollyhock, Hills* (1935); *Summer Days* (1936); *Mule's Skull
with Pink Poinsettias* (1936); and *From the Faraway Nearby* (1937).

F. Alfred: Growing Older

Although Alfred Stieglitz and Georgia O'Keeffe lived rather
independent lives after her recovery from her breakdown in the early

[25] See Georgia O'Keeffe: "About Painting Bones," *Exhibition Catalogue* (New York, NY: An
American Place, 1939); *Georgia O'Keeffe: Painting – 1943* (New York, NY: An American
Place, 1944).
[26] See *Georgia O'Keeffe*, statement opposite plate 74.
[27] *Georgia O'Keeffe*, statement opposite plate 74.
[28] *Art and Letters*, 206.
[29] See *Georgia O'Keeffe*, 206.

1930's, they remained married. A deep affection and a genuine respect for each other prevailed. During O'Keeffe's months in New Mexico they corresponded regularly. Stieglitz was O'Keeffe's sole reason for spending a portion of each year in New York.

Throughout the 1930's and 1940's a reversal of roles occurred in the O'Keeffe-Stieglitz relationship. In 1937 failing health forced Stieglitz at the age of seventy-three to give up doing photography. He suffered a heart attack in 1938, followed by a bout of pneumonia. As Stieglitz grew older, O'Keeffe assumed increasing responsibility for his care and for their business affairs. It was the sale of her paintings which provided them with financial support. One letter written by O'Keeffe to a friend is especially revealing of her relationship with Stieglitz during his declining years:

> I see Alfred as an old man that I am very fond of –
> growing older .... Aside from my fondness for him
> personally I feel that he has been very important to
> something that has made my world for me – I like it
> that I can make him feel that I have hold of his hand
> to steady him as he goes on –[30]

On June 5, 1946, O'Keeffe began her annual sojourn in New Mexico. Stieglitz's doctor urged her in early July to return to New York City because of Stieglitz's deteriorating condition. She declined. On July 10, 1946, O'Keeffe received a telegram informing her that her husband had suffered a massive stroke. She returned immediately to New York City, and was at his bedside when he died on July 13, 1946. After a simple funeral service in the city, O'Keeffe took Stieglitz's ashes to Lake George. She buried them beneath a tree where he could hear the lake that he had so loved. O'Keeffe was then fifty-nine years of age, completely alone and decidedly free.

---

[30] *Art and Letters*, 244.

CHAPTER 27

Alone with Earth and Sky

The death of Alfred Stieglitz marked another critical threshold in the life of Georgia O'Keeffe. After his passing, O'Keeffe had to choose where and how she wanted to spend the rest of her life.

In this chapter we examine the life and the work of Georgia O'Keeffe from 1946 to 1986, with attention to the interrelationship of transcendence, self-actualization and creative expression. We focus on these themes:

- O'Keeffe's option to move permanently to New Mexico;
- her expanding visual language: patio wall-with-door of her home in Abiquiu, rivers, roads, sky and clouds, rocks;
- her final years.

A. The Call of the Mountain and the Desert

Mount Pedernal was part of Georgia O'Keeffe's "faraway nearby" within her New Mexican environment. That mountain fascinated her. She was so enthralled with it that she included it in numerous landscape paintings. She once joked that God told her if she painted it often enough she could have it.[1] On September 13, 1968, Thomas Merton noted in his journal that during his visit with O'Keeffe she was asked what a person sees from the top of Pedernal. Her reply was: "You see the whole world."[2]

O'Keeffe considered the desert of New Mexico to be the

---

[1] See Amei Wallach, "Georgia O'Keeffe," in *Newsday* (30 October 1977).
[2] *The Other Side*, 175.

most beautiful country in the United States. The badlands of New Mexico rolled away hill after hill outside her door. Many people saw that wilderness as useless. But O'Keeffe saw in it all the colors of the earth: light Naples yellow through the ochres; orange, red, purple; and the soft earth greens.[3]

O'Keeffe described the mountain and the desert as calling her.[4] "Calling" was thus an image to describe the lure of "the unexplainable thing in nature,"[5] so clearly manifest to her in her New Mexican surroundings. "Calling" was a metaphor to describe her perception of immanent transcendence. O'Keeffe experienced the call of the mountain and the desert to be persistent, demanding and irresistible.

In his will Stieglitz had named O'Keeffe as prime beneficiary and sole executrix. Consequently, she spent most of 1946-1949 in New York City, settling her husband's estate. O'Keeffe helped organize two simultaneous exhibitions – one of Stieglitz's art collection and the other of his photographs – for the Museum of Modern Art, New York City, in 1947 and for the Art Institute of Chicago in 1948. From 1946-1949, O'Keeffe and an assistant organized Stieglitz's papers and catalogued his work. O'Keeffe distributed his art collection to seven institutions. During those years her responsibilities as executrix left her little time for painting.

The work on Stieglitz's estate gave O'Keeffe occasion to look back over her life and times. She found the review interesting and complex. Many decisions regarding the Stieglitz collection confronted her. Most of those decisions entailed several viable options from which to choose. Moreover, it was a time for letting go what remained of her life with Stieglitz, for grieving her loss, for moving on. O'Keeffe described herself as having come to a point in her life where many things and many relationships no longer held meaning for her.[6]

That loss of meaningfulness was in large part a result of O'Keeffe's persistent attraction to the mountain and the desert of New Mexico. After Stieglitz's death O'Keeffe perceived the unexplainable thing in the mountain and the desert calling her ever more clearly and irresistibly. When she had completed her work on

---

[3] See *Georgia O'Keeffe*, statement opposite plate 26.
[4] See *Art and Letters*, 200.
[5] See *Georgia O'Keeffe*, 100.
[6] See *Art and Letters*, 246.

Stieglitz's estate in 1949, O'Keeffe chose to reside permanently in New Mexico. Thus, at the age of sixty-two she left her New York life and friends behind, gave away most of her valued possessions, and moved to New Mexico. There, "alone with the earth and sky,"[7] O'Keeffe continued becoming herself and expressing her transcendent experience in artistic form.

During the winter and spring months of each year O'Keeffe resided at her home in Abiquiu. In summer and autumn she lived at her Rancho de los Burros home. As O'Keeffe attempted in her art to reduce a subject to its essence, so also she aimed to create a lifestyle and a living space stripped down to the beautiful essential. In New Mexico she fashioned for herself an environment and a way of life centered around her art. Although her life was basically solitary, O'Keeffe maintained warm relationships with family and friends. She welcomed them for occasional visits to her home, especially during summer months.

Some people viewed O'Keeffe's permanent relocation to New Mexico negatively. They saw her move as a deprivation of the excitements of New York City living and as an option for a confined or withdrawn existence. In truth, her lifelong spiritual adventure into the unknown had brought her to that choice of permanent residence. The solitude and the simplicity of her lifestyle in New Mexico became her doorway to the experience of an ever widening and more wonderful world. It was the milieu in which she further carried forward her work of making known her unknown, while yet keeping the unknown always beyond.

B. Willingness to Stay Her Course

With Alfred Stieglitz's death and her departure from New York City, Georgia O'Keeffe experienced a new form of solitude in her personal life. With the support of Stieglitz and his circle of artists gone, she stood alone also in her professional life.

By mid-twentieth century O'Keeffe's approach to art appeared to be out of step with the times. Given that reality, O'Keeffe could have proceeded in any number of directions; for instance: doing what was popular, reverting to the classical style of painting in which she had been trained or even ceasing to paint at all. Instead, O'Keeffe was willing to bet on herself, even when the world

---

[7] *Art and Letters*, 263.

was going another way.[8]   She continued to see the world in her unique way; that is, from her center. She kept on expressing in her visual language what she saw and felt. The strength of her self-identity as it continued to actualize can be seen against the backdrop of changing trends in the art world from the beginning of the 1940's through the 1980's.[9]

During World War II distinguished artists from the School of Paris such as Marc Chagall, Salvador Dali and Jacques Lipchitz fled the Nazi occupation of France and came to New York City. Consequently, the influence of the School of Paris declined, the attraction of American artists to Paris waned, and New York City became the focal point of avant-garde art.

The mid-1940's marked the emergence of abstract expressionism and the New York School of artists. These artists – for example, Jackson Pollock, Willem de Kooning, and Robert Motherwell – wanted to make intensely personal statements that were not constrained by the rules of earlier artistic traditions. Automatism, chance, risk, expansive gestures and large canvases were integral to the activity of painting for those artists. They believed self-definition and confrontation with the existential world occurred in the painting process itself.

In the late fifties color-field painters gained prominence. While abstract expressionists of the 1940's and 1950's accentuated the activity of painting, color- field painters like Mark Rothko, Clyfford Still and Barnett Newman formed images from vast expanses of intense color.

O'Keeffe felt no resonance with the abstract expressionism of the 1940's. Moreover, the popularity of that trend overshadowed her work in the eyes of the art critics and the general public. Some affinities did exist between her work and that of the color-field painters; for example; use of vibrant color, shapes reduced to essential lines, suggestion of large space, and intensity of experience. When an exhibit of O'Keeffe's 1916-1917 watercolors was held in 1958 at The Downtown Gallery in New York City, some critics charged that O'Keeffe was trying to jump on the latest bandwagon. The owner of the Gallery suggested that those critics check the dates

---

[8] See *Art and Letters*, 253.
[9] With regard to the historical trends in American art from World War II through the 1980's, see: H. H. Arnason, *History of Modern Art*, third edition (Englewood Cliffs, NJ: Prentice Hall & New York, NY: Harry N. Abrams, 1986), 359-698; Edward Lucie-Smith, *Visual Arts in the Twentieth Century* (New York, NY: Harry N. Abrams, 1996), 183-361.

on the paintings. O'Keeffe's work anteceded by decades the color-field approach. Some color-field painters such as Kenneth Noland and Paul Feeley have acknowledged O'Keeffe's influence upon their work.

By 1960 O'Keeffe's art had regained public attention, especially in light of the large retrospective of her work that year at the Worcester Art Museum in Worcester, Massachusetts. Throughout the 1960's a number of new art trends came to the fore. In addition to the continuing popularity of the color-field painters, other groups such as minimalists, op and pop artists attained recognition. The minimalists were concerned with reducing a form to its essential shape as an end in itself. Op artists attempted to use abstract optical illusions for effect. Pop artists took their images from billboards, comic strips, advertisements and everyday life. They presented those images as art, often using caricature and irreverence. They were concerned with the fabrication of the object itself, without any indication of meaning, emotion or commitment. Typical of those trends were Andy Warhol's soup cans and Roy Lichtenstein's blown-up comic strip frames. O'Keeffe's creative self-expression pushed forward, not significantly affected by those currents.

By 1970 pluralism characterized the visual arts in the United States. The understanding of art itself went beyond traditional forms. For example, people spoke of land art, performance art, conceptual art, video art, body art and process art. All those currents in art did not detract from the renewed interest in O'Keeffe. Her newfound endearment to the American public only increased over the remaining two decades of her life. The large 1970 retrospective of her work at the Whitney Museum of American Art in New York City set the current decisively in that direction.

A number of forces operative in American society enhanced O'Keeffe's appeal; for example: renewed scholarly interest in modernism; the feminist movement, many leaders of which looked to O'Keeffe as a founding mother; awakening interest in ecology; an aging segment of the population searching for models of qualitative living in their elder years; young people impressed by O'Keeffe's independence and clarity of vision. Together with those factors was the charismatic public persona that O'Keeffe had so carefully cultivated over the decades.

Throughout the last four decades of her life, O'Keeffe was the recipient of many honorary degrees and awards in recognition of her contribution to the arts. Of special note are the Medal of Freedom Award in 1977 from President Gerald R. Ford and the National Medal of Arts in 1985 from President Ronald W. Reagan.

C. Expanding Visual Language

When Georgia O'Keeffe lived in New York, she struggled to secure time in New Mexico. However, after taking up permanent residency in New Mexico, that source of tension vanished. She could drink in all that she desired of her cherished landscape. Her needs for colorful surroundings, for privacy, silence and solitude, for a home of her own adequately met, O'Keeffe developed a new interest. The distance called her in a new direction: global travel.

From her home base in New Mexico O'Keeffe undertook these journeys by plane: Mexico in 1951; France and Spain in the spring of 1953; three months in Spain during 1954; three months in Peru during the spring of 1956; another three months in Mexico during 1957; in 1959 a three and a half month trip around the world, including the Far East, Southeast Asia, India, Middle East and Italy; a six-week trip to Japan, Formosa, the Philippines, Hong Kong, Southeast Asia and the Pacific Islands in the fall of 1960; a rafting trip – the first of several – down the Colorado River in August 1961; travel to Greece, Egypt and the Near East in 1963; England and Austria in 1966.

O'Keeffe's travel by plane in the 1950's coincided with the dawning of the Space Age. In 1957 the Soviet Union launched the first earth satellites, Sputnik I and II. The United States launched the first moon rocket in 1958, and the USSR's Luna II reached the moon in 1959. O'Keeffe's air travel broadened her perspective on the earth, and provided her an opportunity to ponder humankind's expanding notion of space. Her travel enhanced her sense of the wideness and wonder of the world in which she lived.

From the mid-1940's to the early 1970's O'Keeffe's experiences of New Mexico and world travel provided new images. Her repertoire of visual themes expanded to include the following:

- the patio wall and door of her Abiquiu home;
- aerial and ground views of rivers;
- roads;
- sky and clouds;
- rocks.

O'Keeffe's broadening experience of global space corresponded with her exploration of new depths of inner space. On her outer and inner journeying she plumbed further the unknown. Thus, the images which she chose from her living express both the within and the without of her transcendent experience.

(1) Patio Wall-with-Door Images

When Georgia O'Keeffe first saw what became her Abiquiu home, it was a ruin situated in a garden. An adobe wall, broken in one place by a fallen tree, enclosed the property. O'Keeffe entered the site through the opening in the wall. Walking around the ruin, she found a good-sized patio. On one side of the patio was a long wall with a door in it. That wall with the door captivated O'Keeffe. It was actually the wall and door that led her to eventually purchase the property. She experienced the wall with the door in it as something she had to have.[10]

Between 1946 and 1960 O'Keeffe did approximately twenty-four paintings of the patio wall-with-door.[11] In most of those works she explored the relationship of the door to the long wall. She included in a number of those canvases something from the surrounding environment; for example: sky, snowflakes, or a line of flagstone steps. O'Keeffe set the geometric shapes that constitute the wall and door in a floating space that evokes a feeling of infinity. Calmness, silence and peace pervade the images. O'Keeffe's approach in her patio wall-with-door paintings contains a certain external likeness to the minimalist painters of the 1960's. However, while those artists viewed reduction and simplification as ends in themselves, O'Keeffe used those techniques to balance forms in an open-ended field stretching to infinity.

(2) Rivers Seen from the Air and the Ground

In the late 1950's Georgia O'Keeffe began using images of rivers seen from the air.[12] She expressed surprise at the number of desert areas with large riverbeds running through them. As she

---

[10] See *Georgia O'Keeffe*, statement opposite plate 82.
[11] See *CR*, 1146, 1159-1162, 1211-1213, 1224, 1263, 1265, 1271, 1279-1284, 1291-1293; 1445; also 1687, 1688; Georgia O'Keeffe, plates 80-83; O'Keeffe: in the West, 76-78.
[12] See *CR*, 1338-1360; 1417, 1440-1444, 1486; Georgia O'Keeffe, plate 103; O'Keeffe: in the West, 85-87.

looked out the window of an airplane during her travels, she did tiny drawings, about one and a half inches square, of meandering rivers below. On returning home, O'Keeffe then made enlarged charcoal drawings from the miniature pencil sketches. Eventually, she made paintings from those charcoal drawings. It was the shapes of the riverbeds that fascinated O'Keeffe. As for her choice of colors, they did not necessarily come from what she had observed. Rather the colors came to her as she painted.[13]

Beginning in the summer of 1961, O'Keeffe's interest in rivers led her to go on several raft trips down the Colorado River. From that experience came a series of Canyon country sketches and paintings.[14]

(3) Roads

Related to O'Keeffe's visual imagery based on her aerial views of rivers were her paintings of the road which she could see from her bedroom window: "the road toward Española, Santa Fe, and the world," as she described it.[15] Her view of the road is from the perspective of looking down from a higher elevation. Especially striking is *The Winter Road I* (1963),[16] a work of oriental simplicity in which she represented the landscape with a dark calligraphic line – seemingly without beginning or end – coursing through a field of white. The two 1964 paintings, *Road to the Ranch* (also known as *Road Past the View I*) and *Road Past the View* (often designated as number *II*)[17] take up a similar line form, this time with the road sweeping, curving and disappearing into the purple, blue and mauve hills of the Sangre de Cristo mountains and the sky beyond.

(4) Sky and Cloud Paintings

The sky had always been an important visual image for Georgia O'Keeffe. For instance, among her paintings during 1916-1918 were the *Evening Star* series and the *Light Coming on the Plains* series. The 1920's O'Keeffe renditions of New York City

---

[13] See Georgia O'Keeffe, statement opposite plate 103.
[14] See *CR*, 1499-1504, 1577.
[15] *Georgia O'Keeffe*, opposite plate 104.
[16] See *CR*, 1477 (for a similar image, see 1471, painted in 1962); *Georgia O'Keeffe*, plate 105; *O'Keeffe: in the West*, 93.
[17] See *CR*, 1487, 1488 (for a similar image, see 1461, painted in 1961); *Georgia O'Keeffe*, plate 104; *O'Keeffe: in the West*, 92.

included the sky as a reference point. Sky is a familiar image also in her landscape paintings of New Mexico.

The image of sky became especially prominent in the 1960's in relation to O'Keeffe's air travel. While her aerial views of rivers were from the perspective of sky to earth, she shifted her vantage point in a 1960-1965 series. In those canvases O'Keeffe expressed the fruits of her experience of beholding the sky from above the clouds as she looked out an airplane window.[18] She described her original inspiration for this theme with these words:

> One day when I was flying back to New Mexico, the sky below was a most beautiful solid white. It looked so secure that I thought I could walk right out on it to the horizon if the door opened. The sky beyond was a light clear blue. It was so wonderful that I couldn't wait to be home to paint it.[19]

O'Keeffe completed her sky-and-cloud work in 1965 with an eight-foot by twenty-four foot painting, the largest canvas that she ever filled.[20]

O'Keeffe's sky and cloud paintings have a unique ambience. The beholder is drawn into a space where there are no footholds or reference points. That space has a floating, infinite quality. The participant has a sense of dynamic presence in a vibrant void of utter transcendence. The experience of the nothing and the all is fraught with unrestricted freedom of spirit, boundless tranquility and endless joy.

(5) Rocks

In 1944 Georgia O'Keeffe did a pastel on paper rendition of two smooth black stones, which she entitled "My Heart."[21] Her choice of the title came from her observation of the hardness of the rocks.[22] Perhaps at the time of the painting she felt herself to be "hard-hearted" in that honoring her own needs meant a certain lack

---

[18] See *CR*, 1460, 1473, 1474, 1478-1479,1484, 1498; *Georgia O'Keeffe*, plate 106; *O'Keeffe: in the West*, 89-91, 94.

[19] *Georgia O'Keeffe*, page after plate 105.

[20] See *CR*, 1498; *Georgia O'Keeffe*, plate 106; *O'Keeffe: in the West*, 94.

[21] See *CR*, 1074.

[22] See Laurie Lisle, *Portrait of the Artist*, 261.

of availability to significant people in her life.

In 1970 Georgia O'Keeffe began a series of oil paintings of black rocks that she had collected from the road to the Glen Canyon dam near her home. Those rocks had been fashioned over time by the sun, wind and blowing sand into something precious to O'Keeffe's sight and touch. They became for her a symbol of "the wideness and wonder of the sky and the world."[23]

After moving to New Mexico, O'Keeffe did not produce as many paintings as previously. In part, that decrease in productivity was an outcome of her investment of considerable time and energy in travel. The physical diminishments that accompanied her aging process also contributed to reduction in the quantity of her artistic works. Yet, O'Keeffe's self-actualization continued as she journeyed ever further into the unknown and as she gave creative expression of that mystery.

D. The Road Past the View

Road Past the View, the title of an O'Keeffe painting from 1964, provides an apt linguistic and visual image for O'Keeffe's life throughout the 1970's up to her death in 1986.

In early 1971, when O'Keeffe was eighty-four years old, she suffered macular degeneration. She lost her central vision, and retained only peripheral sight. No longer could she revel in the color and the light of her cherished natural world. For the remainder of her life, O'Keeffe traveled "the road past the view" in a twofold sense: (1) She was undergoing a depth of mystery at work within her that transcended her capacity to grasp or to express. (2) She revealed to other persons little of what she did comprehend of her inner experience.

O'Keeffe's loss of vision was a catalyst that took her beyond all that was familiar. In fact, she entitled one of her last paintings *The Beyond* (1972).[24] The horizontal bands of color in that oil on canvas work suggest land and sky. A totally black area, which looks like the surface of the earth, covers more than one-third of the canvas. The remainder of the canvas – possibly sky area, "the

---

[23] See *CR*, 1485, 1578-1580; 1690, also sketches 1517-1522; *Georgia O'Keeffe*, plates 107-108; comment opposite plate 107; *O'Keeffe: in the West*, 95-97.
[24] *CR*, 1581.

beyond," – has gradations of blue, with a narrow horizontal slit of white running across the entire surface. Perhaps the painting is an expression by O'Keeffe of her experience that from beyond her darkness the distance was still always calling her, the unknown of infinity was irresistibly beckoning to her, the faraway was even now nearby.

Georgia O'Keeffe's loss of vision led her to become increasingly dependent upon other people for her care. One such person was a young potter named Juan Hamilton. He arrived at O'Keeffe's door early one morning in the fall of 1973, looking for work. Hamilton soon became her assistant, close friend and representative.

With the loss of her central vision, O'Keeffe had ceased painting. Hamilton encouraged her to begin painting again, first in watercolor, then in oil. He urged her also to try her hand at pottery-making.[25] He made it possible for her to continue her travels: Morocco (1974); Antigua (1976); the Pacific coast of Costa Rica and Guatemala (1979); Hawaii (1982); the Pacific coast of Costa Rica (1983).

With Hamilton's help O'Keeffe undertook several new creative projects. For example: She participated in a film about her life and work, which was produced by Perry Miller Adato and televised in 1977. She completed the text for *Some Memories of Drawings* (1974), and composed a book about her paintings entitled, *Georgia O'Keeffe* (1976). She designed a series of abstract sculptures (1982-1983).[26]

Because of O'Keeffe's deteriorating health and the need to be near medical facilities, Juan Hamilton moved her and his family in 1984 to a new home in Santa Fe. O'Keeffe lived there for approximately two years. In early March 1986 Hamilton took his family on a vacation to Mexico. While they were away, Georgia O'Keeffe's condition worsened. On March 6, 1986, she was admitted to St. Vincent's Hospital in Santa Fe. Georgia O'Keeffe died several hours later at the age of ninety-eight. In accordance with her wishes there was no funeral or memorial service. Her body was cremated and her ashes were scattered over the land that she had so cherished.

---

[25] See *CR*, 1691-1701.
[26] *CR*, 1702-1707.

Conclusion

Conclusion

The Letter to the Colossians speaks of the mystery hidden for generations and now revealed. From a Christian perspective that mystery is Christ in us, our hope of glory (see Col 1:27).

Jesus, the human, divine and cosmic Christ, who underwent death and resurrection embodies God as mystery. Jesus is God concealed yet manifest. Jesus is God beyond us, yet with us – so present as to abide within each person, every community, the entirety of creation. The author of the Letter to the Colossians proclaims our situation in light of that truth:

> Now your life is hidden with Christ in God,
> but when Christ, our life, is revealed
> you will be revealed with him in glory (Col 3:3-4).

The Risen Christ indwelling all creation is for Christians the way to God hidden yet revealed. As we behold Jesus, we are drawn ever more deeply into the mystery of God. Hidden with Christ, we yearn for the complete revelation of him, together with the fullness of our unique identity and that of all creation in him. Losing our life, we find in Christ who becomes our Life the consummation of our personal individuality and uniqueness.

We have referred to that hidden life as the transcendent dimension of our identity – indeed, as the numinous aspect of all creation – which opens out to God's transcendence. Our growth in that hidden life constitutes the process of self-actualization.

From the moment we come into being, we are children of our parents, children of the cosmos, children of God. As enfleshed beings becoming, we encounter in daily living the numinous dimension of ourselves and of our world. We experience that those transcendent depths open out to God as Mystery. With our bodily inward/outward/above/below movement, we join in the great cosmic dance. That dance is a participation in the divine dance of trinitarian relatedness; to use a masculine metaphor, God as Father, Son and Spirit; or, to use a feminine metaphor, God as Spirit-*Sophía*, Jesus-*Sophía* and Mother-*Sophía*.

Throughout our lifespan our experience of mystery and our consciousness of it evolve. We encounter mystery: as primal unity; as magic and wonder; as conflict and confusion; as light and knowledge; as unknowing and dark night; as wisdom and freedom; as transforming union. All those experiences of mystery bespeak to us something of God's immanent transcendence.

Self-actualization is itself a work of creative expression. However, when we drink from life at its source, we develop a need to communicate in a variety of creative forms something of our experience of transcendence and self-actualization. God's own wisdom at play within us impels us to express ourselves in word, image, movement or sound.

In this study we have explored the interrelatedness of transcendence, self-actualization and creative expression. We have also fleshed out that theme with reference to the lives and the works of Thomas Merton and Georgia O'Keeffe.

Merton and O'Keeffe witnessed, each in a unique manner, to the interrelationship of transcendence, self-actualization and creative expression. To some extent, Merton personifies the contemplative as artist, while O'Keeffe exemplifies the artist as contemplative.

Up to a certain threshold in his life, Thomas Merton proceeded generally from wordless, imageless, loving encounter with God to awareness of the divine presence in nature and in the world around him. In other words, he went from communing with God in an apophatic way to a sense of God's presence in the created realities around him. As Merton matured spiritually, his manner of approaching the divine presence expanded. He continued to move from encounter with God in darkness and emptiness to beholding the mystery of God within the created world. Yet, increasingly his involvement with creation became itself an opening for encounter with the transcendence of God. Moving back and forth in a rhythm between those two basic approaches to the divine, Merton developed a sense of God's immanent transcendence everywhere, in everything and in everyone. His whole life became a contemplation of God.

Judging by her self-expression in painting, Georgia O'Keeffe's experience of transcendence occurred consistently through her communion with nature. The Mystery shining through creation revealed itself ever more brilliantly to her. Or, to put it another way, O'Keeffe passed through the Mystery which she beheld in the beauty and wonder of nature to ever new depths of Mystery. As to how she experienced transcendence in her final years on her "road past the view," O'Keeffe revealed little. Given her physical deterioration – blindness, deafness, and at times mental confusion – it is reasonable to conjecture that her experience of her hidden self and of divine transcendence proceeded primarily along the apophatic way.

Merton had to struggle for decades to resolve certain dichotomies that he experienced within his personhood and within his life. While there were at times considerable tensions related to balancing the various aspects of her life, O'Keeffe always possessed a certain simplicity of being and a basic sense of integration.

Both Thomas Merton and Georgia O'Keeffe came from families that did not stress membership in an ecclesial tradition or staunch loyalty to an organized religion. Yet, as a young adult Merton became affiliated with a religious institution. His experience of transcendence, self-actualization and creative expression thenceforth unfolded in the context of Roman Catholicism and the monastic order known officially as the Cistercians of the Strict Observance. As Merton matured spiritually, his relationship with both the church and his religious community underwent radical transformation. He moved from an initial stance of almost blind religious obedience to an emphasis on dialogical discernment with those persons in authority. He broke with the church's silence on critical political and social matters in the early 1960's, and he engaged in prophetic discussion of those issues. Merton evolved from a neophyte monk to one who held positions of leadership in his community. He remained a Roman Catholic and a Trappist monk, but he did so as a spiritual adult who experienced within himself increasing freedom of spirit.

Throughout her life Georgia O'Keeffe remained free of ecclesial structures. Three factors in particular helped to set her on her course of encounter with mystery outside the framework of organized religion. They were: (1) her love of nature, which was evident even during her years of growing up on a farm in Wisconsin; (2) her exposure to several Christian affiliations in her family of origin, which awakened perhaps an initial intuition of the broadness of truth and the innate limitations of any institution; (3) the spirit of modernism, with its accent on the individual person as a locus of truth, self-determination and creative enterprise.

Thomas Merton's search for the beyond had as a whole a rather consistent anguished dimension to it, even as he experienced profound joy and peace. In his last few years Merton was well on the way to becoming "the universal person." Yet, he was still searching right up to his untimely death to discover how to continue to live out his calling.

Georgia O'Keeffe's lifelong quest for the unknown of infinity appears to have had in general a peaceful quality. To some degree that impression of tranquility may stem from her tendency to suffer in silence. O'Keeffe was not prone to discuss her struggles in detail with other persons, even those closest to her. However, the fact that O'Keeffe truly underwent considerable pain does not belie the impression of her tranquility of spirit. From her earliest years she had a clear sense of the basic direction in which to go with her life. Her entire life was an unfolding, expanding and deepening of her fundamental direction.

As we conclude this study, an image comes to my mind that had appeal for both Thomas Merton and Georgia O'Keeffe. Each one used it completely independently of the other. Moreover, Merton employed this image in linguistic form, while O'Keeffe expressed it visually. This image has come to symbolize for me the relentless thrust toward transcendence, self-actualization and creative expression which burned like a fire in both their hearts and kept them pressing forward to the completion of their spiritual journeys. It is the image of a ladder reaching toward the moon.

Thomas Merton concluded his book, *The Sign of Jonas,* with a masterful piece of poetic prose entitled, "Fire Watch, July 4, 1952." It is a description of his journey alone through the entire abbey, as he fulfills his duty of watchman during the peaceful silence of night. At one point Merton stands in the tower of the monastery. As he breathes in with his whole being the wind that is blowing through the belfry, he has his hand on a door through which he can see the heavens. Then the door swings open upon what he describes as an immense sea of darkness and of prayer. At that moment Merton poses to God these questions:

Will it come like this, the moment of my death?
Will You open a door upon the great forest and set

my feet upon a ladder under the moon, and take me
out among the stars?[1]

In 1958 Georgia O'Keeffe, then seventy-one years old, did a
painting that she entitled, *Ladder to the Moon.*[2] One evening
O'Keeffe was waiting for a friend. She stood leaning against the
ladder by her house, looking at the long dark line of Mount Pedernal.
The sky that evening was a pale greenish blue and the high moon
looked white. She explained later:

> Painting the ladder had been in my mind for a long
> time and there it was – with the dark Pedernal and
> the high white moon – all ready to be put down the
> next day.[3]

As for the painting itself, the upper nine-tenths of the canvas
is sky. At the bottom of the canvas is a narrow band of landscape
that includes the Pedernal. At the top near the edge is a half moon.
A ladder floats in space centered vertically between the Pedernal and
the moon. As expressive of O'Keeffe's experience, the canvas
intimates her journeying increasingly further into the unknown of
infinity. Moreover, it suggests her intuition that her attraction and
response to the distance always calling her was but a participation in
a vast cosmic reality. O'Keeffe painted *Ladder to the Moon* at a time
when humankind was beginning to penetrate further the unknown of
outer space. Perhaps O'Keeffe was expressing awareness that she,
together with the whole of creation, shared a yearning for and a
journeying toward the consummation of a destiny unimaginable but
nonetheless beckoning – the calling to participate fully and eternally
in Mystery hidden yet revealed.

Sic finis libri,
non autem mystérii.

---

[1] *Sign of Jonas*, 360.
[2] See *CR*, 1335; *Georgia O'Keeffe*, plate 103; *O'Keeffe: in the West*, 84.
[3] *Georgia O'Keeffe*, opposite plate 102.

Select Bibliography

I - Transcendence and Self-actualization

Berry, Thomas. *The Dream of the Earth*. San Francisco, CA: Sierra Club Book, 1990.

Brown, Raymond E. "Mystery (in the Bible)," *New Catholic Encyclopedia*, vol. 10, 148-151. New York, NY: McGraw-Hill Book Company, 1967.

Brown, Raymond E. *The Semitic Background of the Term "Mystery" in the New Testament*. Philadelphia, PA: Fortress Press, 1968.

Carroll, Denis. "Creation," *The New Dictionary of Theology*. Eds. Joseph Komonchak, Mary Collins and Dermot A. Lane. Collegeville, MN: Liturgical Press, 1987. 246-258.

Casel, Odo. *The Mystery of Christian Worship and Other Writings*. Westminister, MD: Newman Press, 1962.

Culliton, Joseph T. *A Progressive World View for Pragmatic Christians*. New York. NY: Philosophical Library Inc., 1975.

Dionysius (Pseudo-). *The Divine Names* and *The Mystical Theology* in *Pseudo-Dionysius: The Complete Works* (The Classics of Western Spirituality Series). Trans. Colm Luibheid. New York, NY: Paulist Press, 1987.

Dulles, Avery.   "Mystery (in Theology)," *New Catholic Encyclopedia.* vol. 10, 151-153. New York, NY: McGraw-Hill Book Company, 1967.

Empereur, James L.   "Paschal Mystery," *The New Dictionary of Theology.* Eds. Komonchak, Collins and Lane. Collegeville, MN: Liturgical Press, 1987, 744-747.

Francoeur, Robert T. *Perspectives in Evolution.* Baltimore, MD: Helicon Press, 1965.

Gallagher, Kenneth T. *The Philosophy of Gabriel Marcel.* New York, NY: Fordham University Press, 1962.

Gilkey, Langdon. *Naming the Whirlwind: The Renewal of God-Language.* Indianapolis, IN: The Bobbs-Merrill Company, 1969.

Gleeson, Philip. "Mystery," *The New Dictionary of Theology.* Eds. Komonchak, Collins and Lane. Collegeville, MN: The Liturgical Press, 1987. 688-692.

Gottlieb, Roger S., ed. *This Sacred Earth: Religion, Nature, Environment.* New York, NY: Routledge, 1996.

Johnson, Elizabeth A. *She Who Is: The Mystery of God in Feminist Theological Discourse.* New York, NY: The Crossroad Publishing Company, 1992.

Johnston, Charles M. *The Creative Imperative: A Four-Dimensional Theory of Human Growth and Planetary Evolution.* Berkeley, CA: Celestial Arts, 1984.

Joranson, Philip N. and Butigan, Ken, eds. *Cry of the Environment: Rebuilding the Christian Creation Tradition.* Santa Fe, NM: Bear and Company, 1984.

Lonergan, Anne and Richards, Caroline. *Thomas Berry and the New Cosmology.* Mystic, CT: Twenty-Third Publications, 1987.

Moltmann, Jürgen. *God in Creation: A New Theology of Creation and the Spirit of God.* San Francisco, CA: Harper and Row, 1985.

Marcel, Gabriel. *Being and Having.* Trans. Katherine Farrer. Boston, MA: Beacon Press, 1951.

Marcel, Gabriel. *The Mystery of Being* (two volumes). Chicago, IL: Henry Regnery Company, 1950.

Macquarrie, John. *Mystery and Truth.* Milwaukee, WI: Marquette University Press, 1973.

Nemeck, Francis Kelly and Coombs, Marie Theresa. *Called by God: A Theology of Vocation and Lifelong Commitment.* Eugene, OR: Wipf and Stock Publishers, 1992.

Nemeck, Francis Kelly and Coombs, Marie Theresa. "Christian Prayer," *Exploring the Catechism.* Ed. Jane E. Regan. Collegeville, MN: The Liturgical Press, 1995, 138-163.

Nemeck, Francis Kelly and Coombs, Marie Theresa. *Contemplation.* Eugene, OR: Wipf and Stock Publishers, 1982.

Nemeck, Francis Kelly and Coombs, Marie Theresa. *Discerning Vocations to Marriage, Celibacy and Singlehood.* Eugene, OR: Wipf and Stock Publishers, 1994.

Nemeck, Francis Kelly and Coombs, Marie Theresa. *O Blessed Night: Recovering from Addiction, Codependency and Attachment, Based on the Insights of St. John of the Cross and Pierre Teilhard de Chardin.* Staten Island, NY: Alba House, 1991.

Nemeck, Francis Kelly and Coombs, Marie Theresa. *The Spiritual Journey: Critical Thresholds and Stages of Adult Spiritual Genesis.* Collegeville, MN: The Liturgical Press, 1987.

Nemeck, Francis Kelly and Coombs, Marie Theresa. *The Way of Spiritual Direction.* Collegeville, MN: The Liturgical Press, 1985.

Otto, Rudolph. *The Idea of the Holy*. Trans. John W. Harvey. New York, NY: Oxford University Press, 1958.

Rahner, Karl. "The Concept of Mystery in Catholic Theology," *Theological Investigations*, vol. 4, 36-73. Trans. Kevin Smyth. New York, NY: The Seabury Press, 1974.

Sontag, Frederick and Bryant, M. Darrol, Eds. *God: The Contemporary Discussion*. New York, NY: The Rose of Sharon Press, 1982.

Teilhard de Chardin, Pierre. *Christianity and Evolution*. New York. NY: Harcourt Brace Jovanovich, Inc., 1971.

Teilhard de Chardin, Pierre. *Science and Christ*. New York, NY: Harper and Row, 1968.

Teilhard de Chardin, Pierre. *The Divine Milieu*. New York, NY: Harper and Row, 1960.

Swimme, Brian. *The Universe Is A Green Dragon: A Cosmic Creation Story*. Santa Fe, NM: Bear and Company, Inc., 1984.

Swimme, Brian. *The Hidden Heart of the Universe: Humanity and the New Story*. Maryknoll, NY: Orbis Books, 1996.

II - Creativity

Adams, Doug and Apostolos-Cappadona, Diane, eds. *Art as Religious Studies*. New York, NY: The Crossroad Publishing Company, 1990.

Apostolos-Cappadona, Diane, ed. *Art, Creativity, and the Sacred*. New York, NY: The Crossroad Publishing Company, 1985.

Arnheim, R. *Art and Visual Perception: A Psychology of the Creative Eye*. Berkeley, CA: University of California Press, 1974.

Arnheim, R. *Toward a Psychology of Art.* Berkeley, CA: University of California Press, 1966.

Arnheim, R. *Visual Thinking.* Berkeley, CA: University of California Press, 1969.

Cameron, Julia. *The Artist's Way: A Spiritual Path to Higher Creativity.* New York, NY: G.P. Putnam's Sons, 1992.

Cameron, Julia. *The Vein of Gold: A Journey to Your Creative Heart.* New York, NY: G.P. Putnam's Sons, 1996.

Chung-yuan, Chang. *Creativity and Taoism: A Study of Chinese Philosophy, Art and Poetry.* New York, NY: Harper Torchbooks, 1963.

Dillenberger, Jane. *Secular Art with Sacred Themes.* New York, NY: Abingdon Press, 1969.

Dillenberger, John. *A Theology of Artistic Sensibilities: The Visual Arts and the Church.* New York, NY: The Crossroad Publishing Company, 1986.

Edwards, Betty. *Drawing on the Artist Within.* New York, NY: A Fireside Book, Simon and Schuster, 1987.

Edwards, Betty. *Drawing on the Right Side of the Brain.* Los Angeles, CA: J. P. Tarcher, 1979.

Frank, Frederick. *The Zen of Seeing: Seeing/Drawing as Meditation.* New York, NY: Vintage Books, 1973.

Gardner, Howard. *Creating Minds: An Anatomy of Creativity Seen Through the Lives of Freud, Einstein, Picasso, Stravinsky, Eliot, Graham, and Ghandi.* New York, NY: Basic Books, 1993.

Gardner, Howard. *Frames of Mind: The Theory of Multiple Intelligences.* New York, NY: Basic Books, 1983.

Gardner, Howard. *Intelligence Reframed: Multiple Intelligences for the 21st Century.* New York, NY: Basic Books, 1999.

Izutsu, Toshihiko. *The Interior and Exterior in Zen Buddhism.* Dallas, TX: Spring Publications, 1975.

Kadinsky, Wassily. *Concerning the Spiritual in Art.* Trans. M. T. H. Sadler. New York, NY: Dover Publications, Inc., 1977.

Lipsey, Roger. *An Art of Our Own: The Spiritual in Twentieth Century Art.* Boston, MA: Shambhala Publications, Inc., 1988.

London, Peter. *No More Secondhand Art: Awakening the Artist Within.* Boston, MA: Shambhala Publications, Inc., 1989.

Maritain, Jacques. *Creative Intuition in Art and Poetry.* New York, NY: Pantheon Books, Inc., 1953.

May, Rollo. *The Courage to Create.* New York, NY: Bantam Books, 1976.

Neumann, Erich. *Art and the Creative Unconscious.* Princeton, NJ: Princeton University Press, 1959.

Rank, Otto. *Art and Artist: Creative Urge and Personality Development.* New York, NY: Alfred A. Knopf, Inc., 1932 and W. W. Norton and Company, 1989.

Richards, M. C. *Centering: In Pottery, Poetry and the Person.* Middletown, CT: Wesleyan University Press, 1962.

Storr, Anthony. *The Dynamics of Creation.* New York, NY: Atheneum, 1985.

Suzuki, Daisetz T. *Zen and Japanese Culture.* Princeton, NJ: Princeton University Press, 1970.

Taylor, Joshua C. *Learning to Look: A Handbook for the Visual Arts.* Chicago, IL: University of Chicago Press, 1957.

Teilhard de Chardin, Pierre. "The Function of Art As An Expression of Human Energy," *Toward the Future.* New York, NY: Harcourt Brace Jovanovich, Inc., 1975.

Zinker, Joseph. *Creative Process in Gestalt Therapy.* New York, NY: Vintage Books, 1977.

III - Thomas Merton

Breit, Marquita E. and Daggy, Robert E. *Thomas Merton: A Comprehensive Bibliography.* New York. NY: Garland Press, 1986.

Biographies

Furlong, Monica. *Merton: A Biography.* San Francisco, CA: Harper and Row, 1980.

Mott, Michael. *The Seven Mountains of Thomas Merton.* Boston, MA: Houghton Mifflin Company, 1984.

Shannon, William H. *Silent Lamp: The Thomas Merton Story.* New York, NY: The Crossroad Publishing Company, 1992.

Writings of Thomas Merton Published after 1986

A Search for Solitude: Pursuing the Monk's True Life (Journals III). Ed. Lawrence S. Cunningham. New York, NY: HarperCollins Publishers, 1996.

A Vow of Conversation: Journals: 1964-1965. Ed. Naomi Burton Stone. New York, NY: Farrar, Straus and Giroux, 1988.

Dancing in the Water of Life: Seeking Peace in the Hermitage (Journals V). Ed. Robert E. Daggy. New York, NY: HarperCollins Publishers, 1997.

Entering the Silence: Becoming a Monk and Writer (Journals II). Ed. Jonathan Montaldo. New York, NY: HarperCollins Publishers, 1996.

"Honorable Reader": Reflections on My Work. Ed. Robert E. Daggy. New York, NY: The Crossroad Publishing Company, 1989.

Learning to Love: Exploring Solitude and Freedom (Journals VI). Ed. Christine M. Bochen.   New York, NY: HarperCollins Publishers, 1997.

Run to the Mountain: The Story of a Vocation (Journals I). Ed. Br. Patrick Hart, OCSO. New York, NY: HarperCollins Publishers, 1995.

The Courage for Truth: Letters to Writers. Ed. Christine M. Bochen. New York, NY: Farrar, Straus, Giroux, 1993.

The Intimate Merton: His Life from His Journals. New York, NY: HarperCollins Publishers, 1999.

The Other Side of the Mountain: The End of the Journey (Journals VII). Ed. Patrick Hart, OCSO. New York, NY: HarperCollins Publishers, 1998.

The Road to Joy: Letters to New and Old Friends. Ed. Robert E. Daggy. New York, NY: Farrar, Straus, Giroux, 1989.

The School of Charity: The Letters of Thomas Merton on Religious Renewal and Spiritual Direction. Ed. Brother Patrick Hart. New York, NY: Farrar, Straus, Giroux, 1990.

The Springs of Contemplation. Notre Dame, IN: Ave Maria Press, 1992.

Thomas Merton in Alaska. New York, NY: New Directions, 1989.

Turning Toward the World: The Pivotal Years (Journal IV). Ed. Victor A. Kramer. New York, NY: HarperCollins Publishers, 1996.

Witness to Freedom: The Letters of Thomas Merton in Times of Crisis. Ed. William H. Shannon. New York, NY: Farrar, Straus, Giroux, 1994.

IV - Georgia O'Keeffe

Bry, Doris, and Callaway, Nicholas, Eds. *Georgia O'Keeffe: In the West.* New York, NY: Alfred A. Knopf, Inc. in association with Callaway Editions, 1989.

Callaway, Nicholas, ed. *Georgia O'Keeffe: One Hundred Flowers.* New York, NY: Alfred A. Knopf, Inc., in association with Callaway Editions, 1989.

Castro, Jan Garden. *The Art and Life of Georgia O'Keeffe.* New York, NY: Crown Publishers, Inc.,1985.

Cowart, Jack, Hamilton, Juan, and Greenough, Sarah. *Georgia O'Keeffe: Art and Letters.* Washington, DC: National Gallery of Art, 1987.

Eisler, Benita. *O'Keeffe and Stieglitz: An American Romance.* New York, NY: Doubleday, 1991.

Eldredge, Charles C. *Georgia O'Keeffe.* New York, NY: Harry N. Abrams, Inc., 1991.

Georgia O'Keeffe (Catalogue of the Georgia O'Keeffe Exhibition in Santa Fe, 1990). Santa Fe, NM: Gerald Peters Gallery, 1990.

Georgia O'Keeffe (Catalogue of 1988 Georgia O'Keeffe Exhibition in Japan). Santa Fe, NM: Gerald Peters Gallery, 1988.

Giboire, Clive, ed. *Lovingly, Georgia: The Complete Correspondence of Georgia O'Keeffe and Anita Pollitzer.* New York, NY: A Touchstone Book; Simon and Schuster, Inc., 1990.

Hassrick, Peter, ed. *The Georgia O'Keeffe Museum.* New York, NY: Harry N. Abrams, Inc., in association with The Georgia O'Keeffe Museum, 1997.

Hoffman, Katherine. *An Enduring Spirit: The Art of Georgia O'Keeffe.* Metuchen, NJ: The Scarecrow Press, Inc., 1984.

Hogrefe, Jeffrey. *O'Keeffe: The Life of an American Legend.* New York, NY: Bantam Books, 1992.

Kuh, Katharine. "Georgia O'Keeffe," *The Artist's Voice.* New York, NY: Harper and Row, 1962.

Lisle, Laurie. *Portrait of an Artist: A Biography of Georgia O'Keeffe.* Albuquerque, NM: University of New Mexico Press, 1986.

Lynes, Barbara Buhler. *Georgia O'Keeffe: Catologue Raisonné (Volumes I and II).* London and New Haven: Yale University Press, The National Gallery of Art, The Georgia O'Keeffe Foundation, 1999.

Lynes, Barbara Buhler, with Bowman, Russell. *O'Keeffe's O'Keeffes: The Artist's Collection.* New York, NY: Thames & Hudson, 2001.

Lynes, Barbara Buhler. *O'Keeffe, Stieglitz and the Critics, 1916-1929.* Chicago, IL: The University of Chicago Press, 1991.

Merrill, Christopher and Bradbury, Ellen, eds. *From the Faraway Nearby: Georgia O'Keeffe as Icon.* New York, NY: Addison-Wesley Publishing Company, 1992.

Messinger, Lisa Mintz. *Georgia O'Keeffe.* New York, NY: Metropolitan Museum of Art, 1988.

O'Keeffe, Georgia. *Georgia O'Keeffe.* New York, NY: The Penguin Group, 1976.

O'Keeffe, Georgia. *Some Memories of Drawings.* Albuquerque, NM: The University of New Mexico Press, 1974.

Patten, Christine Taylor and Cardona-Hine, Alvaro. *Miss O'Keeffe.* Albuquerque, NM: The University of New Mexico Press, 1992.

Peters, Sarah Whitaker. *Becoming O'Keeffe: The Early Years.* New York, NY: Abbeville Press, 1991.

Pollitzer, Anita. *A Woman on Paper: Georgia O'Keeffe.* New York, NY: A Touchstone Book, Simon and Schuster, 1988.

Robinson, Roxana. *Georgia O'Keeffe.* New York, NY: Harper Perennial, 1990.

Stieglitz, Alfred. *Georgia O'Keeffe: A Portrait by Alfred Stieglitz.* New York, NY: The Metropolitan Museum of Art, 1978.

Udall, Sharyn R. *O'Keeffe and Texas.* San Antonio, TX: The Marion Koogler McNay Art Museum, in association with Harry N. Abrams, Inc., Publishers, 1998.

Wood, Myron and Patten, Christine Taylor. *O'Keeffe at Abiquiu.* New York, NY: Harry N. Abrams, Inc., 1995.